The Doc Aiken Story
Memoirs of a Country Doctor
George Russell Aiken, M.D.

First Edition, 1989

To Nita,
For the good times - and the bad

45-91,
J R Clark M.D.

Library of Congress Catalogue Card Number: 89-090326
ISBN   0-938473-01-8

Book cover and text design by Matt Brown and Kathryn Vilips-Jackson.
Editing and research by Kathryn Vilips-Jackson.

First Edition, Limited to 1,000 copies, May, 1989

CONTENTS

ACKNOWLEDGEMENT

There are so many friends that I should thank, but the memory of an old man would be sure to leave someone out. So, to all the patients and friends over the years who helped and encouraged me, tolerated me, and gave advice; I thank you.

To Bob Perrin, one of my dearest and oldest friends, and his lovely wife, Ina, I owe so much! The two of them gave of their time, their talent, and their encouragement. We had Bob with us for several years, from the time he was twelve years old. My sister, Ann, sent him to us when he had been ill with typhoid, and had had his appendix removed. She hoped that the fresh air in the West would get him back on his feet.

Bob traveled alone, across the country on a train, to Utah. When he arrived, the local boys in Hurricane tried to bully him, but Bob out-witted them. He charmed them with tales of his cross country trip. He appeared in a huge Indian headdress, and told them tales of his Boy Scout activities. He told them about places they had never seen, except in picture books. Bob has been charming people ever since.

When his failing eyesight made it impossible to continue the long drive from Green Valley, Arizona to Utah; he graciously turned over the editing of the manuscript to Kathryn Vilips-Jackson, offering advice and encouragement. We both thank him for that.

To Norma Anderson of Salt Lake City, and others, who encouraged me to write the book in the first place, I thank all of them.

I thank my sister, Catherine Harps, of Sevier, Utah, and my neice and nephew, Jerry and Richard Knight, of southern California, who have supported my efforts, and the work of Kathryn.

To Mardean Pugh, and her sister Lyall McDonald, who, when I was in the hospital, worked like no one has ever worked before, and who were friends and supporters to Kathryn during the difficult period of putting this book together; they are a part of this book.

To Ina Fae Hamblin Frost, who was also supportive, and encouraged us not to give up the book. Mardean, Lyall and Ina Fae were the reason Kathryn hung in there when she found me too difficult to work with at times.

Kathryn edited my manuscript, wrote the stories for publicity, contacted publishers, wrote letters, telephoned and wrote *Johnny Carson Productions* and the *William Morris Agency* to publicize the book, and to try to develop it into a television series. I have never met anyone who fought so hard to make me look good, even when she was ready to quit.

The two of us fought and argued over what she considered my *macho* attitude. Dr. Howard Roberts said she was one of the few people who ever talked back to me, and although it made it difficult for Kathryn, he thought it was good for me. I know that I got a kick out of getting a rise out of her, and she would take the bait every time.

To Marlin and Matt Brown, Publishers of *Southern Utah News*, I owe a special thanks. If it were not for Marlin, and for the *Sun Book Store* and the newspaper; I would not have received as much publicity in the town where it all happened. Through the good times - and the bad, it has been worth it all.

CHAPTER ONE
Looking Back

I have been asked how a farm boy from Ohio, a Presbyterian, ended up in one of the most remote sections of the West, occupied mostly by the Mormons, Navajos and Paiutes; and now, more than sixty years later, consider this my home, and these people my people.

This is the story of those people, that land, the struggles of a country doctor and his wife, sometimes with only a dollar between them, and with a young baby and a dog to feed. I have also been asked why a doctor would put himself and his family through these struggles.

At one point, my wife, tired of pioneering, divorced me and went back East, then remarried me two years later. We had another son, and went on to celebrate our fiftieth anniversary in the little Mormon town we both learned to love.

The nurse I married, after I graduated from Medical School in Columbus, Ohio, now lies buried near the red rock cliffs that overlook Kanab. More than fifty years ago, before WWII, the two of us planted water lilies in the second lake of Three Lakes, on Highway 89 outside of Kanab, Utah. The water lilies live on, and bloom, like the memory of her.

Beneath the Patawotomi plum trees, plum trees brought to Utah by pioneer Mormons in the mid-1800s, and among the tulips and other spring flowers, growing in the garden of the Heritage House, I placed a plaque in memory of Juanita Hauer Aiken. And now, after having lived almost a century, I look back and remember, the good times - and the bad.

Now that I am old, and my eyesight is dimmed by time, I find that the memories come back with even more intensity. I miss my friends and family, and the patients who have gone on before me. I miss the past, and have concerns for the future.

Being old does not lessen the longing to be loved, by family and by friends. Perhaps, age makes you even more aware of the fragility of life, and more appreciative of those you have loved, and those who have loved you. It is only now, as I sit before the fire, my legs sometimes barely able to support me, with the help of my manzanita cane (a gift forty years ago from Lester Little, long before I ever knew I would live long enough to need one), that I ache with frustration, knowing that I cannot cast that line ever again, or ride and throw that rope to catch a wild mare, or exchange tall tales around a campfire with my friends, who have gone on ahead of me.

I miss the long drives in the snow to deliver a baby, or care for someone I knew was depending on me. My patients were my friends, and despite my gruff manner, I loved them all.

My family, like most families I suppose, make courtesy calls. My friends, who are still living, visit and talk of the old times, and it is like a blood transfusion to me, giving me life and the will to go on, to perhaps write another book. But, those are the dreams of an old man. Dreams and memories are all that we really have left when we are old, and each night when I close my eyes and I lie in the dark, and listen to my heart beat, I ask myself if I am selfish to have lived so long, and to want to go on living. I have done much in my life, but it never seems enough.

There are cases I would have handled differently. I would have been a little less gruff, especially with my nurses, who, God knows, put up with a lot from me. Someone told me I always made the nurses cry. Perhaps it was my own sense of insecurity, knowing that someone's life was depending on me, and I took my insecurity out on those that were closest to me.

Occasionally, I will talk to an old friend in another town, or state, by telephone; someone I have practiced medicine with, like Dr. Joseph Sanella, or Dick Riley, to verify facts for this book. It brings back a flood of memories, and I sometimes find it difficult to realize that I have almost lived a century, and have watched so many changes in the field of medicine, styles, and mores.

I live alone, or almost alone. Two cats, Alley and Tiger, who had been abandoned when they were still too young to leave their mother, share my modest home; an old brick home built in 1879. I am not sure who built the home, but early Mormon pioneers, Frank Hamblin and his wife Elizabeth Rhodeleigh Hamblin, who ran the dairy for the United Order of Kanab in Swallow Park, near Johnson Canyon, lived here.

I am sure that Hamblin comes back to visit his old home. Doors open and sounds are heard in the night, but he is always friendly. He has been especially active lately, after a friend suggested growing mushrooms in the dirt floor basement that Bob used to use as a dark room. Either his ghost doesn't like mushrooms, or he simply objects to disturbing the old soil in the basement. It is presently the abode of spiders and friendly ghosts.

The house is at 59 East First South, and is close to the old Chamberlain Heritage House. I spent twelve years helping to restore the house. I planted fruit trees and flowers, that will live on long after I am gone. I helped build a stone walk, the stones uneven, leading to the front of the house. This is where I fell, years after the stones were laid.

I purchased the house I live in now, and a half block of property, more than twenty years ago for my youngest son Bob, and his first wife, Jan. The house was traded back to me in exchange for my larger home on Main Street when Bob married his second wife, Lenore, about four years ago.

Alley and Tiger do their best to entertain me, snuggle up to me, and show their affection, without restraint. Whoever said that cats were aloof, never met cats like Alley and Tiger. They were scrawny kittens, their fur matted with burrs, and half-starved, when their pitiful cries awakened me and kept me awake most of one night. Lonnie, who cleaned for me, found them in the deep weeds across the street the next morning, and brought them home.

When spring flowers bloom, flowers planted by friends, and the weather is nice, I walk. As soon as the cats hear my walker clicking on the pavement that leads away from the patio, they come running and rub up against my legs and purr, and walk along beside me like two old friends. I talk to them, and after the three of us have walked down to the end of the sidewalk and back, they chase each other up the elm trees and down again. They seem to know that they must not run when they are close to me, since I am almost blind, and my legs are weak.

Shortly after I moved into the smaller house, I fell, and was hospitalized for three weeks. My long-time friends, Mardean Pugh and her sister Lyall

MacDonald, contracted to have a patio and sidewalk put in for me. They made some much needed repairs, cleaned, hung curtains, planted flowers and put in a strawberry patch.

Mardean used to work for me, and literally did the work of three people. Louise Bell took over the bookkeeping after Mardean left, and I had to hire two more women to do all the work Mardean did alone. She is a very special person, and so is Lyall. I could not have made it without them.

When summer comes, and I sit on the lovely stone patio they had built; I think how fortunate I am to have friends that do so much, without ever being asked. I have found that it is my friends who do the most, and ask the least.

Neldon Earl, "Mr. Earl," soft-spoken and gentle, comes by every week, and sometimes even more often in the winter, to see that I have wood and coal, and in the summer to mow the lawn, haul the weeds, paint and do repairs.

Frank Davis used to mow my lawn (as a courtesy) and did so much for me before he retired, and started traveling. Even now, when he is in town he comes to visit, and we discuss local and national politics. In the summertime, Frank brings me the sweetest corn I have ever eaten, grown in his garden in Kanab.

Ina Fae Frost, a great-granddaughter of pioneer Mormon, Jacob Hamblin, comes often, on her way to and from the Heritage House. She took over as hostess, after my fall prevented my going back and forth. She sometimes takes me over for special events, and each summer shares news of the people who come from all over the world to visit the Heritage House.

Pearl Little, who lives across the street, and next to the Heritage House, planted some of the strawberries, according to Mardean. Pearl occasionally bakes a pie, and brings over a slice, or brings over a basket of fruit and cookies for Christmas.

Kay Willardson, whose voice is as beautiful as her cooking is good, brings over fresh vegetables from her garden, or a special dessert. Her husband Tom, although he is half my age, comes to visit, and I enjoy talking with him.

I look forward to my trips to the barber shop every two or three weeks. Val Tait has been my barber for almost as long as I can remember. He is a musician and a poet, and a good coversationalist. Sometimes, when I am not sure of a name, I check with Val.

Recently, when a friend dropped me off to have my hair cut, Val told him not to pick me up for at least an hour, to give us time to visit. When the friend returned, Val said, "While you were gone, we fought the Indians, roped wild horses, chased some women, and drank a jug of moonshine! Not bad for one hour, huh?"

Friends who have moved away, come to visit when they are in town. Some of them seem surprised to find that I am still alive, and writing a book. It is always nice when they come, and we can sit and reminisce about the past.

But, I must get on with my story. An old man's mind tends to wander, not so much because he is old, but because there are so many years of memories stored, that once he starts remembering, he savors the warmth they bring to his old bones, and to his heart.

Tiger and Alley are curled up in front of the fire, and I envy them their agile limbs, as they stretch every now and then. I nudge them with my cane and growl at them, but they are used to my gruff voice, and after opening one eye to let me know they heard me, they go back to their dreaming.

And so shall I; I will pretend that I am a young man again, back on the old Doan farm in Madiera, Ohio. That is where it all began.

CHAPTER TWO
Where It All Began

Grandad Bain had bought the Old Doan farm in Madiera, Ohio, when I was two or three years old. That was to become my home until I was five; when my parents bought their own farm. My grandparents had lived in Milford, Ohio, but the Miami River had claimed the lives of their two older sons, and they wanted to get away from the painful memories the river brought back to them.

The Bains were a large family; their ancestors having come from Scotland. I had been the first child born to Clarence and Margaret Aiken on April 7, 1896 in Milford, Ohio. They would later have two daughters, my sisters Ann, and Catherine.

The farm sat atop the Old School Hill overlooking the main road, about one hundred yards away, and across the road from the schoolhouse. The house was large, with several rooms upstairs, used as bedrooms, and three rooms downstairs, in addition to the living and dining rooms, that were used by my parents as an apartment.

All of us ate together. When we all sat down; it looked like a Thanksgiving feast, with much laughter and teasing. As I grew older; I did much of that, and sometimes found myself in trouble with my father, because of it.

Grandad Bain had twelve children, so there were always several aunts and uncles around to join in the lively discussions around the dining-room table. I was a happy child, and loved being surrounded by so many relatives.

Grandma Bain was a frail looking 4'10", who weighed, possibly 80 pounds, sopping wet. She wore her grey hair pulled back in a bun, and always clutched a shawl around her shoulders, summer or winter. Despite her fraility, and her stooped shoulders, she used her cane to get action, and someone's attention. I don't recall that she ever hit me with her cane, but she used it on the girls quite frequently.

After we moved away, and I would come back to visit, Grandma Bain would pull me up to her and say, "Russell, you've been away so long!" The girls would complain that they stayed on the farm to do the work, and all they got from her was whacks from her cane.

Strong sons were important to farm families. Every son meant an extra hand at harvesting time. The nearest neighbors were a German family, the Ramenschneiders, who exchanged hands at harvest time. Other than exchanging work there was not a lot of socializing between the two families.

There was a tragic accident when one of the Ramenschneider's boys lost his life. The father and sons were digging a well, and had dynamited to break a limestone deposit about twenty feet down. They went in to eat their lunch after the blast, and left the well to let the deadly carbon monoxide and nitrous oxide settle.

The youngest son, anxious to get the work completed, finished his lunch ahead of the others, and went back to the well. He let himself down into the well on a bucket. When his father and brothers found him, he had lost consciousness. An older brother, in attempting to rescue him, also lost consciousness.

The Bain's were called, and my uncles rushed to the Ramenschneider farm to help in the rescue operation. Both the Ramenschneider boys were brought out, unconscious, but I believe, only the younger one died.

It was the cave-in of a bank of the Miami River, after a severe rain storm, that claimed the lives of the two older Bain boys. Families were brought together during these tragedies, but it was a hard world and one had to go back to the realities of life, and running a farm.

Mother and her sisters; Christine (Teen), Mary, and Catherine (Kate), helped with the household chores. The boys, Will, George, Kenneth, Jim, Frank, Alec and Sinclair helped outside, although "Sinc", who was my youngest uncle, was usually my *partner-in-crime,* when it came to getting into mischief.

We were close to the same age, and one time tried to sell some out-dated tickets to old Mrs. Armstrong. We didn't know that people could read what was written on them, and we did not know that the tickets were not for an up-coming *pie social* as we had told her they were, in our sales-pitch.

She must have had it in for young *entrepreneurs*, because she told our parents. Not only did we get our first lesson in finance, but we also received a couple of hearty wallops on the back-side to make the lesson stick!

There were several old farm buildings nestled on the one hundred acres, with farm machinery, and ponds, that were sometimes the cause of accidents. The old buildings also provided shelter from inquisitive parents when one wanted to mimic their older uncles. Sinc and I had watched them smoke cornsilk behind the barn, so we tried it, out behind the straw-stack, and burned it down!

Then we watched the older uncles suck cider through the long, dried stems of the tiger lilies. If they could do it; we could do it, we thought! All I can remember is that we were two sick little boys, and we both had to be put to bed with cold cloths on our heads. After that, we could never understand what our uncles saw in cider through a tiger lily stem!

If Sinc and I were not busy getting into mischief; we were busy deciding what we were going to be when we grew up. Uncle Joshua, who had married Dad's sister, Aunt Bessie, was an engineer on the Baltimore & Ohio Railroad.

On my way home from school I would stop by and wait for his train to pull into the station. He would climb down out of the cab and ask me how I did in "problems" that day. Then he let me climb aboard where I could watch the fireman open the big boiler and throw in a few shovels of coal.

Sometimes, Uncle Joshua would let me pull the cord that made the whistle blow. I loved that, and felt like I was really grown up, to be allowed to perform such an important task. I decided I wanted to be an engineer.

Later, Uncle Joshua's train was in a wreck, and he lost one of his legs. That ended my desire to be an engineer.

Then Sinc and I decided we wanted to be a *Rag Man*. We were thrilled when we saw the rag man turn off the main road into our lane. As he rang his big bell he would holler "Any rags, any iron, any old paper today?"

Sinc and I would race around to see what we could scrounge and sell. On a farm there are always old pieces of iron lying around, but sometimes we tried to sell a brand new piece of machinery that Grandad Bain had just purchased. That is when Grandad would step in and ruin our chances for making a fast buck. It seemed that *grown-ups* were always stepping in and ruining our chances to get rich quick.

And we were convinced that to become a rag man meant we were sure to get rich. We would watch *bug-eyed*, as the leathery-faced old rag man weighed what we had to sell, on a pair of scales he carried with him. As he weighed and re-weighed, mumbling to himself; we would squirm with impatience until his gnarled fingers dug slowly into the long sock-like purse he carried. He'd close one eye, and watch us as he brought out those few pennies to pay us. He seemed reluctant to let the money go, and we'd lick our lips, already thinking of how we were going to spend all that money.

When he finally let go of the money, and dropped it into our out-stretched hands, one coin at a time; we would dash into the house clutching our wealth. Yes siree, we were going to become *rag men,* and carry a long sock-like purse, and when we rang the bell and hollered, we wouldn't let go of our pennies either - until we absolutely had to. We were going to become *millionaires!*

Had we been older we would have realized that he could not have had much money. His poor horse was scrawny and underfed; just as he was. All *we* could see, was that long sock and all those pennies!

There is a lane across the street from where I now live, and as I sit on the patio, I can see, in my mind's eye, the rag man coming down the lane; and two small boys running to meet him. Off to the right is a large, weather-beaten barn, and rusted farm machinery. It reminds me of my childhood, and Sinc.

In-between planning our careers as rag men; we were investigating the machinery Grandad Bain had on the farm. He had purchased a large farm wagon called a *jolt-wagon,* because it had no springs. It had a high-sided box bed with a spring seat on top for the driver. It was painted green and had the name *Bain* in large letters in the middle of the panel.

We took a pair of reins from a set of harnesses and tied them to the end of the wagon-tongue. Sinc climbed into the driver's seat, and I handed him the reins. We pretended that we were *off to market.* There was a foot-brake he could push on and off as he *drove* to market.

Grandad had a *fodder-chopper* in the barn to cut up cornstalks for the cows. This was a machine you could turn by hand, or you could operate the large fly-wheel on the opposite side with a belt from an engine, or a horse-driven carousel. I decided, while Sinc was driving to town, that I would chop fodder for the farm animals.

When Grandad, or the older uncles were home, Sinc and I, and sometimes Alec, had the job of keeping Old Frank, the horse, on the move to keep the fly-wheel turning. A belt ran from the one-horsepower machine to the fly-wheel on the chopper.

Sinc soon tired of the drive to market, so he climbed down to help me chop fodder. We took the belts off the chopper so we could turn it by hand. I found that I could really get it spinning by using both hands, then letting it go. Then we got some stalks of corn and started shoving them into the box.

Sinc climbed back onto the driver's seat and left me to continue with the chopping. I was having such a good time that I reached in too far to push the cornstalks in with my left hand. There was no place to put my right hand, so I accidentally put it on the double-mesh gears and my hand was pulled into the cogs.

The handle struck me as it came around, and fortunately kept my hand from going through. I screamed, and Sinc climbed off the seat, white-faced, and turned the handle back to release my hand. He ran to get Aunt Teen, and although I don't remember any pain; when Aunt Teen, sympathetic and her face twisted in worry, saw the blood and started to cry; I did too.

All my uncles and Grandad were gone, so Aunt Teen called my Dad at work. When he arrived, out of breath and excited; he hitched up Nelly, a Texas cow-pony, to the breaking-cart, a long-shafted, two-wheel cart. Nelly had a way of objecting to this kind of locomotion and would kick hell out of the front of a buggy, so that is why we used the cart.

Dad was yelling and waving his whip to make Nelly hurry. I was more terrified of Dad's driving than I was of the pain in my hand. Just as we crossed the old stone bridge at the *Crazy Jug,* the hub of our cart hit the hub of a buggy going in the opposite direction; knocking the wheel off the other buggy, and sending it rolling down the incline.

The buggy did not turn over, but the man jumped off and threatened to change the contours of my father's face. My father shouted back, and after several minutes of fist-waving and shouting; my father climbed back on the cart and sped on, leaving the poor man to figure out what to do about his buggy.

When we arrived in Madisonville, Dad carried me in and started giving instructions to Dr. Heir, who calmly went about his preparations for surgery. He gave me chloroform, then sewed up my mangled hand. Although I never suffered any disability from the accident; I still have an impressive scar, more than eighty-five years later.

CHAPTER THREE
Growing Up

There was always much to do on the farm for all of us. In addition to the farm buildings and the barn with stables; there was a blacksmith shop and carpenter shop at the end of a large shed. On the other end was a cider mill and a rack for drying fruits and vegetables, along with a smokehouse.

In the fall, after the cider mill was cleaned up and the apples were crushed and squeezed through the mill; the cider was then collected and stored in barrels for making vinegar. It was after the cider had aged for a few days that the older boys would get some long dried stems from the tiger lilies that lined the lane, and used them to suck cider through the straws. Sinc and I remembered our first experience and the terrible hangover we had from drinking too much cider, so we were happy to leave the tiger lilies and the cider to the older uncles.

During the summer, my mother and my aunts were busy drying apricots, peaches, apples and vegetables on the drying racks for the winter. The dried fruit was then stored in paper sacks in an open space above a large cupboard in the kitchen. There was a board loose on the outside of that portion of the kitchen; so Sinc and I figured out a way to get to the fruit without being caught.

We pulled a ladder over to where the loose board was, and while one of us acted as a look-out, the other one would climb the ladder, reach through, and steal the dried fruit. I am sure that we would have been given some fruit if we had asked, but somehow the fruit was sweeter when we went to so much trouble to get it.

We would take turns cutting a small hole in the back of the sack, so that from the front no one could tell that the sacks were being emptied. When Aunt Teen went to the cupboard to get dried fruit to make a pie, she would find empty bags. When we were questioned, Sinc and I put on our most *angelic look* and tried to convince her that there was a rat loose that had made the holes in the bags.

When the first frost came in the fall, the hogs were butchered. A large wooden barrel would be set in the ground at an angle, and filled with water. A large fire would then be built close by and stones of granite would be placed on the fire. The heated stones would then be placed in the barrel to heat the water. One of the boys would shoot the screaming pig between the eyes with a .22 caliber rifle, and then hang the pig up, head down, and cut the throat to drain the blood from the body into a clean pan. The blood was then saved to make blood pudding.

I have been asked how I could possibly stand to be a part of the butchering, but I didn't think anything about it at that time. All I could think of was how good the bacon and the ham were going to taste. Perhaps my sisters cried, or were upset; I don't know, but the boys were not affected by it, to my knowledge. Maybe it would bother me now; now that I am older and mellowed.

After the pig was hung and drained, a cooling period followed; usually one night. Then the pig was placed on a table and cut up. There was a large smokehouse near the garden gate where the cut-up pig was hung and smoked, using hickory or apple wood. The lard was rendered in a large iron pot that hung on a crane in the large fireplace built on the rear wall of the lean-to kitchen. This was before the days we knew about the dangers of cholesterol.

The lean-to kitchen extended across the back of the house and had a stone floor. Windows extended along the outer wall, with a long table under them. At the end of the room, opposite the well, was a large cupboard used for storage.

To the right of the kitchen entrance was the well-box where a windlass raised and lowered a large iron water bucket. There was a latch on the windlass to keep it from dropping too fast. If you were not careful the large handle would hit you as the bucket was lowered, and that wallop would wake you up in a hurry.

The well-water was used mostly for drinking and cooking. There was a cistern outside the kitchen which had a pump on it and this water was used for the laundry.

Women in those days used to put out containers to catch rain water for washing their hair, and if you were a brunette; you rinsed your hair in vinegar water to remove the soap, or if you were a blonde; you used the juice of a lemon in the rinse water. Perhaps it worked, because as I recall, women had thick, shiny hair.

The chicken house was Grannie's domain. She made pets of the chickens, and gave them names. She would let them out from time to time to pick up loose grain around the corn-crib, and as she walked and talked to them; they would make clucking sounds in reply.

The eggs they laid were large, with orange yolks that stood high, and rarely broke in the cooking. Hens today that are kept in pens, do not produce the eggs that were laid by hens raised in a natural environment, nor do they have the same flavor.

The corn crib was built with open-slotted sides so that the grain could get plenty of air. The upper part of the crib was built wider than the lower part, in order to keep out the snow and rain. It stood on stilts to keep it away from the moisture on the ground.

The wagon shed was a large rectangular building with just a roof on it, but no sides. You could drive through, un-hitch the horses and leave the wagon or buggy under the roof, and out of the weather.

The privy, or out-house, was a two-hole model that had plenty of use with such a large family. Newspapers and catalogues from Sears & Roebuck, or Montgomery Ward, served as bathroom tissue. There was no *Charmin* nor *Angel Soft* for us!

Sinc and I would sit and leaf through the pages, and it was from the underwear illustrations, that we first learned that we were different from the girls. We would laugh and point out illustrations that we considered quite *racy*.

This was in the early 1900's, and in the summertime, Grandad took in a few boarders; city folks who liked to visit a farm and get away from the city. Sinc and I always loved it when we had boarders. They might be a little uppity, and dress funny, but they usually had a good supply of firecrackers, rockets and roman candles that they brought along for the Fourth of July.

We considered them a little *sissified,* but we kept our opinions to ourselves, since we wanted those fireworks they brought. We learned through trial and error what we should and should not do to get what we wanted. I can't exactly say we were *conniving,* but then again, I can't say we weren't!

The cash crop on the farm was tomatoes, which were contracted to a cannery. The ground was plowed and harrowed in the Spring, then deep furrows were plowed in straight rows.The older uncles would drive down the rows with a wagon full of stable manure, then toss a fork-full into the furrows about every three feet. Then the younger ones, Alec, Sinc and I, would put dirt over each pile of manure, and make a hill.

When the tomato plants arrived, the younger kids would drop a tomato plant on each hill, and the older boys would come along with a *dibble,* poke a hole in the hill, and drop in the tomato plant. Dirt was then packed around the root. The planting was done late in the afternoon, even if it rained a little, Since there was no irrigation system, the survival of the plants depended on the rains.

The rest of the farm was in pasture, with large fields of oats, and wheat. They were planted in the fall, and harvested the following summer. Harvest time meant lots of activity and excitement. When the grain was cut, it was tied in sheaves, and these were stacked in cocks. Four or five sheaves were stood on end, then one or two were placed on top to bind them to keep out the rain. Later, the sheaves would be brought into the barnyard and piled in large stacks so that the thresher could pull in between them, and the sheaves could be thrown in to thresh the grain.

The grain was then put in sacks weighing between fifty and eighty pounds each, then carried into the barn where the grain bins were located, and emptied. That was one of the jobs the kids helped with at threshing time. We didn't mind, because all of the time Sinc and I could be talking, and planning our next escapade.

When the grain was harvested, men from neighboring farms would come to help, and were helped in return. The women would fry chicken, bake pies, and put on feasts for the harvesters. We always looked forward to the extra food, and Sinc and I would try to slip in and get an extra piece of pie; relishing the stolen pie, as we did the stolen fruit.

CHAPTER FOUR
Keeping Them Down On The Farm

The old Doan Farm was a nice place, but it was hard to keep the boys on the farm, the same as it is today. I remember how sad we were, and yet how excited, when Uncle Will left the farm to go to Alaska to seek his fortune. Alaska at that time seemed like one of the most remote parts of the world, and Sinc and I envied the adventures that we knew Uncle Will would have so far away from home. We pictured polar bears and Eskimos, and great fortunes of gold.

Occasionally, someone in the family would get a gold nugget from him, just to prove that he was doing alright. He sent postcards, and we would all gather around the table and talk about what an exciting life he must be living. It made the farm seem a little less enchanting, despite all of the fun we shared as a large family.

Uncle Kenneth went to the city and took up the plumbing trade. He would commute by train, and later on; the traction line, but some of the boys chose to stay on the farm and help Grandad Baines. Uncle George, Jim, Frank, Alec and Sinc stayed and worked on the farm. Mary, Teen, and Kate also stayed on the farm, so there were still enough relatives to make us feel part of a large family. My father worked in the city, and commuted daily on the train while we lived there.

When I was about five, we moved from the farm to a cottage on Carmargo Pike on the outskirts of Indian Hill. My hand was still bandaged from the fodder chopper accident, when I had another mishap. I was playing with my dog when my shoe lace became un-tied. I had a friend, Roeberg, that had his dog there as well, and we were all playing together. As I leaned over to tie my shoelace I tried to balance myself by putting my foot on my dog's back. Thinking I was hurting his friend (my dog), Roberg's dog attacked me, biting the hand that was still bandaged. I still have a dimple at the base of my thumb from the dog's tooth print.

When I began school we lived in the large farmhouse in Madiera. On my first day in school we were asked what we wanted to be when we grew up. By this time I had decided that maybe being a rag man wasn't going to be the most exciting career in the world, what with Uncle Will off in Alaska, and Uncle Kenneth and my Dad working in the city.

My Dad had started out helping in the *Boericke and Tafel Pharmacy* on Fourth Street in Cincinnati as a young man. He later became a salesman for the firm, and eventually became Manager. He met many doctors, so perhaps his conversations with them, and what he relayed to my mother at home, influenced me in my decision to become a doctor. Dad went to work for them when he was only sixteen years of age, and worked for them for almost fifty years. Long after I became a doctor; he was still with them.

The schoolhouse was small, with only two rooms downstairs, and one room upstairs. First, second and third grades were in one room, and taught by Miss Rude. Fourth and fifth grades were in the other downstairs room and were taught by Miss Major.

The sixth, seventh and eighth grades were upstairs and taught by Mr. Demar. The upstairs room had two large pot-bellied stoves to provide heating, and one stove each in the two downstairs rooms. When it was cold, the fires were started and kept burning with coal and wood. If it became too warm, the windows were opened; a simple ventilating system.

Public school days were happy times for me for the most part, but I was a bit of a show-off, and full of mischief. Our teacher, Miss Rude, was a strict disciplinarian, and had to be; there were around forty students in one room.

Usually the room was pretty quiet despite the large number of students. She wore a large ring on her left hand which she used to tap on the edge of her desk as a signal to settle down and be quiet. She also used it on the top of our head if we didn't get the message the first time. Everyone feared that ring, and only had to have it used on their head once to know she meant business.

Miss Rude ran the classroom on signals, and we learned them all. If we wanted to speak; we raised one hand with all the fingers extended. If we wanted a drink of water (or an excuse to get out of the room), we extended two fingers. The well was just outside in the schoolyard, so Miss Rude knew just about how long it took to pump a cup of water, and how long it took to drink it, so we had better not dilly-dally too long or we were in danger of getting the old ring treatment!

When we wanted to go to the out-house, we held up our hand with only the index finger extended. The boy's toilet was a two-hole model located down the hill in a grove of locust trees. We often made excuses to get out of the room to the out-of-doors simply because we had so much pent-up energy that we found it difficult to concentrate on studies when there was so much to attract our attention outside.

The girl's toilet was up the hill, also in a grove of locust trees, but behind the school, and any boy caught near there was in for trouble. It was a *no-man's land* between the two out-houses. The boys were not allowed to go out at the same time one of the girls went out. If one was gone too long, or what the teachers believed was too long; we would be reprimanded.

When the school bell rang to dismiss us for the day, Miss Rude would tap a small bell on her desk. That was the signal to put our work and books into our desk, neatly. When the next bell rang we turned in unison, slid out of our seats, and stood by our desks. When the third bell rang, we walked out quietly. Miss Rude ran the class like a Marine Drill Sargeant, and we listened most of the time.

Like most kids, my favorite part of school was recess, or after school. We played leap-Frog, did broad-jumping and played baseball in the summertime and the fall. When winter set in and the snow covered the schoolhouse hill, we would sled down the steep hill, shouting as loud as we could, pushing and laughing as we rolled, fell off; then climbed back up the steep hill to repeat the performance.

The sleds often spilled everybody when it hit the traction line crossing and took a wild leap into the air. The sleds were like boxes with a steel runner. The bobsled held about twenty of us, but it took someone who was older to guide it down the sledding hill, which was trisected by a highway cross-roads, the traction car line, and the Baltimore & Ohio railroad. I don't recall that any of us were ever seriously hurt, because we always laughed and started all over again.

Sinc and I sat across from each other in the third grade. Miss Rude had gotten married a few weeks before school was out that year, so her older sister substituted as our teacher. With Miss Rude and her over-size ring out of the way we decided to relax and have a little fun. We didn't know that compared to Miss Rude, her sister was like *Attila the Hun!*

I have forgotten what mischief we were up to, but it amused the class, so that was all the encouragement we needed. The trouble was, we didn't see *Attila the Hun* coming down the aisle behind us. She grabbed each of us by the back of the shirt; lifted us out of our seats, shook us like a dog would shake a rat, then cracked our heads together, and threw us back in our seats!

To add insult to injury, after school, she walked across the road, and up the lane to the farmhouse to tell our folks about our misbehavior. In those days, parents supported the teachers, and if you got into trouble at school, you were sure to get it when you got home.

Sinc and I both liked E.T. Demar, who taught the Sixth, Seventh and Eighth grades. He was a grey-haired, grey-bearded schoolmaster who had taught my Dad when he was in school, then stayed long enough to teach me and my two sisters, Ann and Catherine. We all loved and respected him.

He expected us to know how to read and write properly, and taught the *Spencerian* style of writing, which was accomplished by using the whole hand in free movement. He emphasized knowing how to spell, to add and subtract, and to know geography as well. On Friday afternoons he would hold *spelling bees,* or mental arithmetic and geography questions. He made learning fun, and did not have to hit us in the head to accomplish it.

Mr. Demar would play baseball with us, preferring to bat above anything else. He would play until a ball he had hit broke one of the school windows; then he would quit. He would throw down the bat and walk away with a smile on his face; until the next game, and the next broken window.

Soccer was a little bit rough for him, but he stood on the side-lines, cheering us on. I guess Sinc and I would have done just about anything for Mr. Demar. We decided we liked men teachers more than flippity teachers with rings on their fingers, or ones with the strength of a prize-fighter!

CHAPTER FIVE
Halleys Comet, and the Move to Indian Hill

It was the time of Halley's Comet in 1910, that my parents moved out of Madeira to a ten-acre farm on Indian Hill. I remember my father getting us all out of bed to point out the comet that blazed across the sky in a fiery path. I was frightened and wondered if the world was coming to an end, and tried to recall what Sinc and I might have done to keep us out of Heaven.

I missed the farm with all of my relatives, but I now had my own horse, Old Bess, who had been given to my father when her owners bought a car and no longer needed a *carriage horse*. She trotted, and was a smooth horse to ride. She had one idiosyncrasy when she was hitched to a buggy or a cart. Once she was hitched, she did not like to be kept waiting. If we lingered after church to talk with friends, and my Dad had the reins in hand; Bess became impatient.

On one occasion he had been talking for some time, all the time holding the reins, and Bess was waiting impatiently. When he was finally ready to go, he snapped the reins and said "Giddyap, Bessie!" and she did. She bolted, pulling him off the buggy.

On other occasions, she would rear up on her hind legs when she felt the conversation had gone on long enough. She was one lady who did not like to be kept waiting.

Secretly, we were happy that Bess did not like long conversations. Neither did we. Sinc and I were anxious to slip away while everyone was visiting, grab a pair of old bib-overalls we had stashed away in the barn, throw a blanket over Bess, and take off for the old swimming hole, riding bareback in our Sunday clothes.

Sometimes, someone would find the overalls and take them in to wash, and at those times, we were forced to go "skinny dipping" We'd take off our Sunday clothes, and hide them, in case anyone came by and decided to take them, leaving us to ride Bess home like *Lady Godiva*.

Old Bess had a taste for flapjacks. When I was in my mid-teens I used to ride to Milford to the Little Miami River on Bess, and go fishing. I'd find a riffle, turn over a few rocks and catch some crawdads to use as bait. I soon learned that bass would take a soft-shelled crawdad for bait quicker than a hard-shelled one. The channel cats would eat the tails when I used the hard-shelled crawdads.

Sometimes I would stay overnight on these fishing trips. I had a formula for making flapjacks that were easy to make, and delicious to eat. I'd put some sugar in the batter so I didn't have to carry any syrup with me. I even learned to flip them in the air without using a pancake turner.

On one of these trips I had been out fishing early and came back to camp with a taste for a big stack of flapjacks. After I had finished making them I went to a spring nearby to get water to make coffee. I was thinking how delicious they were going to taste. They smelled so good I could hardly wait to get the coffee made so I could start eating.

Well, I told you that Bess was a lady who did not like to be kept waiting, and that included waiting for breakfast. When I came back from the spring with the water to make coffee, there was Bess finishing the last flapjack! She raised her head as I walked into camp, eyed me cooly, whinnied and sauntered back to where she had been standing. I'm not sure, but that whinny sounded just like "*Sucker!*" I had just coffee for breakfast that morning.

There were several ice ponds where we could ice skate in the wintertime. Summer's Pond was not very large, but it was located in town, behind the saloon. The saloon keepers used to cut blocks of ice from the pond in the winter, then store it in the icehouse for keeping the beer cool in the summertime.

Cutting the blocks of ice always left a square pool of open water. The skaters used to dare each other to see how close one could skate to the edge of these open pools without falling in. One time we were playing follow-the-leader when I skated close to the edge of the pool on my left skate, with my right leg extended over the open water.

I don't recall what girl I was trying to impress, but I found the open pool and the danger enticing. The first couple of times I made it, which only added to my desire to be daring and show up the other boys.

On the third go-around I looked away from the pool to see if everyone was watching, and my skate caught on a stick of willow. Down I went, right into the pool of icy water! I had to have help getting out, and I was soaked. Blue from the cold, but red-faced, I hurriedly took my skates off, then ran down the railroad tracks to the station where I knew there would be a warm fire.

Mr. Ozier, the railroad station master, kept a fire going in the large pot-bellied stove. I rotated around the stove; my teeth chattering, trying to dry my clothes before my Dad came home on the six o'clock train.

My clothes had shrunk about three inches above my wrists, and the legs were high above my shoe-tops. I was a pitiful looking sight as I ran all the way home, after I heard the train whistle. I knew my Dad would be following a few minutes later.

I expected a scolding, but no one said anything to me. Warm clothes were provided and I was simply told to come and eat supper. The memory of the two uncles who had drowned in the Miami River a few years before, was still fresh in their minds.

Hosbrook's Pond was a long stretch of water with a bridge across the upper end. This was our favorite pond. In the summertime we would catch frogs, or fish, and would sometimes chase the water snakes. At the deep end of it we could swim, shouting and splashing and pushing each other.

We would search the woods around the pond and watch for trees with branches that had a bend in them to use as hockey sticks in the winter. We would whittle the sticks and use a tin can or a block of wood for a puck. There were no special rules to our game of hockey; we would just skate and see who could hit the puck the most often.

Some of the older boys, like Boots Reeder and Pete Morrill specialized in figure skating, but that was too tame for Sinc and me. When we were in high school we would skate there at night. It was the one time you could put your arm around a girl and not be called a sissy.

We would place lanterns around the holes that were left after the ice blocks had been taken out for the icehouse. This was to warn the skaters to avoid that area. One night, someone moved the lanterns by the edge of the pool. Pete Morrill was skating alone. As he skated behind the lanterns he went into the pool. He didn't even stop to take off his skates but ran all the way home in his wet clothes. It was a foolish prank that could have cost him his life. No one ever admitted moving the lanterns, but I am sure they never forgot it.

Aunt Kate, the youngest aunt, who taught school, and was one of the breadwinners for the family, had a long-time boyfriend, Jim Erskine. For twenty years, Jim was Aunt Kate's beau, but they never married. He would come *courtin'* in his buggy, and bring her small gifts. They never dated anyone else, and the last I can remember of Jim is that he just sort of shriveled up. My aunt Kate never left the farm, and Jim never looked for anyone else.

Jim's younger sister, Maggie Erskine, fell in love with my Uncle George, but unlike Aunt Kate and Jim; they married and settled down on a farm in Madeira.

Aunt Teen never married, and as I remember, never had a boyfriend. She seemed content to stay on the farm and cook for the boys, although I can't see why, when Grandma Baines used to whack the girls with her cane. Perhaps Grandma Baines destroyed any self-confidence the girls might have had.

Aunt Mary married a Swede named Gus, and moved to Bayview, Long Island. She did not stay there more than a year when she decided that Long Island, and married life, were not to her liking. She divorced Gus and came back to the farm.

Uncle Jim joined the Navy and made it a career. He had been stung by a bumble bee and had an allergic reaction when he was a young man, so his doctor advised him to move to the city to get away from bumble bees. He later married a girl from Edgewater, New Jersey, and bought a home there. When I was taking medical training, and was down to my last dime in New York; I used that dime for the ferry, to visit Uncle Jim, and stayed with them for awhile.

Sinc, whom I was so close to while I was growing up, married a school teacher named Woodsey. Sinc never went to college. Alec, who was close to our age, roomed with me in my first two years of college. He majored in agriculture, then went back to Madiera after he graduated, and he and Sinc bought a farm together. Alec never married.

Will, who had gone to Alaska to seek his fortune when we were just kids, left Alaska (apparently with money) and married someone in Yakima, Washington, and settled there. Later, when I was a doctor in the Navy, Nita and I visited with them in Yakima.

Uncle Frank never married. He was always sickly, and later died of Bright's disease when he was still a young man, about thirty-five. He could never do heavy work, so when Alec, Sinc and I picked berries and packed them in boxes; Frank would hitch up Nellie, the Texas cow-pony, and take us in the spring-wagon to Norwood; a wealthy residential area, to sell the berries.

We would go to the back door where the kitchens were located, and give our sales-pitch to the cook. She would usually buy the baskets for about fifteen cents. Frank would make change for us, and after we had sold all the berries, he would stop and buy us a *double-dipper* ice cream cone. We always looked forward to our pay, in the form of a cone. We sometimes stopped off at the ol' swimming hole after we had ice cream, and went skinny dipping.

We were still a close-knit family, and in the summertime; I would go back to Grandad Bain's farm with my uncles. On Saturdays, I would return to our own place to clean the yard and the chicken coops, then get ready for church the following day. After church, I would go back to Grandad's farm. These were happy times for me, and apparently for most of the family, because few of us ever wanted to leave.

I was growing up, and my chores and responsibilites were multiplying. Dad had built a large house on his ten acres, and it was my responsibilty to take care of the farm animals, the barn and a large chicken house.

Dad started raising fancy Wyandottes and entering them in shows. He and Mother would wash the chickens, then dry them in the warmth of the open oven door. They would clean the dirt from under the scales of the chicken's legs with toothpicks, and the chickens loved it. Snow White, a large rooster, especially liked the attention, and would pose proudly when Dad placed him on the kitchen table. He and Mother won numerous blue ribbons with their Wyandottes.

Sinc and I no longer had the time to get into mischief. I had decided that I was going to become a doctor, and I had chosen classes in high school that would prepare me for my entry into college. Although I played football that first year, I was studying Latin, English, algebra and history. I would practice football after school, then catch the six o'clock train for home, do my chores, eat supper, and then study.

I had joined a literary club in high school, and was later elected president. Ray Dunning, the new president was hurt in a football game, and I regret that I was the cause of his broken leg. The coach had asked me to do a rolling block on Ray in football practice. When I threw the block, I hit Ray in the lower legs, and heard the bones in his right leg snap.

Someone called Dr. Knight, and after he arrived, several of us held Ray in the seat of Dr. Knight's car, while others extended his leg to try and hold the splint in place. We took him home and got him into bed. Two flatirons were used as weights for traction, and hung over the bed.

Johnny Clippinger and I went to the literary meeting after leaving Ray at home, in traction, and miserable. It was then that I learned this was to be Ray's first meeting as president. His leg was never right after that, and years later when I met his wife she said "So! *You're* the one who broke my husband's leg!"

I knew nothing of parliamentary procedure, and did not feel confident after I was nominated, and elected president. Mr. Ayres, who sponsored the literary club, was a great help in guiding me, and I credit his help in giving me confidence and experience. I feel that it was helpful to me when I became a member of the Utah State Legislature later in life.

On Thursday nights, when the club met, I would hurry home from school; do my chores, then ride Bess back to Madisonville, a distance of three miles. There was no other transportation at that time of the evening.

Sometimes, the city kids would borrow my horse and race her around the track while I was in the meeting, and by the time I was ready to ride home, poor Bess would be so exhausted I would have to lead her all the way home.

In 1915, Dad bought our first Ford, and what a beauty she was! It had a copper radiator, flat fenders, and a rag top, which *almost* always let down. Dad, his Panama hat folded back against his forehead in the wind, would hold his head high, arms out-stretched; clutching the wheel, and drive, mostly with the top down, so everyone could see who was driving!

My mother would clutch her hat, and caution Dad to look out for horses and buggies. She was not sure she approved of this new-fangled contraption that you could not talk to, like you did to Bess. My sisters and I loved it, and were anxious to travel.

That first summer, we drove to Angola, Indiana, about three hundred miles from Madeira. After much coaxing, Dad finally consented to letting me drive, but when I reached a speed of about twenty-miles an hour (I don't think the car had a speedometer); Dad would say, "All right! That's fast enough!"

There were no toilet facilities in the garages in 1915, so we used the out-houses outside the schools that were closed for the summer.

We stopped in a small town in northern Ohio that first night, and drove to Angola and Lake James, the following day. A three hundred mile trip was quite an undertaking then.

It was while we were at Lake James that I learned to cast for bass. We had taken a cabin at the lake and I would spend most of the day in a row boat. I would follow the lower basin up to the second basin, through Jimerson Lake to Nevada Mills. Sometimes, I would row up to Snow Lake where there was a spring, and the bass fishing was good.

After I became a doctor, and the pressures of my practice kept me awake; I would get into a *fantasy* boat; trace the shoreline of these lakes, and before I had returned to the cabin, I would be asleep.

It was that same year, when Dad bought the Ford, that I graduated from high school, and applied for admission to Ohio State in Columbus, Ohio.

CHAPTER SIX
Medical School

After graduating from high school in 1915, I entered Ohio State in Columbus, Ohio. Alec had applied for Agricultural College, so we roomed together. To make ends meet, and to help pay for my tuition; I worked as a waiter at Mrs. Joyce's Boarding House.

One of my professors, H.C. Heil, whom the students nicknamed "Old Acid Face" took his meals at the boarding house. I was instructed to bring him a cup of hot water in the morning, as soon as he appeared. He was quiet, and rarely spoke to anyone, but the simple fact that I rushed to get his hot water, put me in good standing with him. He suffered from ulcers, which may have accounted for his dour countenance.

I took pre-med, so the first two years were filled with physics, chemistry and biology, and an arts and science course. I also signed up for French, but I was so bad that the Chairman of the French Department said that he would pass me (so as not to interfere with my medical studies) *only* if I promised never to take French again!

Miss Beech, who was my professor, told me, after written exams, that I did not know as much French as she thought I knew. I had made it a point to sit in the front row, and when I knew the right answer to a question my hand would fly up, and I would answer. I flirted with her outrageously, trying to charm her so she would not know how little I knew.

Even after traveling through Mexico for more than fifty years, I still do not know how to speak Spanish, except for a few words, that I have difficulty in pronouncing. I took German in high school, and despite studying Latin, I still have difficulty with the Romance languages.

In addition to my working, I also led an active social life, and my grades reflected it. When I went to register for the second semester, Dr. Landacre brought up the subject of my poor grades. "You are not very smart are you?" he growled. "You would make a better farmer than a doctor." He then told me he would recommend me to Dr. Vivian at the Agricultural College, and told me that I should give up medicine.

I had left the farm to become a doctor, and I was upset that Dr. Landacre thought I should go back to the farm. I told him so. He thought about it for awhile, then suggested that I take only one course at a time; concentrate on that, and said that I *might* make it through medical school, if I followed his suggestion. I agreed.

It wasn't long after I registered for my second semester, and made my promise to Dr. Landacre that I would cut back on my social life, and study more, that I met my future wife.

I was walking down the hall when I spotted someone up on a ladder. She was a tiny, pretty little girl, with legs to match the rest of her. I introduced myself, and from that moment on; we became inseparable. She was Juanita Hauer, who was taking nurses training. I had been dating someone else, but she had gone off to a different college, and after I met Nita; the other girl and I drifted apart.

We were both freshmen, but Nita's course was three years, and mine was four; so she graduated the year before I did. During my junior year in 1917 some of the senior students were leaving to join the army in WWI. They were being offered commissions and would make more money than they would practicing medicine as civilians.

Internship was not required in 1917 to get an M.D. degree, so all of the seniors, except Harry Caufield, left, but Harry stayed on as a senior intern. Paul Grove and I were appointed student interns and lived at the university hospital the last two years of our training.

We had not yet studied obstetrics or surgery, nor did we have training in eye, ears, nose and throat at the time, but as student interns we had the opportunity to attend all clinics and assist in all the surgery. We took turns; one of us would give the anesthesia, and one of us would assist in the surgery.

We had completed courses in anatomy, and had done basic work in physiology and neurology. We delivered babies, and took care of numerous emergencies that came into the hospital. We both gained good practical experience that helped me when I became a country doctor and had to handle emergencies alone, without a hospital or a laboratory nearby.

Nita and I were dating, despite a rule forbidding the student nurses to go out with any of the interns. We had been going together for more than a year when Nita was put in charge of obstetrics and pediatrics. The building she worked in was across from the university hospital; an old building that did not have a cook. Since she worked the night shift someone had to take a midnight lunch to her.

The night nurse in charge of the hospital did not like to leave the new building to take a lunch to Nita in the middle of the night, so she would call me. She always had an extra lunch made so I could eat with Nita. Both of us always looked forward to our time together.

On a couple of occasions, the superintendent of the hospital walked in while Nita and I were having our midnight snack together. Since that was taboo she would "punish" Nita by having her continue on the night shift. She would try to look stern when she meted out Nita's punishment, but we all knew she was doing us a favor, by letting us continue to spend a few minutes together at night.

One night, the bells started ringing upstairs in the obstetrics ward. Nita and I left our half-eaten lunches and raced upstairs. Sarah Joiner, a large black lady, was down on her knees beside a rocking chair. Sarah had given birth to her baby while she was on her knees, and the infant had fallen to the floor. The infant was tangled in the umbilical cord, and was sliding back and forth in the water that had broken. She was kicking, and squalling loudly.

We hurriedly got some clamps, tied off the cord and cut it to release the child from the mother. We then put Sarah back into the bed. We asked her why she didn't call for help. She said "Well, I've been here before, and I didn't want any of those medical students examining me, so I decided to have it by myself!"

Sarah named her baby girl after Juanita. Later that night, when the two of us delivered a little boy; the mother named the baby, George, after me. However, the poor little infant was premature and died. I don't remember the name of the mother.

About the time of Nita's graduation in June of 1920, there was a typhoid epidemic near Portsmouth, Ohio. Nita had been working with some private nursing cases at the university hospital, but after receiving a call from the Red Cross, she left for Portsmouth to help.

Before leaving for Portsmouth, Nita had a typhoid shot, but in two weeks she became gravely ill. No diagnosis was ever made as to whether or not she had contacted typhoid fever. After two weeks she was brought home with a high fever. She developed night sweats and ear trouble and remained ill for the entire summer. She continued to have problems and I don't believe she ever fully recuperated from the illness, even after we married.

During my senior year there were many extra-curricular activities; medical conventions, school plays, fraternity dances, and other formal dances. Nita was unable to attend many of the affairs because of her illness, so to keep tabs on me she appointed her younger sister Louise go with me.

Louise was a cute kid, petite like her sister; a good dancer, a good singer, and a good conversationalist. We got along fine, and later after Nita and I married, and Louise lost her husband; she would travel with us. I never met two sisters who were so compatible, and both Nita and I were to enjoy her company for more than fifty years, on trips through Mexico and Central America.

Nita and I planned to be married the day after I graduated, so I had to find a place to practice. An old doctor friend of my father's, Dr. Streuble, passed away before my graduation, leaving a practice in Dayton, Kentucky, across the river from Cincinnati.

The town of Dayton had a population of approximately eight thousand. There were about ten thousand more in the adjoining town of Bellvue, and about twenty-five thousand in Newport, Kentucky. There was a small hospital, Spears Memorial where I could send my patients; so Nita and I decided to take over Dr. Streuble's practice.

I had passed my Kentucky State Board Exam in May, 1921, so Nita and I were married the day after my graduation from Ohio State, June 14, 1921. My parents came to Columbus on the train to attend the small wedding, held in Nita's family home. I borrowed $8.00 from Dad to buy the plain gold band I placed on Nita's finger. I don't know who paid the minister, or if he even got paid!

I don't even remember what Nita wore, but I wore my old Sunday suit that had seen me through college and medical school. My mother, who had wanted me to marry someone else, was aloof, and did nothing to make my new wife feel welcome.

We all went back on the train together, and our wedding night was spent in my old bedroom at the farm. Nita met the Baines for the first time. My father liked her, and so did Grandma Baines. The aunts and uncles tried to make up for my mother's coldness. Grandad Baines had died while I was in medical school.

The next day, we went to Cincinnati and picked out furniture to be shipped to Dayton, and from there, we took the train to Kentucky.

All of Dr. Streuble's instruments were still in a cabinet in his office. He had been dead for almost a year, so our first day in the office was spent cleaning and sterilizing. His old black bag became my first doctor's bag. We spread out the instruments and equipment in the kitchen and shined them the best we could.

We had bought furniture but it had not been delivered, so a mattress that we found on the floor was our first bed in our new "home."

There was another doctor in town who was quite old, Dr. Weber, so he referred a confinement case to me shortly after we arrived. We were tired from the move, the cleaning, and the discomfort of sleeping on a lumpy mattress on a hard floor. We were scarcely awake when we heard the doorbell ring, then a whistle, out in the hall.

We were still upstairs, and after some scrambling around; we learned that Dr. Streuble had a speaking tube on the porch downstairs. When someone wanted the doctor, they would blow on the tube and could talk to anyone upstairs.

A tall, lanky man with a shock of black hair, said his name was George Ilg, and his wife was having a baby. He told me that Dr. Weber said I should go to this address right away. He scrawled an address on a piece of paper, and after some difficulty making out the address; I hurriedly dressed and ran to pack my bag. Nita and I gathered up instruments and after re-checking the address I took off down the street. I had no car, so I had to walk rapidly several blocks away to where the mother was in labor.

When I arrived, out-of-breath; I found that I did not have anything that I needed; no scissors, no hemostats, no ergotrates, no pituitrin, no syringes, and no cord tie! I raced into the kitchen and gathered some newspaper for the mother to have her baby on, then got a paring knife and two pieces of string to tie the umbilical cord. I was embarrassed, that on my first case, in a new town; I had so little to work with.

Despite everything, the baby was delivered without complication, and the mother was good-natured about the primitive tools. I cannot remember whether I delivered a boy or a girl.

It turned out to be a rough summer for us. We did not take a vacation that year because we had to stay home and try to build up a practice. Things were slow and the economy was in a depressed state in 1921. People were out of work and there was no insurance or medicare as there is today.

On Sundays, we would go to the Presbyterian church, and after church, Dr. Ervin (whose son would later marry Nita's sister, Louise), would introduce us to help us get patients. The trouble was, no one ever got sick!

In July of that year, Mr. Perry, one of the parishoners who was on the City Council helped me get appointed City Physician, or City Health Officer. It paid the grand total of one hundred dollars per year! Since I had no car; I had to walk, or take a streetcar to visit my patients.

My mortgage was sixty dollars a month and it was six months before I earned enough money to make the payments without help from Dad. There were nine or ten other doctors in Dayton so when they did not want to make a house call; they would refer patients to me. This is the only thing that kept me going in the beginning. I took the cases they did not want.

Dr. Senior, who was about eighty-five, asked me to take care of one of his confinement cases since he had to go out of town to take care of a gun-shot wound in someone's abdomen. When I arrived at the expectant mother's home, I gave her a little chloroform to ease her pains a bit.

It was three or four o'clock in the morning, when the old doctor arrived; very tired. He was a stuffy looking little old fellow; starched collar, starched cuffs and a starched front on his shirt. While he was scrubbing up he started a conversation with the girl's mother.

Dr. Senior said, "You were the first baby I brought into this world, when I first came here. Let's see, is your name Violet?" She replied "Yes, doctor, and you brought my daughter into this world too, and her name is Violet. And now we want you to bring us another girl."

"Well, do you have a name picked out for this baby?" the old doctor asked. "Yes," said the girl's mother. You see, my mother's name is Violet, my name is Violet, and my daughter's name is Violet. So, when this baby is born, we will name her Violet too."

After awhile, when the baby was delivered, and Dr. Senior was holding the baby up to give it a little spank to get it to cry; he said, "Well, Violet, you are going to have to change the baby's name. *This* violet has a stem on it!"

CHAPTER SEVEN
The Anti-Medical Liberty League

As City Health Officer, part of my duty was to take care of the calls on welfare patients. There were many poor people living along the Ohio River-front in house-boats, or shanty-boats. That summer we had five cases of typhoid from the river people. They got their drinking water from a spring on the side of the river bank, which I suspect was the outflow from someone's sewer.

When I first told the Health Department that we had some cases of typhoid fever, the man in charge of the Health office turned to the others in the office and sneered, "Everytime we get a new doctor in town; we have an epidemic." I held evidence in my hands, but I do not recall that the man ever apologized for his insolence.

That fall, we decided to try and enforce immunizations. Most of the people had not been vaccinated, making any outbreak of smallpox or diptheria serious. A loosely-knit group of people calling themselves *The Anti-Medical Liberty League* began to oppose us on immunizations. The group included chiropractors. Tempers flared on both sides and sometimes pistols were used to make a point.

There was a confrontation between a teacher and a parent over a smallpox immunization where both of them were waving pistols in the schoolroom. These people were more afraid of shots than they were of the diseases they might get.

During the period of upheaval, I received an anonymous letter saying that the writer was going to climb up to the second floor (where I lived) and choke me to death. For a few days, I looked over my shoulder, but then I forgot about it. I suspect that the letter-writer was the one who threatened the principal of the school with a gun. All this over immunizations!

We took the case to court, and lost. We learned that we could not legally force someone to have immunization against their will. There was one positive aspect to the court battle, people learned that I was in town.

Most doctors dispensed their own medicines. Detail men from various pharmaceutical companies called on doctors and gave their sales pitch on medicines. We always had samples on hand, so I would give them to those I felt could least afford to buy them.

My Uncle Will, who had practiced medicine on the Ohio river bottoms before me, always threw in a few quinine pills for malaria, along with a physic. He said that they all had a little malaria, and that a good physic never hurt anybody.

One day one of my welfare patients, Sally, stopped by the office to get some pills for her mother; whom I had seen earlier in the day. She said, "I ain't got no money for the medicine, Doc." I assured her she did not need any; that I was going to give her the pills anyway.

The only bottle I had to put the pills in was a large one. Sally watched me as I poured out the few pills needed for her mother's illness. As I handed her the partially filled bottle she said, "Doc! If you are going to *give* them to me, Why didn't you fill 'er up?"

One of my jobs as City Health Officer was to treat the welfare and indigent patients at Spears Memorial Hospital. One night I was called to treat a man who claimed to have been injured by a streetcar. The brakeman and conductor had called a patrolman to take the man to a hospital. When I received the call; I was suspicious. I told the patrolman to hold the man because I was sure he was someone I had seen before.

"It isn't possible" the patrolman told me. "He is not from this area." It was the middle of the night when I arrived at the jail. The man was standing up in the cell; a cap hiding part of his face. "I know you," I exclaimed. I turned to the policeman and said "Bring him out into the light so I can see him better."

Without having the man remove his cap I described a scar behind his left ear, in the left occipital region. I told them there would be a depression in the middle of it where the man had undergone a trephine operation.

I then told them the man standing before me had pulled the same trick three years before while I was interning at University Hospital in Columbus. He had faked a convulsion at the end of the Neal streetcar line, and we had kept him overnight when the brakeman brought him in for observation.

He had told us that he had been injured, and that the streetcar people would send up information on the accident. He said that they would be responsible for his medical expenses. When we took him to the ward to put him to bed he made such a fuss that we gave him a hypo and told him to quiet down. That was just what he wanted. When we found out the next day that the address, and the information he had given us was false; we threw him out of the hospital. The faked accident was simply a ruse to get morphine.

The policeman checked the man and found that the scar I described was where I had said it would be. "Well, what shall we do with him?" he asked. "As far as I'm concerned, I'd just give him a nickel for carfare and send him off down the road," I answered. So, that is what we did. It was a coincidence that he happened to come to someone three years later who had a similar experience with him in another city, and in another hospital.

There were occasions when I packed a gun in my belt. Some of my calls were made late at night in a bad section of the city. I would walk down dark hallways to call on someone who had been injured, or was ill. It was at times like that, I asked myself why I ever became a doctor!

When school started in the fall, there were three teachers, Denny, Bobby and Polly, who came to our house and said they needed a place to live. That helped us pay our mortgage.

That winter, I was appointed to the Eye Staff at Spears Memorial. I had more patients now, and with three tenants, our finances were improving. The winter of 1921-1922 we had a flu epidemic and we were kept busy making house calls and seeing patients in our office.

By the end of the the second year, our two-room office was too small to handle the number of patients. A new store was being built across from the bank on the main corner of town. We decided to sell the house and lease the other half of one of the stores owned by Mr. Rifkin.

We could live upstairs and have our practice downstairs. That would give us a waiting room, two treatment rooms, and a consultation room. We were now doing prenatal care and well-baby clinics for Metropolitan Insurance Company, as well.

At the end of four years, we had a nice apartment, a large office, and a thriving practice. We had little leisure time. Sometimes on a Sunday afternoon, we would take off a few hours to visit our family across the river, twenty miles away.

Louise, Nita's sister had a job singing on the vaudeville circuit. She developed singer's nodes on her throat, so she had to give up singing. She came to visit us in 1922 and got a job with Proctor and Gamble while she was there. We invited her to move in with us that winter.

It was while she was living with us that she met her future husband, Morris Ervin, who was the son of our minister. In 1924, they married, and moved to Columbus, Ohio. Morris was the political correspondent for **The Cincinnati Times Star,** and was later transferred to Washington, D.C. where they lived for the remainder of Morris' life.

Our first son, George Russell, Jr. (Duke) was born on September 24, 1924. Prior to that time, two baby girls were born to us. The first one died after a premature birth, and the second one was born dead; a knot tied in the umbilical cord.

Duke was only three or four months old when Louise became pregnant and began having difficulties in her first pregnancy. Nita went to Washington to help her younger sister. After the baby was born; Louise developed complications, so Nita extended her stay.

When Nita came back in May of 1925, she had lost so much weight that she was down to eighty-five pounds. Her normal weight had been one hundred and ten. She was suffering from extreme weakness, night-sweats, nervousness and was unable to care for our baby.

I was concerned, and took her to see Dr. Wiggers in Cincinnati to have x-rays taken of her chest. Dr. Eha, the x-ray specialist, felt there was involvement of the lungs. He suspected tuberculosis. At that time, the treatment was to put the patient in a TB sanitorium, and all I knew of TB patients is that they died. The doctors advised a change of climate, perhaps Phoenix or Tucson.

Our practice was thriving; we had a home; we were close to a hospital. Both of us were discouraged. We decided, after much discussion to seek a climate similar to Phoenix or Tucson, but where we had family.

Nita's sister Glenna, had married Jack Wilson in Las Vegas, Nevada, and they were struggling to get a small ranch going in the desert. We sold our practice in Dayton, and our lease with Mr. Rifkin, then headed west in early June, 1925.

We wrote Jack and Glenna to tell them we were coming to see them. Then, just before we left, we sent a telegram that we would be arriving by train in two or three days. We had sold our car so the trip would not be as hard on Nita.

I still remember the evening our train pulled into Las Vegas. The thermometer at the station registered 117 degrees. The trip had been hot and miserable. There was no air conditioning in the train, and whatever air we got was from the open windows, which blew cinders into our eyes, and smoke, when we went through a tunnel. It was especially hard on Nita and the baby.

No one was there to meet us. We found lodging for the night in a room that had no cooling system. The baby was cranky, and Nita and I were ready to turn around and go back to a cooler climate.

Boy, our airedale, that we had brought with us from Kentucky, growled his displeasure everytime someone went near his crate to give him water during the long train ride. The porter would put his dish down and run. When our train stopped for any length of time, I would go back and walk him along the station. I have never seen an animal so happy to get into a room, air-cooled or not, as Boy was. He jumped on the bed, raced around the room, and barked his approval after getting out of the crate that had been his home for several days.

The next morning, we looked up the sheriff. In some of the letters we had received from Glenna, she had mentioned a friend, Spud Lake, who was the local sheriff. He said he would be glad to drive the three of us, and the dog, out to Glenna and Jack's ranch. The ranch was twenty-five miles out in the desert, west of Las Vegas and at the foot of the Charleston Mountains.

Neither the letter, nor the telegram, had ever reached them, so they were surprised to see us. They quickly made us welcome and were delighted with our young son. There were no cows on the ranch, and no milk. Duke was on the bottle, so we drove back into town in Jack's Ford and bought a Toggenberg milk goat. The goat provided milk for all of us.

Jack was the number-one brick mason in Las Vegas. The Union Pacific had hired him to reline their boilers with brick. One of the things they had given him, in addition to his pay, were all the three-inch tubes that were removed from the boilers.

Jack conceived the idea of using the boiler tubing for a project to get some irrigation water into his garden. Two others, before Jack and Glenna, had tried to homestead that place and gave up when they could not get water from the two small streams into the garden area. There was a quarter-mile of gravel and sand to go through, so the water would be lost before they could get it to the garden.

Jack found that by taking a no.3 can (we had gone to the dump and picked up the large cans thrown out by restaurants), he could cut both ends of the can out and make a tube, or valve that would slip over the ends of the three-inch boiler tubing.

We had stopped at Von Tobles garage and got some old inner tubes that we cut into wide rubber bands; then slipped the rubber bands over the tubing. This made a contractable, and waterproof joint. He then built piers on which to run this tubing down to the garden.

Each day, I would drive into town in the old Ford and haul the tubing back to the ranch. The tubing had a one-eighth bend in it, which I cut off, then I would carry it up to where Jack was building the piers to lay the pipes on. After weeks of work we managed to get the water into the garden. We also planted an orchard, which was quite an accomplishment in all that heat, and with rattlesnakes a part of the scenery.

We had used part of the tubing to carry water up the hill and close to the house, to make bathing a little safer. Before that, bathing was done in the creek. One day Glenna and Nita were in the creek where there was a hole full of water that they had been using as a bathtub. As they climbed out of the creek to get dressed, they found their clothes being guarded by a large rattlesnake.

From their screams, we thought someone had been bitten, so we raced down the hill with shovels in hand. There were the girls screaming and pointing, while trying to cover their nakedness. Jack killed the rattlesnake with a shovel, and the next day we built the shower near the house.

We were at the ranch for almost three months, and in the meantime, I had been looking around for a possible residency in Las Vegas. A doctor was leaving Sunrise Hospital, and I had been assured of a residency in September of that year, 1925.

The garden, the orchard and the tubing and shower were in, so in August, we decided to take a trip into cooler country before I started my residency. We bought an old Ford truck with a Ruxell mountain-gear, an old miner's tent, and some grub. Nita's health had improved in the fresh air, and on the goat milk, but she still had not gained much weight. Before I made my final decision on where I wanted to practice we decided to drive to Cedar City, and look over Panguitch Lake.

Nita, Duke and I, and Boy, set out in the old Ford to seek our future home and practice. If we didn't find a place that was cooler; I always had the residency in Las Vegas I could go back to. We did not know then that we would spend the rest of our lives, or most of it, among the Mormons and the Paiutes.

CHAPTER EIGHT
Setting Up Our Practice in Hurricane

We traveled through southern Utah for more than two weeks. We had been in Hurricane, and liked it, then went to Panguitch and Cedar City. The people in Cedar City seemed cold and unresponsive, so we returned to Hurricane. Arden Schaefer, Park Ranger at Zion National Park, told us that he thought Hurricane would be a good place for us to set up our medical practice. It was the population center of about three thousand people within a fifty mile radius.

When we came back through Hurricane we stopped by Petty Mercantile. Charles Petty also owned the Petty Ford Agency across the street from the Isom Hotel. The hotel was situated on the north side of the street and on the other corner was the LDS Ward Hall and the Relief Society Building. Nearby was a small campground with shade trees. We parked our old truck with the miner's tent and equipment under the trees. The tent was simply a piece of tarpaulin that you hung over a limb and tied with a rope.

We walked to the drugstore and asked if the townspeople had a doctor. Iva Stanworth said they ran the last doctor out of town the week before. She suggested that we come back the following day and talk to Charles Petty, who was a Utah State Representative, and to Mr. Emley, who was the mayor.

Nita and I had left the baby sleeping in the tent, with Boy tied to the tree to watch over Duke. As we walked back to the campground we saw several people in front of our tent, held off by Boy. The baby was now awake, and crying loudly. He had crawled out of the tent and Boy had stationed himself in front of him, barking furiously at the nearby campers who were trying to pick Duke up, to comfort him.

Genevieve Isom, the daughter of Tom and Annie, brought over a melon that evening to sell. She wanted to go the movies and was told she would have to earn the money. We bought the melon for twenty-five cents, and that was our dinner.

It was Genevieve, who later taught Duke to walk, by placing his feet on hers and walking with him.

The next morning we went to Petty's store to talk to the two men. I told them I was a doctor and would like to set up a practice in Hurricane. Petty was not very friendly. "We just *ran* a doctor out of town," he said, shaking his finger for emphasis, "and *you* better have some pretty good recommendations to show who you are, or we'll run *you* out of town!"

His attitude and unfriendliness made me angry. I decided I was going to stay, just to show the insolent Mr. Petty. I told him so. I had recommendations, but I stubbornly refused to show them to this man who thought he ran the town. I soon learned that he was aptly named. Petty was only about forty-five years old, but he had the disposition and personality of a scurvy old man. The mayor, who was a sheep man, was all right.

My Kentucky and Ohio medical license were in Nevada with Glenna and Jack, along with some equipment and the rest of our clothing. I moved Nita and the baby into the hotel until I could get back with our things, and collect some money.

I called Paul Groves in Kentucky to send me whatever money he had collected on my accounts. Since we now only had seventy-five cents, after buying the melon; I had to get some money fast. Dad had helped us in the past, but we decided to try to make it on our own. We could stay at the hotel on credit, have our meals there, and we would have a place to take care of correspondence while we set up practice.

The town itself had about fifteen to eighteen hundred people in 1925. There was a residency waiting for me in Las Vegas and we asked ourselves if we should return to the security of a position in Las Vegas, with all the conveniences of a city hospital; or should we gamble, on a new town, with less than one dollar between us? We decided to gamble. I wasn't going to let some impudent upstart like Mr. Petty, stop me. This was in August of 1925.

The baby became ill with *summer complaint* the day after we moved into the hotel. I gave him only boiled water and boiled milk until he was better. Mrs. Isom said it was a good thing, because now people knew I could take care of babies. Babies sometimes lost their lives in those days, by becoming dehydrated from diarrhea. There was no refrigeration, and the bacterial count in the raw milk was high. I treated a number of babies with the boiled milk and water, and still recommend it today.

About 1890, the people on the Virgin River settlements were getting a little crowded for land they could irrigate, so they decided they would have to acquire more land for farming, and possibly for a new town. They made application for a townsite to be established on the Hurricane Bench. Their big concern then was to get water from the Virgin River onto the Bench.

LaVerkin had put in an irrigation system using water from the Virgin River by drilling through the mountain above LaVerkin. The Hurricane Canal people decided they would build a canal on the west side of the Virgin River; down and around LaVerkin Hot Springs, and come out on the bench above the town of Hurricane. Men came from the north fork of the Virgin River, and from the towns of Virgin, Grafton and Rockville, to work on the project.

Many of these men worked only in the wintertime, so it took them about seventeen years to complete the project. They worked for credit on which they could draw when the water came in. The plan was to draw for lots on Hurricane Bench, and the amount of credit they had built up would go towards the lots they drew. No one knew whether they would draw a city lot, or whether it would be farmland.

It was common knowledge that Roan Spilsbury talked some of the men who had a taste for alcohol, into trading their lots, for a keg of Toquerville wine. Some men became landowners - and some men just had hangovers!

Some of the grapes came from Santa Clara, and a winery was built by the road in Toquerville. It still stands today, but in 1925 it was no longer being used as a winery. According to Glade Peterson in the Toquerville postoffice, it was remodeled into a private home six or seven years ago (about 1982). It is a beautiful residence on the left-hand side of the highway as you drive into Toquerville from Hurricane.

Dr. Wes Larson, former professor at Southern Utah State College, who is now writing books and teaching in the SUSC Elder Hostel program, is currently doing research on the area, assisted by Lois Meyer of Toquerville. According to Dr. Larson the winery was completed in 1866, by polygamist

Conrad Nagle. It was believed that he lived there with his seven wives, but they lived in surrounding homes. In 1889, during the persecution of the polygamists, Nagle went to Arizona, and then to Mexico.

In 1892, when the High Council abolished the use of wine in the sacrament meetings; the winery was no longer used as a winery. During the time that Nagle was making wine he also had a license to make brandy. Any surplus was sold to the mining town of Silver Reef.

In The Peoples of Utah, it is written that during the Brigham Young period of Utah history; Swiss Mormons, under the leadership of Daniel Bonelli, were sent to Dixie to establish grape culture to produce wine that could be sold to travelers, and "to be indulged in to a greater or lesser degree by both Mormon and Gentile Utahns." John C. Nagle became the leader of wine production in Toquerville for many years.

Tithes were paid for with kegs of wine, according to Tom Isom, but the Church in Salt Lake City stopped accepting wine for tithing because friends along the way would sample the wine until the kegs were almost empty by the time they arrived in Salt Lake.

To get back to the building of the canal; when the men got to the shoulder of the mountain above LaVerkin Hot Springs, they ran into some problems for which they needed help. They sent a committee to the Mormon Church asking for five thousand dollars for powder and dynamite, and some cement to finish the project and bring the water to the bench above Hurricane.

Tom Isom used to tell me stories about the workers on the Hurricane Canal. In nearly every community there is a person with some peculiarity. The canal crew had a fellow named John who had a cleft palate, and a speech impediment. And in a group of workers there is usually someone who appoints himself the local comedian, and imitates the unfortunate person.

The men were teasing John one day at lunch break, "You know John, Bill sounds so much like you that I'll bet he can get in bed with your wife and make her think it is you." John bristled, and stuttered,"I'll bet my best heifer he can't!"

The bet was made. When the men came home from work each evening most of them would stop off at Henry Cornelius' store after supper to catch up on gossip, and to swap stories. One night, after the men had been aggravating John about how well Bill could imitate his voice the men agreed to try it out.

The two of them approached John's cabin, and as Bill slipped quietly into the house through the back door; John stood by the corner of the cabin where he could hear everything that was said in the darkened bedroom.

John heard Bill stop in the kitchen and fill a tin cup with water. John's wife asked "Is that you, John? Bill answered, "Yes, it's me." She asked if he had stopped at the store, and if Emma had told him that she had bought a new nightgown. From the darkened bedroom she asked if he would like to see it. Bill, pretending to be John, told her not to turn on the light; that he would see the gown in the morning.

Bill hesitated in the kitchen as he slowly drank the water, wondering if perhaps the men had pushed John too far. John's wife called from the bedroom asking what was taking him so long. Bill decided to go through with the joke; no harm could really come of it and all the men would get a big laugh out of it.

John, his ear pressed to the wall outside the house, was becoming nervous. He heard Bill walk into the bedroom, and heard the chair squeak as he sat down. Bill dropped one boot to the floor as he started to remove his boots. When the second boot dropped, and John heard Bill walk to the bed, and heard the bed squeak as he sat down; John bellowed like a bull and came charging into the house; knocking a chair down as he rushed into the bedroom, trying to get the words out. John, out of breath, turned the light on, and as his startled wife tried to cover herself, not knowing what was going on; John blurted out to Bill, still fully dressed, except for his boots, and holding his sides laughing; "Hey! Hey! You take the heifer!"

I had sent my Ohio and Kentucky license to the State office to apply for reciprocity to practice in Utah. Dr. McFarlane from Cedar City, and Dr. McGregor from St George, vouched for me. While I was waiting for my Utah State Medical license I had an opportunity to find out how cheap, and petty, Charles Petty was.

I was helping Mr. Isom load hay into the second story of their barn. It was August and suffocatingly hot in the back of the haymow where I was working. I heard the pickup, and the man in it, yelling, before I saw them. He jumped out of the truck, waving his arms. "A man's been hurt! Where's the Doc? Where's the Doc?" I was happy to get off that haymow and start practicing medicine again. This would be my first case in Hurricane; that is if you don't count Mrs. Campbell's pig.

We sped to where Charles Petty was having a cesspool dug. Charlie Cox, from Short Creek, had lost part of his finger when it was caught in the rope on the winch. Part of the finger had been torn off and had dropped into the cesspool. The tearing of the flesh had left a portion of skin that I quickly folded over, and held, to stop the bleeding.

I did not yet have my equipment from Nevada, so I borrowed a darning needle from Maggie Petty, but the needle would not go through the flesh. I then used a pair of pliers to pull the needle through to sew up the wound, and save the remaining portion of Cox' finger.

After I had sutured and cleaned up the wound, Petty asked me what I usually charged for something like that. "Ten dollars" I replied. "You don't have your Utah State license yet, have you? Petty sneered. "No. but I expect it at any time, and I *am* a licensed medical doctor in two states," I said, already bristling at what I suspected was coming next. "Then, I don't have to pay you," Petty laughed, as he walked away.

Petty had hired someone from Short Creek because he could get them for less money. Few people in Hurricane would work for what Petty was willing to pay. Petty had sent someone for me to save Cox' finger, but he welched on paying for it. There was no industrial insurance, and Petty did not intend paying for injuries suffered by *anyone* who worked for him.

My first case in Hurricane, that I thought would add ten dollars to our seventy-five cents; was never paid for by Charles Petty, Utah State Representative, owner of Petty's Mercantile, and Petty's Ford Agency.

Actually, my first case was Mrs. Cambell's pig. We were having dinner at the Isom Hotel shortly after our arrival when we heard someone whispering to Mrs. Isom; whom everyone called Aunt Annie. "I don't know. Why don't you ask him," we heard Aunt Annie tell the woman. The woman seemed upset, so I got up from the table to see what I could do for her. She asked if I could come to her home; she had an emergency.

I left my dinner, and rushed to get my doctor's bag. On the way to her house she said that she had a sow that was having difficulty delivering a litter. She asked if I knew anything about pigs. I laughed and said my uncle raised pigs and that I had helped deliver a few of them. She seemed satisfied.

When we reached her house, I scrubbed my hands and dipped them in a Lysol solution. When I examined the sow it was obvious that someone else had already been working on her. She was torn, and the little piglet that was trying to be born had its' head crosswise. In a case like that one has to push them back, then try to have their nose come down between their forefeet, coming out the narrow way of the pig, instead of crosswise.

I asked what *butcher* had been working on the unfortunate sow before I arrived. She said, "The old dentist out here thought he could put a wire loop over the pig's head and deliver it by *pulling it out!"*

The "Old Dentist" was an itinerant dentist who traveled around the country in a spring wagon with enclosed sides. A sign on the side proclaimed DENTIST, and his name. This particular dentist covered the area from Panguitch to Toquerville, Escalante, Tropic and Hurricane.

His dental patient would step up on the tailgate of the wagon, onto an improvised dental chair, and pray! To the side of the chair was a small table where he kept various instruments for pulling teeth. He didn't bother draping the patient, and nothing was given for pain. He sterilized whatever tool he was using over an alcohol lamp.

No repairs were ever made. He only pulled teeth, which he threw over his shoulder, and out of the wagon. He tried to deliver the piglets the same way, by *pulling them out.*

I told Mrs. Campbell that the sow was torn inside, and that there was nothing we could do about that, but we did deliver the piglet. After I went back to the hotel; the sow died. From that day on, when anyone was discussing my ability as a doctor, she would snort and say "Doc may know something about people; but he doesn't know a helluva lot about pigs!"

The following Sunday, Nita suggested that we ride around and get acquainted with the country. As we drove through Toquerville, crossed the bridge and started up the hill on the other side; a car pulled up behind us and motioned for us to stop.

A man jumped out of the car and ran to the driver's side and asked if I was the new doctor in Hurricane. When I said "Yes", he said there had been an accident and that he had been sent to find me. We turned around and sped to the scene of the accident, trying to keep up with the car in front of us.

Some drivers liked to coast down the winding road, leading into Toquerville. George Pace, of New Harmony, had lost control of the car he was driving, and had overturned. After examining him, I determined that he had fractured several ribs. There were two girls who had been in the car with him; one of them had a broken jaw, and the other girl had contusions.

George was in a great deal of pain and was having difficulty breathing. He looked like he was going to die. It was Sunday so most of the neighbors had gone to church. We took him to the Naegles in Toquerville, and put him to bed. I found that by putting my hand in back of him I could raise him up enough to breathe. His pulse picked up as long as I would hold him there; which I did, for the rest of the night.

The next morning, arrangements were made for Charles Petty to send over his Buick. He was the only one with a car large enough to transport someone to a hospital. We picked George up with sheets, as gently as we could, then placed him in Petty's car. I then drove George to Cedar City where I met Dr. MacFarlane, and turned the case over to him. I still had not received my license.

That incident made things a lot easier for me, because Dr. MacFarlane said that if I wanted to practice medicine in Hurricane it would be fine. He said that if there were certificates to sign, death or birth; I could sign my name, and his name too, and everything would be all right.

When the people in town saw how sick George was, and that he survived; I was given a lot of credit, whether I deserved it or not. And it did help.

When Paul Groves sent the $60.00 he collected on our accounts in Kentucky, we moved out of the hotel and into a small, but comfortable brick home. We hired a young woman, Erma Hartley, to take care of Nita, help do the housework and cooking, and to take care of the baby.

We had a telephone installed, and traded the old Ford pickup to Mr. Petty for a Model A coupe. He said that when the new models came in I could trade that one back in, but I had to promise to buy all of my gas from him. There were no speedometers on cars in 1925, so the only way he could keep track of the mileage, was by keeping track of how much gas I used. He charged me ten cents a mile, and each month I owed him from fifty to sixty dollars. He was known for his slick deals, in his favor.

Petty later took his dealership to Cedar City, and then to Salt Lake City, where, I am told he went bankrupt. He was in partnership in Hurricane with Stan Bradshaw, and when Petty went to Cedar City Bradshaw had a Chevrolet dealership in Hurricane.

I learned recently that Maggie Petty and one of her daughters was killed in an accident, while vacationing in Europe. I was sorry to hear that, because Maggie was a pleasant woman, and we liked her. She was not at all like her husband.

After buying the new car, we heard there was going to be a celebration for the opening of a new bridge in Ashfork. The opening of a bridge sixty-five years ago was a big event. Again, just as we reached Toquerville, we were stopped. Someone had telephoned ahead and said there was an emergency and that I should return at once, to Hurricane.

A boy, Jerome Leroy Gifford, about ten or twelve, had been brought in from Springdale. His foot had almost been severed by a mowing machine. His mother, Fanny Crawford Gifford, had sent him into the field where his father was mowing hay to tell his father to come in for lunch. The boy, thinking to play a trick on his father, hid in the hay. John Jones Gifford did not see his son, and as the mower approached the boy, the sickle bar hit him above the ankle, almost severing the foot.

It was a bad wound, but I could not tell how bad until I got all the bandages off the foot. Mrs. Dennett, the mid-wife and practical nurse in the area, had bandaged the foot before she, and the boy's grandmother, (I don't recall if it was Grandmother Gifford, or Grandmother Crawford) brought the boy to Hurricane.

Before I had seen the extent of the wound I thought I might be able to suture it. I gave Mrs. Dennett a small bottle of chloroform to administer a few drops to the boy. It is a difficult anesthesia to administer and before long, the boy stopped breathing. We had to use artificial respiration to revive the little fellow. I then told Mrs. Dennett she could help me, and I'd have my wife administer the anesthetic.

The tendons were severed; the Achilles tendon, and the tendons in the front of the foot. The fibula had been broken, as well as the tibia. There was just a small amount of skin that had not been severed. I knew we had to get him to a hospital. I bundled him up and drove him to St. George, but found that there was no doctor there that night. He was admitted, and kept in the hospital overnight. I drove back to Hurricane and early the next morning I drove back to the hospital and helped Dr. Woodbury suture the foot.

Some doctors would have recommended amputation, and it would have been easier, but we spent hours suturing the foot to save it. Mrs. McGregor gave the anesthetic, very lightly. The foot was then put in a cast, and I drove him back to Hurricane. We kept him at the Isom home for about ten days before taking him back to Springdale. We wanted to keep him near us so we could change dressings and make sure that he had proper care.

The boy's foot finally healed, but he was left with a limp. Years later, shortly before I stopped practicing medicine, about 1974; I received a check from Mrs. Dennett for $150.00, and a letter saying that she knew the parents had never paid for having the boy's foot taken care of. I was touched by her letter but the most important thing was knowing that the boy's foot was saved. In the life of a country doctor, it is knowing that you have saved a life, or in this case, a foot, that means more than money.

Jerome Leroy Gifford never married, and I am told that he had a lame foot for the rest of his life. He died on April 18, 1988 in Toquerville, according to his sister Sylvia, who still lives in Toquerville.

CHAPTER NINE
The Smallpox Epidemic

The night before we moved out of the Isom Hotel and into the little brick house, I delivered Florence Isom's first baby. She was my first confinement case in Hurricane.

Dr. Wilkinson, the doctor who had been *run out of town*, was considered a saint by half of the town, and a devil by the other half. Our methods of delivery were different, and I soon learned that some of the women preferred his method.

I used to use a Kelly pad and bathed the patient with sponges dipped in a lysol solution. I used rubber gloves for examinations. I would sit down at the side of the bed and examine my patient occasionally to see how the baby was progressing.

Apparently, Dr. Wilkinson just sterilized his hands in hot water, then stood with his hands over his head. He never exposed the prospective mother until the baby, hopefully, cried. He would then reach under the covers and take the baby out without exposing the woman at all.

In contrast, I always did an episiotomy and re-sutured the perineum after the baby was born; sometimes before the afterbirth was delivered, or certainly after the afterbirth. I can understand how the modesty of the mother would make her prefer the method used by Dr. Wilkinson.

After Florence Isom's baby was born and I was getting ready to go back to the hotel, Mrs. Hinton, the nurse, brought in two large four-by-four posts about 18 inches high. She wanted to put them under the foot of the bed to tip the patients feet up, and her head down. When I asked what that was for, she said that Dr. Wilkinson did that to keep the patient from bleeding.

I said, "If a patient bleeds, I surely want to know about it, but she can't sleep comfortably in that position, practically standing on her head! I had given Florence ergotrates and pituitrin so there was no reason for her to bleed. I used to give a teaspoonful of ergotrate every four, six, or eight hours depending on the amount of pain or cramps the patient had. This cut down on the amount of bleeding and helped the uterus go back into place.

I went back to the hotel and don't know if they used the posts under the bed or not. The next morning while we were eating breakfast I heard someone running up the street. There was a pounding on the door and I heard Herbert, father of the new baby, yelling "Hurry down to the house. The cord came off!"

I tried to calm him down long enough to find out if the cord came off the baby, or if the cord came off the cord. I asked if there was any bleeding. He said there was not, so I told him if there was no bleeding I would finish my breakfast, and then come down and take a look. He did not seem happy that I chose to finish my breakfast, and slammed the door as he left.

The apartment where they lived was upstairs. When I arrived, Herbert was standing in the doorway down by the street telling several people what a *louse* I was. I ignored them and started to go upstairs. He blocked my way and said "You can't go up there. I'm going to fire you!"

I pushed him aside and said "She is my patient, and my responsibility, and I am going to see what happened." He didn't try to stop me, but when I reached the upstairs and passed the bedroom; there were three or four buxom women sitting there with their arms folded over their bosoms. They were scowling, but I went past them and into the kitchen where Mrs. Hinton was bathing the baby. I looked at the baby's navel, and the cord had come off all right, which is the only time it ever happened in my fifty-odd years of practice.

Mrs. Hinton, (whom we called Aunt Mina) had gotten excited about the string coming off the cord, so she had run to the store and called Dr. Wilkinson. She told him that the new young doctor didn't know what the hell he was doing. I don't believe he came (he had been run out of town, according to Petty), but it provoked me.

When I walked out of the kitchen, and into the bedroom to examine the mother; I was ready to express my anger. I decided against it because I was new in town. They had been used to Dr. Wilkinson and his ways; they didn't know me and I didn't know them. I would simply have to prove myself, and in time perhaps, they would learn to trust me as a doctor.

By the time I opened my practice in Hurricane I had practiced for four or five years and had delivered a lot of babies. I was confident of my ability as a doctor. I looked at the sullen women and said "Dr. Wilkinson has been here for a number of years and you have gotten used to his way of doing things. For instance, putting beds up on posts which I think is ridiculous. There is no reason for it. As far as the cord is concerned, I don't know how the string came off, because it has never happened before. In the hospital we did not put a string on the cord but waited until the cord stopped pulsating, then cut, and we'd get just a few drops of blood, and that was it.

"The episiotimy is one of the things that is being done today that wasn't done in the old days. They used to let the mother tear wide open, causing a prolapsed uterus, and other problems. We do not have as many problems today because there is better care during the delivery.

(There was a theory at one time about icterus in newborn babies in which people supposed that the blood left in the cord went to the baby's liver and caused icterus."

"You people are all stock people," I continued. "Now, who ties all the belly-buttons on all the sheep, cows and horses? They have umbilical cords too.What happens to them? Nobody ties them off, and you really don't have to tie them off on babies either. In this case, Florence is all right and the baby is all right, so we don't have any problem."

I was glad I held my temper. The women had simply been upset and concerned for the new mother and for the baby. We became good friends after that, all of us. It simply took time to build up a mutual trust.

Shortly after that, Alvin Allred called me from Springdale, and said that the midwife, Mrs. Dennett had a patient with placenta praevia, and wanted me to hurry over. It was quite a distance from Hurricane to Springdale, and the roads were not as good as they are today.

Alvin later told me that from the time he called me, until the time my car sped past his store in Springdale, only 55 minutes had elapsed. He said that it was the fastest it had ever been driven. Perhaps it was at that time that my reputation as a fast driver began, and followed me for the next sixty years, until an accident, when I was in my nineties, put an end to my driving. I am told that there were many residents in Kanab who breathed a sigh of relief when "Ol' Doc Aiken" traded his car in for a cane, and an easy chair.

When I arrived at Lyle Winter's place, I found that his wife had, indeed, a placenta praevia. I was surprised and wondered how a midwife could have known what it was. I have learned, during the next sixty years of my life, that nurses, midwives and women in general, know more than we men have given them credit for in the past.

The patient was hemorrhaging severely when I arrived. I quickly scrubbed and prepared to do what I could for her, and for the baby. In a placenta praevia it is best to go through the placenta and get hold of the baby's foot, or both feet, or whatever you can get hold of and pull down to stop the bleeding. However; in the length of time that it took for Alvin to call me, and for me to arrive, the patient had bled so profusely that the baby was born dead, from exsanguination.

The mother needed a transfusion to replace the blood she had lost, but there was no blood to transfuse. I had read in *The Horse and Buggy Doctor* that when you stop the source of bleeding, no patient dies. I don't see how they could claim that no patient dies, but it improves their chances of living if the hemorraghing is stopped. After the baby was delivered, and the placenta removed, I gave the patient ergotrates and massaged the uterus and clamped it. The bleeding was stopped, and the patient lived.

After the emergency, and the patient was resting, I asked Mrs. Dennett how she knew it was a placenta praevia. She said that Mr. Winter's first wife had died of it, and so had the baby.

There were many babies being born in the Hurricane area. When Uncle Tom and Aunt Annie Isom's daughter-in-law was due to be delivered I was called to the hotel to check on her. She said that Dr. McGregor had been taking care of her but did not want to drive from St. George for the delivery. He had suggested that she call me.

She asked if I would deliver her in the Sim's position, which I did, later in the week. In the Sim's position the child is delivered while the mother is lying on her side. It is the only time that I delivered a baby in that position, but I respected the young mother's modesty, and her wish not to be exposed.

When school opened in the fall of 1925 in Hurricane, I was upset to find that the children had not had pre-school immunizations. Early in the fall I got a call from George Spendlove whose little girl had come down with the croup. She had been ill for two or three days and while looking at the child's throat I could see a vast membrane in the back of the throat. It covered the tonsils and spread down into the larynx. The poor child was croupy and obviously ill.

I was going to St. George that evening to help Dr. McGregor with an operation, so I took a smear of the exudate to examine under the microscope in his office. If it proved to be diptheria, I could get the anti-toxin, which was a new serum for diptheria, at the drugstore in St. George. There was not yet a drugstore in Hurricane.

Both of us examined the specimen under the microscope, and it confirmed my suspicions. I purchased the anti-toxin and drove back to Hurricane, arriving about ten or eleven that evening. I drove straight to the Spendlove's home and explained the use of the anti-toxin, and the dangers involved.

Due to the toxicity of diptheria, and weakening of the muscles, the heart muscles especially; a baby can collapse and die even after being given the anti-toxin.We did a sensitivity test, and I explained that even after she showed no sensitivity and we gave the anti-toxin; we would have to be very careful that the baby did not choke when the membrane came loose.

Tragically, during the night, the baby apparently got up, walked across the floor to the mother's bed, and fell over dead.

The parents were beside themselves with grief. They called me, and I went over immediately. The mother, crying and heartbroken, ran at me, screaming. She beat me with her fists, striking my head, face, and shoulders. I don't recall what the husband did, but I found myself down in the dust; still being beaten, and denounced for giving the child the anti-toxin.

When their anger was spent, I pulled myself up from the ground, dusted myself off, and went back to practicing medicine. I was crushed by the child's death. It is the part of being a doctor that I never got used to, losing a patient. No matter how long you practice, you cannot help but feel the grief the loved ones go through, when a patient is lost. I was sick at heart about the baby.

Later in the fall, Homer Englestead brought his boy in with what appeared to be smallpox. I didn't want to alarm anyone since I didn't know of any cases in the vicinity. I remembered my experience in Kentucky when the Head of the Health Department in Kentucky sneered and said that evey time a new young doctor came into town; they had an epidemic. In that case, I was proven to be right. And I was right this time, but I was reluctant to say so.

The boy did not appear to be ill. He was active and running around. No one had been immunized against smallpox, but if I was wrong and sounded the alarm, I would be ridiculed. I still was the new doctor in town and everyone was just waiting for me to make a mistake. So, I didn't say anything. I realize now that I should have had the courage to speak up and take my chances on being ridiculed.

Homer took his son home and the boy later went to a social where he let his friends play his harmonica. At the end of the incubation period, which I recall was about two weeks; we quarantined one hundred families with smallpox!

The early outbreak was among the kids, and wasn't severe. The little Wood boy had just one pustule on his back. He had a two-point fever at first, which they normally have before they break out. Then when the temperature goes down to about normal, the little pox which is similar to chicken pox, appear.

Not many of them had the pox on their faces, but mostly on their backs, arms and hands. When the small pustule gets pus in it, the temperature spikes again to a high degree. Fortunately, we had no loss of life in the epidemic.

In one of the cases among the adults, Hy Nielsen, the brother-in-law of Homer, was out with the sheep herd when one of his kids came down with smallpox. He was notified and asked to come home. I have never been able to understand it, but it was almost impossible to get these people to accept vaccinations. They were like Leola Button, who did laundry for the Nielsens. She said, *"Well, I don't see any bugs. I don't know why I should be vaccinated!"* Leola later came down with smallpox - bugs or no bugs.

Hy's wife was 8 or 9 months pregnant when she came down with smallpox, after her children had it. Her temperature rose to 102 degrees when she was delivered. The baby felt so hot in my hands that I checked his temperature and found that it was between 105 and 106 degrees! We wrapped the child in wet cloths to cool his body and try to get the temperature down.

Since the mother was suffering from smallpox when the baby was delivered I had hoped that the baby would have developed an immunity. But, after the two week incubation period, the baby came down with smallpox.

In some diseases a child develops an immunity for the first six months of life, but apparently this is not true of smallpox.

Hy, too, came down with smallpox after the incubation period. He was especially sick. I had warned him, when he was first notified that his children had smallpox, to be vaccinated. He refused, insisting that he was not going to get sick.

Hy had reason to regret not being vaccinated. His feet were so swollen that he couldn't walk. He told me he wished he could die, but he was too sick. In his miserable state he would count the pox on his hands and feet, which only made him feel worse. He said he counted eighty-seven pox on each hand. He begged for relief.

The pox had coalesced under the callouses on the soles of Hy's feet. There was a large bag of pus under the sole of each foot. I sterilized my pocket-knife and cut away the calloused soles of his foot, alleviating the pus collected there. I have never seen such a mess.

Despite Hy's wish that he could die, he eventually recovered. Jess Bliss and some of the other men were also extremely ill. It seemed to hit the men the hardest. I don't know why, but no one died in the epidemic.

The smallpox epidemic lasted about six weeks in Hurricane. Near the end of it, people in the upper Virgin Valley, Rockville and Springdale, were asking my wife and I to vaccinate them. We charged one dollar each for the vaccinations. Many of the men worked on the trail in Zion Park, so they had cash. We vaccinated one hundred people, and came away with one hundred silver dollars. We needed it, since most people paid us in trade. I splurged, and bought a gramophone with part of the money.

When we first opened our practice in Hurricane we did not have many office calls. People lived too far away to come into the office. The majority of our calls were house calls from three to fifty miles away. We did some operations in the office, such as taking out tonsils, but any other surgery was done in St. George or Cedar City.

On Christmas, in 1928, we received a large box from my parents in Ohio. After distributing presents to Nita and to Duke, I found there was a large obstetrical bag for me. In the bottom of the bag was a large copper pan, sixteen inches long, in which I could sterilize my instruments. It also contained a Kelly pad to be used on a patient's bed. In the upper compartment of the bag I could carry scales for weighing babies, and all the medication for home deliveries. It provided a complete set-up. I cannot remember a Christmas when I was more delighted with a gift.

We were starting to settle down and get acquainted with people in the area. That first Christmas horse races were held in the early afternoon. After the races we asked Claud and Annie Hirshi to accompany us to Cedar City where the show *Ramona* was playing. We stopped in Kanarraville to eat, and then went on to Cedar City for the show.

When we left Dixie it was warm and pleasant, but when we reached Cedar City there was snow and ice. We had left Duke with Erma Hartley, the girl who worked for us. While we were enjoying the show Pete from Petersen's drugstore in Cedar City tapped me on the shoulder and said that I was needed back in Hurricane for a confinement case.

There was a mile or more of sheet ice that had formed in Kanarraville, while we were in the show. Water had overflowed from a ditch onto the main highway, making driving hazardous. When we reached Hurricane we were told the case was in Short Creek, not Hurricane, an additional forty-five miles away, over the Arizona line. The distance was greater on the old road, than it is today.

The expectant mother was convulsing when I arrived. I was told that she had started convulsing early that morning when she first went into labor. They counted sixty-eight of them.

The mother was the eighteen or nineteen-year-old, polygamous wife of Price Johnson. This was her first child. She lay on a low double bed in a room so small there was scarcely room for me and the nurse, Mrs. Coleman. She was covered with four or five heavy quilts made of denim. A coal-oil lamp provided the only light in the unheated room.

Her entire body was swollen, and in-between convulsions, the poor girl was conscious. Faced with an eclampsia in a home without proper equipment I knew that we had to get the girl to a hospital, but the nearest one on the old road, was too far away.

Since Short Creek (the name was later changed to Colorado City) was a polygamous colony, the inhabitants were unwilling to be hospitalized. Despite the law against polygamy, the polygamists were not usually arrested, unless they went out of Short Creek.

Had the patient been in a hospital we might have been able to perform a caesarian section. Getting over convulsions, or eclampsia, depends on the delivery of the child. One of the questions asked when I took my Ohio State Medical Board exams was "If you should have an eclampsia case out in a farmhouse, what would you do? What procedure would you use?"

I was now confronted with just such a case. My answer to Dr. McCann, the examiner when I was taking my State Board, was that "I would *not give the patient chloroform or morphine*, but that I would get her to the nearest hospital."

But in this case, it was impossible. I did give her a sedative, a quarter-grain of morphine, which was contraindicated, but it was the only thing I had to help stop the pains. I gave a few drops of chloroform, to help stop the convulsions, but I had no other anesthetic.

I silently cursed the futility faced by these young women, in this remote section of Arizona, and wondered why any woman would let herself be a part of this. I cursed the men, the religious zealots, who married these young women, knowing that they would have no prenatal care, and that they could die, and the children they bore could die (and oftentimes did). It was a difficult life for the women, and I felt compassion for them, while hating whatever it was that made them put up with it.

The elders of the church stood in the kitchen warming their backsides, while we shivered in the cold bedroom. The husband was nowhere to be seen. I knew the baby could not live more than twenty or thirty minutes. When the baby was delivered and we knew that it was breathing, we called the elders, who gave the premature child their blessing. The baby died within a few minutes.

After the baby was delivered, the convulsions stopped. I sat with the mother and tried to console her. As I drove back to Hurricane I fought to control tears of anguish over the plight of these women, and anger at the men who put them there.

I had been with the mother most of the night, and now had to struggle to stay awake. The sun was shining into my car, making me sleepy. Several times, during the forty-five mile drive I pulled to the side of the road to sleep. I had been up for more than twenty-four hours, and I was exhausted.

Several years later, in 1931, I had a follow-up on this case after I moved my practice to Kanab. I had opened a small office at Parry Lodge. The Price Johnsons had moved from Short Creek to Lee's Ferry. The young mother who lost her child had not been well, so they moved to Fredonia. I was called, and again, she was swollen. Because of her previous history, I took a large trochar with me. I thought she might have a lot of water in her abdomen.

In eclampsia cases, the patient develops a lot of albumin, making it difficult for the kidneys to excrete the poisons. They develop liver problems in most cases, which contributes to the ascites.

When I arrived, the distraught young woman was sitting up, unable to bend over, due to the swelling. I applied a local anesthetic to her abdomen, then made a small incision and inserted the trochar. I drained off three or four gallons of fluid.

We did not have the diuretics that are available today, so I put her on digitalis. I drove back to Kanab, and then went back the following day to check on her. She was in poor shape, suffering from high blood pressure, and a deteriorating liver. The young woman died, along with the child she was carrying, that evening.

CHAPTER TEN
Rustling on the Arizona Strip

It was in the latter part of November, 1925, that I was called to assist in a coroner's inquest in Short Creek. The town marshal, Andrew Isom, said there had been a killing the day before, in a dispute over an alleged rustling of cattle.

Shortly after breakfast, Isom picked me up, and on the way out to Short Creek he told me as much as he had been told about the killing. Mr. Wells had shot his neighbor, Mr. Roner, after Roner accused Wells of stealing a calf. It was believed that Roner had been shot in the back, with the bullet coming out the victim's shoulder. The men in Short Creek were convinced there had been foul play.

The men had believed for some time that Wells had been stealing their cattle, although they had no evidence. They figured if they could pin a murder rap on Wells, they could get rid of him for good.

They found out later that Wells and his boys would drive a few head of cattle and their calves into a canyon; hold the calves in a corral, then drive the cows back out. After about two weeks, Wells and his boys would turn the calves loose; the cows would no longer claim them, so they were considered *long ears,* or *orphans,* and Wells would then put his brand on them. This was common practice among some men, and they built up their herds this way.

Roner was a one-legged fellow who drove a team of burros that pulled a spring wagon; just like the old covered-wagon days. It was said that he had previously been on the show *Covered Wagon Days,* and had come to the Arizona Strip to live out his life as a pensioner. He lived on the Utah side of the Strip.

Roner's body had been taken to Short Creek and placed in a granary. The body lay wrapped in a horse blanket, on its' back, the victim's hat had been placed over his face. There was bloody, frothy fluid from his mouth, along with some dirt, on his face.

Just as I pulled the horse blanket back from his left side his left hand came up, hitting me in the face. That raised some goose pimples on the back of my neck since I had not expected any motion from a dead man. I then reached across his body and pulled the blanket off the other side and his right hand came up in the same manner.

Roner had been shot early the previous day. He had pitched forward as he fell off his horse, landing on his face with his arms extended in front of him. The first shot had gone into the shoulder, then into the chest; which accounted for the bloody froth from the mouth. The second shot went into his back at the left lumbar region and came out the right groin.There had not been a lot of bleeding, indicating he must have died immediately.

We removed his coat and sweater, and heavy underwear. On the upper right arm there was a long crease made by the bullet before it entered his shoulder. As we pulled the clothing down over the body we saw a dark lump in the right groin. I took my pocket-knife, cut into the lump, and removed a 30-30 slug.

I needed something I could use for a probe, about two or three feet long, to determine the direction of the bullets. Outside of the granary I saw a fence made with straight wire, with no barbs on it. I asked one of the men to cut some of the wire to use as a probe. The one we put into the shoulder wound went into the chest cavity. We put the other one into the left side of the back where the bullet had entered. That one came out in the right groin where the slug had been removed.

I said, "Roner was shot in the shoulder first, then shot in the back, if Wells' story is true. If he had been shot in the back, with the bullet coming out of his right shoulder; it would have taken his shoulder off. The bullet hole is always larger where it comes out than where it enters.

"From the looks of the crease on his upper arm, Roner must have been a left-handed shooter. He must have had his gun to his left shoulder, with his right arm extended down the barrel for the bullet to make this long crease before it entered his shoulder."

The story was, as told by Wells' daughter, was that Roner had ridden up on his horse, armed, and swearing at Wells; accusing him of killing his calf. Wells was sick at the time, and his daughter had called back into the house that Roner was outside and wanted to see him.

Wells said that he came to the door and Roner had his gun pointed at him. He was swearing and appeared to be in a violent mood. Frightened for his safety, and that of his daughter, Wells reached behind the door and grabbed his .30-30, and shot first, hitting Roner in the right shoulder. Roner's horse whirled, and started to run in the opposite direction when Wells shot again. Roner fell off his horse onto his face where Wells left him until the following day.

I have been asked how Wells had time to reach behind a door and grab a gun and shoot Roner, if Roner had a gun pointing at him. Roner's gun was a .22 Savage (I had owned one like it), and it was difficult to tell by feeling, if the safety was off or on. Roner was wearing cotton gloves and may have had difficulty releasing the safety; or he may not have known that Wells would actually shoot him. Wells had two teenage sons, and they may have provoked Roner into making threats that he may not have intended carrying out.

That evening, some men who worked for the Union Pacific at the North Rim of the Grand Canyon, rode through on their way to Cedar City. Wells called to them, and said that he had shot his neighbor and asked that they go to Short Creek and notify the Justice of the Peace. He was still ill, and was not up to traveling. The sheriff at Kingman, Arizona, was notified, and he in turn had contacted Andrew Isom.

So, it was just Andrew Isom and me, and the men in Short Creek, who formed a small coroner's jury to determine who was at fault.

I think I proved to the men that Wells was justified in shooting Roner; that he had a right to protect himself, and his daughter. Roner was trespassing, armed with a loaded rifle, and yelling that he was going to kill Wells. Whether that was his intention will never be known.

It was discovered later that the calf in question had fallen into a ditch behind Roner's corral, and had died there. Ed Black, the Justice of the Peace, ordered Roner's body buried on the south side of Berry Knoll. It was the only place soft enough to bury him, since everything else was frozen. Berry Knoll was named for the Berry Brothers who were killed there, but are buried in St. George.

Lester Johnson, who was thirteen at the time, along with his brother Glenn (who later died in a ferry accident at Lee's Ferry), helped one of the Black boys bury Roner. He said "We dug down until we hit bedrock at four feet. We wanted to bury him deep enough so the coyotes wouldn't dig him up."

I believe a nephew came a few days later, but I never heard anymore about it and don't know whatever became of Wells. Roner still lies on Berry Knoll just before you reach Short Creek (now Colorado City) coming from Fredonia.

Rustling on the Arizona Strip was a serious problem in 1925. The Arizona Cattlemen's Association, in an effort to curb the rustling hired Art Burch to help track the rustler's down. The New Canaan Ranch near Short Creek, was suspected of being a rustler's hideout. It was first owned by Ben Sorensen, who then sold it to Bill Chanley. Both Chanley and Sorensen were accused of rustling.

Sorensen, it was rumored, borrowed money from Jockey Hale, who then foreclosed on the ranch. Hale then sold the ranch to Lester Johnson's father, who later sold it to the Leithheads. The Johnsons were not involved in the rustling.

Lester Johnson said that the rustlers would hide the calves in a *dugout,* and cover it with brush to deaden the bawling of the calves for their mothers. They did what Roner accused Wells of doing; of building up their herds with the *long ears* or *orphans.*

Bill Hitson, bragged that he never ate his own beef, until he was caught, with nine carcasses. Elmer Jackson laughingly told me how some of the cowhands would tell their foreman, Gid Findlay (who was totally honest), that he could sleep, and they would check the cattle for him. Findlay was foreman for the church-owned cattle herd, and it is rumored that some Fredonia herds were built up by stealing the cattle and calves from the Mormon church herds.

Art Burch would go around to the camps of the National Park Service from Grand Canyon and the Kaibab Forest, and ask the men working on the Cape Royal Road and Forest Service roads if they had any fresh meat, and who they bought it from. Burch would also watch for the tracks of coyotes and follow them to where there had been a kill (by the rustlers); check the brand on the carcass, then contact the rancher to see if he had sold a beef to anyone.

Sixty years later, an occasional rustler is brought to trial, but men don't live by the gun the way they did in the twenties, and rustling, although it is still being practiced, is not as prevalent as it was on the Arizona Strip at that time.

Descendants of some of the rustlers live in southern Utah and live respectable lives, holding positions of trust and importance. The Arizona Strip was as wild as Dodge City, or Tombstone, at times. Some of the men who lived by the gun, and rustled, still went to church on Sundays.

CHAPTER ELEVEN
Chasing the Wild Horses

It was near the end of our first year in Hurricane, about the middle of 1926, when I had my first chance to go out and chase wild horses. They were still plentiful on the Arizona Strip. This was before the cattlemen began killing the beautiful stallions and mares.

We were at a dance when some cowboys invited this "greenhorn" from Ohio, to join them that night in a wild horse chase. This was a new form of excitement for me so I readily accepted. We left the dance about midnight. I took Nita home, kissed her and the baby goodnight and took off, after changing into suitable clothes.

Our destination was Black Rock Canyon about twenty-five miles south of town. One of the fellows, Tad Ruesch, sang cowboy songs the entire distance. Grant Sanders, the other cowboy and I would occasionally join in.

The trail at Black Rock Canyon led down to a pool in the creekbed where the wild horses came to drink. When we reached the canyon we stretched ropes across the end of the canyon and hung saddle blankets on the ropes to keep our own horses from leaving. We then turned them loose on a bench, on a side hill, above the water where the wild horses would come to drink. We hoped our horses would attract them.

Reusch and Sanders argued that since I, as a doctor, was used to staying up all night anyway, they would sleep and I could watch for the wild horses. I was new at all this, so I agreed. I settled into a round stone structure about six feet high that they called the *Fort*. I found that I could sit in the bottom of it and stretch my legs out.

I heard the horses, before I saw them. It wasn't long before a band of them came by, trotting down the trail towards the water. I could scarcely keep from shouting I was so thrilled at being so close to such splendid animals. When they saw the blankets hung across the canyon, they turned; saw our horses on the bench, and ran to join them.

The cowboys had gone to sleep, so I stayed awake to make sure the horses did not come back down the trail and leave. It was daylight before the exhausted *dancers* and *singers* woke up.

The band was led by a magnificent red stallion. He appeared to be nervous, running around the band and acting as if he wanted them to follow him out of there.

I stretched my legs, climbed out of the fort, and joined Reusch and Sanders down in the canyon. We all had our eyes on the stallion. As we saddled up and got our lassoes; the stallion circled, picked out Grant, then laid his ears back, and with a loud scream took out after him. Grant lost no time in getting out of the way.

The stallion ran up the side of the hill to the top of the mesa, stopped, and looked back at the three of us. Silhouetted against the early morning sky in red rock country, he was the most beautiful animal I had ever seen. I had read about wild horses, but had never expected to see anything like that stallion. He was whinnying for his band to join him.

Since we did not want the mares, and the red stallion had evaded us, there was nothing to do but turn around and ride the twenty-five miles back to town; eat breakfast and get some sleep. The boys had their sleep, but I was red-eyed and tired. I looked forward to some hot coffee, a good breakfast and a hot bath.

That summer I met Fern Esplin who was to become a good friend and my patient. He was a sheep man who kept part of his herd on the Arizona Strip. He also had a place at the end of Duck Creek on Cedar Mountain. He lived there in the summertime.

He ran his dry sheep on Cedar Ridge on the Arizona Strip, an area noted for the large number of wild horses there. Fern knew I liked to ride, and I told him about my one experience in trying to chase wild horses. My sister, Catherine, was visiting us shortly after I met Fern, so he invited the three of us to join him at his camp on Cedar Mountain.

We arrived late in the afternoon, the two girls from Ohio were as excited as I was to share a regular sheepherder's dinner, which proved to be delicious, eaten out under the stars and in the fresh air. The dinner consisted of mutton chops, potatoes fried in a dutch oven, homemade biscuits, and canned peaches for dessert. We lingered over coffee, and as the fire died down; we would add enough wood to keep the flames flickering. We kept this up, while exchanging stories and talking, until three o'clock in the morning. Fern had a record player that you cranked, and a scratched record that played "Three O'clock in the Morning" When the record reached the crack it would repeat "o'clock, o'clock, o'clock."

It was five o'clock, when we all got up, and after only two hours sleep, had breakfast, saddled our horses, and rode down to Clay Hole Wash, a distance of about nine miles from camp. Fern didn't carry a canteen with him, but took two cans of canned grapes along, and drank the juice from that. He considered the juice from the grapes the best thirst-quencher he could think of. I had to agree with him.

I was riding Fern's regular saddle horse while Fern rode a horse he called "Old Bud." His idea was to ride down into Clay Hole Wash where there were several pools of water. It was the only water for miles around for the wild horses to drink.

When we reached the wash we took the saddles off our horses and got down under the banks, which were about ten feet high. We then went up on the edge of the bank, took off our hats, and held our heads over the edge of the bank to watch for the wild horses to come in.

We would first see a cloud of dust, then out of the dust would appear a band of horses, two or three hundred yards from where we were. The horses would trot, then stop and look around. They did this several times. In the lead were four or five mares with colts, then came three or four yearlings, followed by the stallion.

We estimated that between four or five hundred wild horses came in to water that day.

About noon, as Fern and I were watching one band come in, Fern spotted a couple of nice yearlings, and suggested that we try to catch them. He said "I'll take the Black one and you take the Bay." I agreed. We left Nita and Catherine at the wash while Fern and I prepared to go after the yearlings.

The mares and colts came up to the edge of Clay Hole Wash, then trotted down into the wash to drink. The stallion did not see us since he was looking out over the horizon, and we were below him. When the mares and the colts finished drinking, they started out the other side, and the stallion started down to drink.

As the stallion started in, Fern said, "Well, this is the time to take two of them." We jumped on our horses, riding bareback. Fern cautioned me to "keep low on your horse and you won't scare them. If you sit straight up, it seems unusual to them, and it frightens them."

When we reached the wash, we took off at a dead gallop, and we were going as fast as we could go when we came up out of there. On top of the wash, we came upon the horses we had seen. When they saw us they took off in a big cloud of dust, obstructing our view and making it difficult for us because the terrain was rough. There were many washes, some of them fairly deep. Trying to ride over that kind of terrain at full speed and find a wild horse too, you had to have a lot of confidence in your own horse.

Fern had told me his method for catching a wild horse, and I was hoping I could remember, while I was looking for the yearling I was supposed to go after. I couldn't find him, but I saw a big stallion right in front of me. Now here was one I could be proud of catching. As I rode alongside him I reached down to get him by the tail, but when he saw me he took off, leaving me spitting dust and coughing.

Fern was off someplace else looking for his yearling, so I was left pretty much by myself. We had apparently disturbed another band of horses, and they were now trying to cross in front of me; a peculiarity of wild horses.

One mare tried to cross in front of me which made it fairly easy for me to catch up to her. Following Fern's instructions, I reached down, got her by the tail, and pulled my own horse off to the left. As I started to pull I began pulling myself off my horse, since I was riding bareback. Rather than holding onto her tail with my hand, I tucked the tail under my right knee, and tried to pull my horse over to the left.

The wild mare got her feet tangled up, and over she went. When I felt that release I jumped to the ground and dropped the reins. As I started back to the mare I saw that she was sitting on her hind legs with her front feet in front of her. I made a flying tackle and grabbed her by the neck. I had a Mormon hobble, a strap hobble worn around the waist as a belt. The horse was struggling and I had trouble trying to hold her head down, so to keep her from moving, I jumped on her front legs with my high-heeled boots. I pulled her head over and put her right ear in my mouth, and hung onto that with my teeth. I then reached down and unfastened the belt from around my waist, and hobbled the front legs.

After I had the mare hobbled, I looked around and found that Irvin, the horse I was riding, had disappeared. When we saddled up that morning Fern said that he was short a bridle, so we had used a Shetland pony bridle on Irvin.

When I jumped off my horse and dropped the reins they didn't drop down far enough to reach the ground, so when the wild band came past, Irvin just joined them.

From up the country a mile or so, Fern saw that I was afoot, and my horse was gone. Fern thought more of Irvin than he did of anything else. He rode Old

Bud down and we began looking at the tracks. Luckily for us, Irvin had half a shoe on one of his feet, making it possible to track him all the way down to the Franklin Heaton reservoir, a distance of about eleven miles. Fern had to catch his horse, separate it from the wild band, then ride him back to camp, so it was a long ride by the time he got back.

We had left the horses hobbled that the two of us had caught, back at Clayhole Wash, along with our saddles, and the two girls. We got our saddles and our lassoes, then went to where the horses were, to release them. To do this, you throw a loop around the horses front or hind feet (it doesn't make any difference), then give him a little *boo,* and when he jumps; you can pull his feet out from under him, and down he goes. The hobble can then be taken off, and when he gets up; he kicks loose from the rope, and is free.

CHAPTER TWELVE
The Anderson Ranch

In Hurricane, most homes were built on about a quarter of an acre, with a barn and a small orchard of peaches, pears, apple and cherry trees. Almost everyone had their own vegetable garden.

The people who had a plot of ground of ten acres or more allotted an acre to sorghum, or sugar cane. Since not everyone had a mill, nor the vat for extracting the syrup from the cane, they would take their produce to someone who did. That was a crop that gave them a cash product.

One time, when I owed a man seventy-five dollars for some work he had done, I gave him one hundred gallons of sorghum from a man in the sugar cane business who owed me seventy-five dollars. The sorghum was valued at seventy-five cents a gallon, so all of us were happy with the trade; especially the man who received the one hundred gallons. He took it up north and sold it at a profit.

The men generally raised alfalfa, as well. A good, irrigated field would produce three or four cuttings; the fourth cutting would be left for winter pasture.

Most families had a milk cow. If the cow had a female calf, the farmer would keep it to produce more milk, and if it was a male calf, it would be butchered when it reached a certain size.

A family nearly always had a team and wagon. In the Fall, the man of the house would team up with other men who had teams, and they would drive to *Smith's Mesa,* or some other mesa for juniper and pine wood for the winter. The wood provided fuel for both cooking and heating, so they did not have to spend much money to heat their homes.

There was electricity in town that came from Southern Utah Power, which had a hydro plant in LaVerkin. This was a fairly cheap source of power.

There were one or two sheepmen, and cattlemen in the towns of Hurricane, LaVerkin, Toquerville, Rockville and Springdale. Springdale, however, was getting to be more of a tourist town, since it was the one closest to Zion National Park.

There were several boys in Hurricane who had a little wagon, and an old horse. Every afternoon, during the growing season, they would knock on the door and ask my wife what garden produce she would like to have. No matter what she ordered: corn, beans, or any other vegetable grown in the area, they would return with her order, and the price never varied; it was always two-bits.

Nita and I both enjoyed horseback riding, and during the Christmas holidays, often raced our horses against most of the horses in town. We would then take them to Toquerville and race there. We had accumulated several horses, in return for medical services, so we were becoming quite horse-conscious. I soon found out though, that when I took a horse in trade; I had to have feed for them, so I traded for feed. That made it a little expensive for us, but we had a lot of fun horse trading.

One time, when Top Stout's kids had quinsy (in those days we didn't have sulfa or penicillin) we waited until the pustule came to a head, and then lanced it. Without the antibiotics it took a little time for healing.

While I was taking care of the kids I noticed a beautiful little black mare in their corral. I asked where in the world they got a beautiful horse like that. Stout told me she was a wild horse, a mustang. They had caught her three years before, but they had been unable to break her enough for the young boys to ride.

I wanted that horse. She would make a nice gift for Nita at Christmas time. I didn't have much money, so I asked if Stout would be willing to make a trade, the horse for taking out tonsils later. The deal was made.

Every Christmas Eve, in Hurricane, the kids had the crazy custom of going around after they got through with the entertainment at night, and opening the corral gates and barn doors, letting all of the animals out. On Christmas morning, there were animals all over the place: cows, horses, pigs, chickens and ducks, running up and down the streets.

When I went to the Stouts to pick up Nita's Christmas present, *Little Marqueta,* was out of the corral, but headed back to Stout's barn. When I tried to get between her and the barn she nudged away from me.

I finally got hold of her long mane, jumped on her back, and away she flew towards the barn. There was a pool of water, which she jumped; then she started to crow-hop. All I could do was to hang onto her mane and pray that she didn't buck any harder.

Rowe Ballard, who ran the grain mill, spotted me hanging on to the bucking mustang. He thought I was a goner for sure, and yelled out, "There goes our doctor!"

Our airedale, Boy, thought that was great fun, so he joined in. There we were, the three of us, me hanging on for dear life; the dog chasing the horse and barking, and Little Marqueta kicking and bucking all the way down the lane. When she reached the barn; she stopped. I quickly reached over, got the bridle, and put it on. She seemed astonished, but let me put the saddle on her, and without further ado, trotted back down the lane to become Nita's horse.

I had acquired another horse that we called *Old General.* Shortly after Christmas, Nita and I went riding, me on Old General, and Nita on Little Marqueta. Suddenly, Nita's horse decided she didn't want to go any farther; wheeled around and started for home, as fast as she could go.

All I could do was to yell for Nita to hang on, when she reached the gate. When I got back to the gate, there was Nita, flat on her back in the corral. Marqueta was a spirited horse; good for racing, but Nita never did ride her much.

Quail hunting in the area was excellent, so in the fall, I learned where many of the coveys were. I borrowed an old model 12 repeating shotgun approximately thirty-three inches in length. The extractor worked, but the ejector didn't. I could pull the shell out of the barrel, but I couldn't flip it out, so I would have to tip the gun over each time. Every time I would take a shot and pull the pump back, I'd have to remember to tip the gun over to get the shell out; otherwise it wouldn't work the next time. Later in the fall, there were ducks and geese, so I spent much of my leisure time on the pond up on the bench.

Joe Simmons had a filling station at Anderson Ranch, but to augment his gasoline sales, he did a little boot-legging on the side. It was about 1926, and Lee Eagar, a young man who hauled freight from Cedar City to Hurricane, occasionally dropped off packages at Simmon's station.

One day, when Lee stopped by to deliver some packages, and while he waited for his money; he became curious about a gun lying on the table. It was an Army issue .45, and was part of Simmon's boot-legging equipment; one he kept for protection.

Lee picked up the gun and was examining it. As Joe handed the money to him, Lee handed the gun back to Joe; and for some reason, the gun accidentally discharged, hitting Lee Eagar. Both of them were surprised and looked around to see where the bullet had gone. Neither of them knew one of them had been hit.

As Lee pushed the screen door open to go out, he felt something wet on the front of his shirt. When he felt it to see what it was; there was blood on his fingers. He had felt nothing.

Joe helped him back into the station and had him lie down on the couch. He hurried to the telephone and called me in Hurricane. The boy's older brother, Walter Eagar, worked at Petty Mercantile; so I rushed over and told him what had happened. I asked him to drive with me to Anderson's Ranch, so he could talk to his brother and be a witness as to what happened. I knew that if Lee Eagar died Joe could be in trouble, unless there was a witness who could tell what happened.

As we drove, I coached him on what questions he should ask his brother. Since Lee had been shot in the abdomen, I knew that it was serious. When we arrived at the station, Lee was on the couch, lucid, but still feeling no pain. He didn't even require a hypo, or an anesthetic, as we raced him back to St. George.

On the way to St. George, I had Walter talk to his brother to verify what had happened. Lee said there was no animosity between he and Joe; they were good friends, and that it had been an accident. He did not know why the gun fired. Joe Simmons told us the same story.

When we reached St. George, Dr. Reichman was there; so we operated on Lee right away. The bullet had coursed downward into the celiac plexus, and had hit two or three large arteries, causing vast hemorrhaging. They were so badly torn, there wasn't much we could do.

Perhaps today, with blood transfusions, modern technique and equipment, and a team of specialists; we might have saved the boy, but in 1926...? We gave him a little anesthetic when we operated on him, because he was almost pulseless, and nearly dead by then. We tied up some of the bleeders, put in a pack, and sewed him up.

On the way out of the operating room, we were met by his young wife, a girl of about sixteen, who lived in Leeds. When she asked about her husband, Dr. Reichman said "I think he's going to be all right." When she was out of earshot, I objected to Dr. Reichman and asked him how he could say that. We both knew that Lee could not live with that amount of distruction. I argued that they both had a right to know the truth, in case there was anything they would like to discuss before he died.

Dr. Reichman agreed, so I told the wife to go into the room; that her husband was conscious and not in pain, and that they could talk. I told both of them there would be a few minutes for anything they wanted to discuss; that the boy could not live. I left them alone, and Lee Eagar died a few minutes later.

In April of 1926, Nita's father, whom we called Grandad Hauer, came out west to visit. He was about seventy years old at the time. He had never been out west, and was curious about the people and their habits, in this part of the country.

We had a desert cooler on the side of the house where we kept our butter and milk. Gunny sacks covered the cooler and water dripped down over the sacks, causing evaporation in the dry air, which kept the contents cool inside. Grandad Hauer had never seen anything like that in the mid-west. When he went back to Columbus he built a cooler like the one we had, but the butter ran and the meat got whiskers. He was quite upset about that. He didn't know that the humid air in Columbus did not evaporate as it did in the desert air, to provide the cooling.

Grandad was excited about the wild horses I told him about, and wanted to go along when the local men gathered their own horses. The men would release their horses south of Hurricane on the Hurricane fault, towards St. Pierce. Jockey Hale had a few stallions loose in the area, so the men would release the mares, hoping they would get bred by one of Jockey Hale's prize stallions.

In May of 1926, half a dozen of these men got together and rode out to Black Rock Canyon to where the roadway went down the side of the canyon. The road was made when the Mormon pioneers hauled timber from Mt. Trumbull to build the temple at St. George.

At the foot of the canyon, there was a place where water collected in the spring of the year. When the rest of the holes were dried up, that one still had water in it, so many of the semi-wild horses from that area would come to water there. It was a good place to catch the horses, because there was a bench at the side of the canyon that we could run the horses onto. After two or three days, there would be a sizeable bunch of horses on the bench. The men could look them over, and see which ones had colts. The mares were branded, so it was easy to establish ownership.

John Sanders was one of the men who initiated this type of wild horse round-up. They were not actually mustangs, but horses owned by ranchers who had turned them loose to graze on the open range. Reed Langston and I, with two or three other men, went along that time.

We suggested that Grandad Hauer ride in the wagon with Ep Ballard, who was closer to his age. He refused, and insisted on riding Old General the twenty-five miles to Black Rock Canyon. Old General was a gentle horse who had been ridden around the sheep camps a lot.

As we rode down the trail towards the canyon, John Sanders spotted a band of horses. Reed and I rode out around them, and drove them back towards the trail. As the horses came down, they would drop in line in back of John. They wouldn't go ahead of him, so he just kept his pace, the horses trotting along in back of him. Once the first horse started, it was easier to handle the next group because they would fall in line with the previous bunch and just follow John down the road.

The wagon was placed cross-wise at the end of the canyon; lassoes were strung across the rest of the canyon, and blankets hung over those. Reed and I rounded up quite a few horses that we led up onto the bench, then blocked the trail so they could only go down to the water, or up on the bench. One of us would sit up on the little fort to keep them from getting out that way.

The horses seemed satisfied for a couple of days on the bench. John looked the horses over, and pointed out a sorrel mare of his that had a sorrel colt. He owed me six dollars, so we made a trade; the colt for the six dollar debt. We didn't take him home that year, but we put my brand on him and came back for him the following year.

It was quite an experience for Grandad Hauer. He had never camped out much, and had rarely been on a horse, but he was game and didn't complain about saddle sores, or aching backs. He could go back to Ohio and tell his cronies about his rounding up wild horses. He took photographs of the round-up, which he shared with us. For the remainder of his life he would remember his trip out west.

CHAPTER THIRTEEN
Navajo Lodge

In June of that year, which was the opening of fishing season, we went up to Duck Creek. Duke was about a year-and-a-half at that time. George Naegle, his wife, Gertrude, Grandad Hauer, Nita, Duke and I, drove down across the Arizona Strip, and into Pipe Springs. From there we went to Fredonia, into Kanab, and up to Long Valley. We then took the Cedar Mountain Road to Dutch Creek on the way to Cedar City. The road from Cedar City over Cedar Mountain had been closed, because of the large amount of snowfall that year.

When we got to Duck Creek we camped where the creek was nearest to the road. We dug a cave in one of the large snowbanks and used that as a refrigerator for our supplies.

Four of us fished on the stream just across the road from our camp. We all caught our limit that morning of brook trout and cutthroat trout, about eight or nine inches long.

Grandad took care of the baby while George and I fished. Gertrude liked to use butter for cooking the fish. Nita preferred Crisco. We decided to have a contest to see which fish tasted better, Gertrude's or Nita's.We would alternate between the ones cooked in butter, and the ones cooked in Crisco. We all ate our fill of fish for breakfast and decided that it made no difference, as long as the fish were fresh.

We later left Duck Creek and went to Fish Lake, but after two days decided it was too cold there, so we returned to Hurricane to thaw out.

One Sunday morning, while Grandad was still with us, Ranger Don Jolley came by to say his dad, who lived on the east rim of Zion Canyon, had been very sick. Don said he would bring a horse and leave it for me at the foot of the East Rim Trail. Grandad wanted to go along, so Don said he'd bring an extra horse for him.

We drove up the canyon to the foot of the East Rim Trail where the two horses were waiting for us. Grandad and I rode from the bottom of the Zion Canyon, where the elevation was about 2800 feet, and climbed another 3,000 feet. This was a spectacular horseback ride, for an old fellow from the flatlands of Ohio.

When we reached Mr. Jolley's cabin, and I checked him over, I found that he had pnuemonia and was running a high temperature, with chills. I had brought medical supplies with me, although we had no antibiotics at that time. I gave him a cough preparation and some liquefying agents for the mucus. He eventually recovered, but pnuemonia was a serious illness in the twenties, and many people lost their lives from it.

The following year, 1927, my mother and dad came to visit. While Grandad Hauer loved the West, and everything about it; my dad hated it. He would stand and look out over the open spaces, unblemished by tall buildings and traffic, and wonder what I saw in this country. He'd peel his nails back and shake his head, and ask how I could give up civilization for this. He'd ask, "Where are all the people?" The things he hated about Utah, were the things I loved.

Dad considered himself quite a stylish dresser, and one day while he was sitting outside Parry Lodge, dressed in wool knickers, argyle socks, and a sweater; two cowboys rode by in their ten-gallon hats, their Levi-Strauss jeans, with four or five inches of the legs rolled back, and boots. When they saw Dad, they started to laugh and to point at "the dude in the funny lookin' clothes." Dad stood up and shook his fist and shouted, "You wouldn't look so damn good yourself, riding down the streets of Cincinnati!"

During his visit he met Fern Esplin. Fern invited Mother and Dad, along with Nita and me, to join him at his sheep camp on Cedar Ridge. He also took us to Toroweap.

It was at Toroweap that I took the picture that is in the book, of the 3,000 foot drop into the canyon. I sent it to *The Saturday Evening Post,* but they returned the picture with a curt note, saying sniffily, that they did not accept "trick photography."

We didn't see any wild horses on that trip, because the *Taylor Grazing Act* had gone into effect, and the wild horses were being slaughtered. When the government began dividing the Arizona Strip into parcels for grazing districts, and allotting these districts to the sheepmen and cattlemen; none of the people with livestock wanted the wild horses competing for the feed and water.

They began exterminating the horses. Some were shot; some were rounded up with low-flying planes, run into corrals and hauled away. Many were sold for dog food.

The cruelest act of all, was by some Short Creek residents who were given money by the BLM to buy bullets to kill the horses. Instead, they kept the money, then rode alongside the wild horses, cutting their throats or slashing their bellies and leaving the terrified horses to bleed to death.

I could never understand the type of bit some men used in their horse's mouths. The curbed bit would tear the flesh of the horse's tender mouths, and would make them bleed. Now that I am older, and look back over the years, I realize that many of the complaints of tender-hearted women were well founded.

When we first located in Hurricane, I thought my fishing days were over. One look at the Colorado River reminded me of what one old-timer said about it, that it was "too thick to drink, and too thin to plow." When we took our first trip to Zion Park and saw the Virgin River, muddy and laden with sand; we were sure we would never find fish there. Later, I learned that at its' source, the three creeks that made up the Virgin River, had excellent fishing; but that was a little distance up in the mountains.

We once camped for a week on the stream that flowed out of Panguitch Lake, and found the fishing there, fairly good. I had not used the proper technique, so caught only a few trout. It was only after I went on the wild-horse chasing trip with Fern that I learned there was good fishing on Cedar Mountain in the Duck, Mammoth and Assay Creeks. Fern had built a summer place at the end of Duck Creek, where it sank into the meadow. It is now called the old movie set. The movie *Flicka* was filmed there.

Fern wanted me to buy a lot up there too, and build a cabin. He helped me pick out a spot near Duck Creek Falls, where a lumber mill once stood. The elevation was about nine thousand feet, so it was cool and comfortable in the summer, but almost impassable in the winter.

That summer, I went to the Forest Service office in Cedar City to apply for a building permit. Orange Olsen, Superintendent of the Dixie National Forest, said they had no building sites available there, and they had no plans of developing the area. He said they were planning, however, to give a permit to someone to build a small lodge on Navajo Lake, which was their development area. He suggested that I apply for that; so I did.

Everybody else who had applied for a lodge permit wanted to build a dance hall, but I said that we would just build a small lodge with some cabins, and provide facilities for eating, horseback riding, and fishing in the summertime. It was such a beautiful area that we felt there would be a nice future for that type of development. Being a boy from the flatlands, the area especially appealed to me.

The permit to build the lodge was granted in the fall of 1926. In the summer of 1927, we began to build. The first year, we built two, three-room cabins, and started the lodge. The following year, we built the main lodge; with a kitchen, a dining room, and a lobby with a large, log-burning fireplace.

The lake was nearly dry in the fall of 1926, and according to Fern, the fish were all dead. There had been only a muddy slough around Breathing Spring. He said that they had speared a few large trout with pitchforks, when the water was low. The water was low on Navajo Lake, and although there were ducks on the lake, we assumed there were no fish.

By the following spring, when we started to build the cabins; the melting snow had filled the lake. The lake was also fed by springs; one up in the meadow, *Breathing Spring*, and at the lower end of the lake, *Navajo Spring*. The latter was part of the run-off from the midway water, which disappeared under a large field of black lava.

We didn't do much fishing in the lake in 1927, simply because we didn't expect the lake to have any fish. One day, while driving along the lakeshore toward the lodge; we saw a large hawk swoop down near the shore and spear a large trout. It was so heavy that the hawk was having difficulty lifting the trout out of the water, so it was skittering along, dragging the trout on top of the water. I took a fast run at it with the car, scaring it enough so that it dropped the fish on the edge of the shore. I jumped out of the car and picked it up before it could flop back into the water. It was a three-pound trout and delicious eating.

When I told the men working on the lodge about my experience, I had to take trout back to their families in Hurricane, every time I left the lodge to go home.

Lyle Winters was not from Hurricane, and even though he was a Mormon, like the rest of the workers who were working at the lodge, he was considered an outsider. The men used to wash up and brush their teeth and shave at an open trough, outside the cabin. Grant Sanders was the cook, and Top Stout, Richard Isom, Alvin Larson and George Campbell, were the workers, in addition to Lyle.

Things started disappearing, like the top to someone's toothpaste, or a razor; and one day, George Campbell's partial plate disappeared. Some of the men came to me and accused Lyle Winters of "stealing" the items, although any logical human being would question why anyone would want to steal someone else's partial plate, or even the top to someone's toothpaste.

I ignored the demands of the men to "fire" Lyle because they considered him a thief. One night, I decided to stay overnight at the lodge after the #1 cabin was built. During the night, I heard a pack rat scurrying around, and got up to chase him. Where the bed attached to the wall, the rat had built a nest; where he had a collection of pine cones, tops to tubes of toothpaste, and the missing partial plate.

Bob Perrin was also one of the workers, and was a tremendous help to both Nita and me. He not only helped with the building of the cabins, but he milked the cow we kept at the lodge, and oftentimes took care of Duke.

In 1930, when Nita came back from Cincinnati to re-open the lodge; it was Bob who drove her out, after replacing the transmission in our car. He was an invaluable addition to our small family, and is still a friend today.

Bob had come to us in the fall of 1926, from Ohio. My sister, Ann, had written to us telling us about Bob, who was the young son of friends of hers. Bob had been ill with typhoid fever and had lost weight, and seemed unable to regain his health. Ann hoped that time spent in the fresh air, out west, might restore his health. We agreed to make him a part of our family.

I will never forget when I first saw Bob, a forlorn, and handsome young man, standing in the small train station in Lund, Utah. It was four o'clock in the morning. The train did not come to Cedar City, so I had driven from Hurricane, to forty miles beyond Cedar City, to meet the Union Pacific train that Bob had taken from Ohio.

When he got off the train (the only one disembarking there), the conductor asked him if he was sure someone was going to meet him; that no one came to that little station. The train was a long one, and I was on the opposite side of the train. I didn't see Bob, nor did he see me, until the train pulled away from the station.

He was holding one suitcase, and a large package. In the suitcase was the large Indian headdress, that hung to the floor; a headdress that would put Bob in good standing with the local bullies in Hurricane.

The next morning, Bob was out on the porch when the Reeves brothers, and some of the locals, came by to pick a fight with the new kid on the block. Bob, who was sophisticated and far more knowledgeable than the boys in Hurricane, said that he was too tired to fight; that he had just completed a three day train trip.

Their eyes widened. They not only had never been on a train, they had never even seen one! He then asked them if they were Boy Scouts. They had never heard of a Boy Scout, so Bob told them about scouting.

He then brought out the magnificent Indian headdress, and modeled it for them. This new kid in town was far too smart and too interesting to beat up, so they made him their leader.

A scouting program was set up in Toquerville by Paul Thurston, one of the Toquerville teachers. It was in Toquerville that Bob Perrin earned his Eagle Scout award. One of the Reeves, who had come to "beat up on him," became one of Bob's best friends. Bob stayed with us until he left to attend the University of New Mexico, in 1930.

In a recent conversation with Bob, he told me that when he used to go out to bring the mother cow in to milk, he would get wet walking in the deep grass growing on the swampy meadow. The cow had a calf that was penned in a log corral that Bob built at the lodge; so Bob devised a plan whereby he would tweak the tail of the calf, making it bawl. Then the cow would come running, saving Bob the task of crossing the swampy meadow to bring her in. When the mother arrived at the corral, Bob would milk her; then he'd put her in with the calf, to let the calf nurse.

It is not difficult to see why former Arizona Governor Meacham, when he was in so much hot water, wanted to hire Bob Perrin to handle his press relations. Bob turned him down.

It was on a camping trip with Bob, when he was a teenager, that he says it was only due to his vigilance, and keeping the campfire burning all night, that we were saved from mountain lions. Their flashing eyes, Bob insists, could be seen in the shadows outside the rim of light of our campfire.

Fishing was exceptionally good during the latter part of 1927, 1928, and 1929. We caught a lot of large brook trout. Although I preferred the cooler temperature at Navajo Lake, I had to keep working to provide money and materials for the workmen.

The cabins were made of logs, but that didn't mean they were cheap to build. It took four men on a log when they were cutting for a three-room cabin. One would always be waiting for the other three, or three would be waiting on the one.

We bought four wooden boats from the Thompson Boat Manufacturing Company during the winter of 1928. The workmen would row over to Breathing Spring after work, and catch a few fish on the spawning beds.

We had phenomenal fishing during the summer of 1929. Most of the local people used bait, and two hooks on the line. They used night crawlers at ten cents a dozen, or salamanders at ten cents apiece. By using two hooks on a line, if they hooked a fish, they would let it swim around a little, and pretty soon they would get another strike.

The limit at the time was ten pounds, and the fish weighed from two to six pounds each, so it didn't take one long to catch your limit. The game warden was also an avid fisherman, so that kept the numbers we caught within legal limits.

While we were building the lodge, we hired Ep Ballard as a teamster to snake logs down from the mountain-top. The men working on the lodge lived in Hurricane, as I did; so every two weeks, they took turns going home to take their water turn, so their fields and gardens could be irrigated.

Water, in Utah, brings out the worst in some people. Men have been shot, women thrown into ditches, and heads cracked open with shovels, because someone thought their neighbor was taking their water turn a few minutes too early. During the week, in their Levi-Strauss coveralls, the men shouted, cursed and shook fists at their neighbor, over a minute or two of water. Even the women became embroiled in something close to fisticuffs.

But, on Sunday, dressed in their Sunday best, the men who were calling their neighbor a *son-of-a-bitch,* and threatening to shoot him a couple of days before, now smiled and called him *Brother.* They changed their disposition with their clothes.

On one of these return trips from Hurricane back to the lodge, I was in a bit of a hurry. We were driving up the highway to Cedar City, at about thirty-five miles an hour. The road was rough, and wash-boardy. Old Ep, whose main transportation had been by wagon, behind a slow-moving team, was soon clutching the car seat with both hands. Finally, in exasperation, Ep growled,

"Gad Doc! If you're in such a dang big hurry to get there, why didn't you leave earlier!"

In 1929, we added two more cabins, a large laundry room, and toilet facilities. I was still practicing medicine in Hurricane to pay the bills, but we were also busy working at the lodge between 1927, and 1929.

Dad had wanted me to be closer to Ohio where he could visit with his grandson, so in 1929, he wrote saying that Dr. McCleary, who had a lucrative eye, ear, nose and throat practice in Cincinnati, was interested in talking to me.

He said Dr. McCleary wanted me to come back to Ohio, and set up a practice with him, so he and his wife could take a trip around the world that winter. Then he planned to retire in Florida. Dr. McCleary said that if I would come back and practice for two years with him, I could take over his practice when he retired. In the summertime, I could go to New York for specialized study.

When we first came out west it was for Nita's health, and we had planned to return to the Midwest, or to practice in the East, when she was well. Her health was much improved, and I knew that it would be more profitable to practice in the city, but I found it difficult to make the decision. Despite the harshness of the weather, and the wildness of the landscape, that very ruggedness of the West, has a way of working its' way into the marrow of one's bones.

In July of 1929, I received a letter from Dr. McCleary, saying that he was coming out West, and would like for us to visit him when he was at Zion Canyon. He said he had a propostion for me.

When Nita and I joined McCleary and his wife in Zion, he said that there was not a large enough population to ever make a go of it in southern Utah. He painted glowing stories of what we could accomplish if Nita and I would come back to Cincinnati and set up a practice with him. He offered me $200.00 a month.

We had started building the lodge, and I enjoyed the fishing. I liked the people in Hurricane, and I enjoyed the horse racing in Toquerville. We had made friends, even if we didn't make much money.

It was easier for Nita to decide to go back East. Her family was there. She would have more of a social life in the East. She was especially close to her younger sister Louise, and she missed her. Since we were not Mormon, except for horse racing and occasional get-togethers, there wasn't much of a social life for her in Hurricane. She had endured the hardships, and the lack of money without complaint.

I asked myself if I was being selfish by wanting to stay in the West. I tried to convince myself that I had always liked EENT work, and the opportunity would be for the good of all of us. I told myself that we could still keep the lodge, run it in the summertime; that we could have our cake, and eat it too. We could have the best of both worlds. So, I accepted.

The lodge was beginning to get busy that summer. I was acting as a guide for those who wanted to ride horseback. Paul Thurston acted as a fishing guide. Paul and I would get up at four o'clock in the morning; go out and catch four or five large brook trout, then come back to the lodge and fix them for breakfast for the guests.

We got in trouble with the game warden though, because the brook trout are a game fish, and we were not allowed to sell them. We also got in trouble because we canned some. They folded over so nicely, and fit into the cans perfectly. We had a canning machine and were doing great, until the game warden stepped in.

After breakfast, Paul would take some of the guests fishing, and I would take those who wanted to ride, horseback riding. We'd ride to Cedar breaks, and down into the North Fork of the Virgin River. I lived at the lodge all of the latter part of that summer.

When we made up our minds to accept Dr. McCleary's offer in Cincinnati, I turned my practice over to Dr. McIntyre, who was from the University of Utah in Salt Lake City. He had been the doctor for the men who were working on the tunnel in Zion Park. I had been practicing in Hurricane for four years at the time we left there.

It was a busy summer for us. Between taking care of the lodge; we were busy canning fruit, and had canned about one hundred pounds of trout (before we were stopped by the game warden), and had canned venison from a couple of deer.

In the fall of the year, we found we have overextended ourselves. I had given up my practice, so we had no money coming in, except from the lodge. Oscar Larson was in the area one day looking for some lambs that had strayed, and when he asked me how things were going, I told him.

Oscar offered me a two thousand dollar loan, which I accepted. This meant I could clear up any debts and go back to Cincinnati with everything clear, except for the two thousand dollar loan. I was grateful for my good fortune. I didn't know then, that it would be another Larson (I don't believe they were related), who would be the cause of our losing the lodge.

We packed our things, and I left a gun collection, furniture, and other valuable possessions, including Indian baskets, in the cabins; because we expected to return. Everything would be safe, until our return the following summer; we thought.

The stock was trucked to Hurricane, where we left the stock for Alvin Larson to find pasture, for Marqueta, Brownie, Alice, Fly, and another little Pacer, and the cow and calf.

We said our goodbyes, thinking we would be back to run the lodge every summer, and headed back to Cincinnati. We didn't realize what lay ahead of us.

CHAPTER FOURTEEN
Cincinnati and New York

We left Hurricane on October 28, 1929. We now had a new four-door Chevy that we had purchased from Stan Bradshaw. We packed the car, (Duke was now almost five) but this time we didn't have our airedale, Boy. Someone had thrown poison meat to him and killed him, along with Tom Isom's old dog that had never harmed a soul. All Tom Isom's dog ever did was to walk alongside Tom's wagon.

The sheepmen, when the lambs were born, were afraid that any large dog would kill the lambs, no matter how gentle the dog might be. Tom Isom and I both suspected who the man was. We missed Boy, and were sad to think he would no longer be a part of our lives.

We stopped in Flagstaff that first night. Roads were rough, and travel slow. It took us a week to reach Cincinnati. There were no radios in the cars then, nor television sets to let us know what was happening in the world.

When we reached Cincinnati, we learned that the stock market had plunged, and that the United States was in the Great Depression. When we arrived, we went straight to my parent's home in Madiera, about twenty miles from Cincinnati. I could either drive into Cincinnati, or take the streetcar, until we could find a place closer to the office.

Dr. McCleary was upset now that I had come. He had been a millionaire one day, and after the crash had lost most of his holdings. He was beside himself and said that he could not afford to retire in two years as he'd planned.

The two thousand dollar loan from Oscar Larson had been used to pay the workmen who had built the cabins, before we left Hurricane, so I had little money left. In 1928, Donald Pierret, from Indian Hill, Ohio, had offered to go in with me to build the two extra cabins at the lodge, and later backed out. That was what had put us in the financial bind that necessitated accepting Oscar's loan.

I had turned over my practice in Hurricane to Dr. McIntyre for what I believed would be a secure future for my family, and now I had less security than I had in Hurricane. We had to find a place to live, so we stayed with my parents until we could find a small apartment in Hyde Park. I could then leave the car with Nita during the day, and take a streetcar to work.

I packed my doctor's bag that first day, and went to Dr. McCleary's office, downhearted, but determined to make the best of it. At least my parents were close by, and we could turn to them if Nita or Duke were in need. That gave me some sense of security.

It was difficult to adapt to Dr. McCleary's way of thinking. He had been the son of a livery stable man in Gallapolis, Ohio, between Cincinnati and Pittsburgh. He told me that he used to watch his father harness horses and bring them to the dudes, who hired the rigs on Sunday. He was bitter over what he considered menial labor for his father, whom he loved fiercely, and he vowed that he would never be in that position; that he would never be poor, nor do menial labor.

He decided when he was very young that he would become a doctor, no matter what he had to do to earn the money. He was going to be wealthy and come back and live in East Walnut Hills in Cincinnati, which was an exclusive residential section. He would show the people he considered snobs, that he and his father were as good as they, or even better; because his father had worked, and he would work.

His eyes would narrow, and his voice become intense, as his fingers clasped and unclasped as he spoke, almost as if I wasn't even in the room; as if he were talking to his father, somewhere, in another place. But then, reality would come back to him, and he would realize that he was no longer a millionaire.

His voice would become brusque, and he'd tell me how he wanted me to act around the patients. He disapproved of my habit of walking in the front door, and stopping to talk to the patients in the waiting room. "Time is money" he would growl, and then he would tell me to come in the back way; direct my patient to the treatment room, then step to the wash basin, wash my hands and dry them slowly, while explaining to my patient that I always wash my hands before examining them. This seemed a strange thing to say, since this should have been common procedure, before examining a patient.

He said that he never spoke to a patient on the street and attempted to avoid them. If he could not, then he would ask, not how they were, but "How is your nose?" or "How is your eye?" or something similar.

He limited each call to exactly six minutes, and he charged six dollars. He told me that as soon as I had treated my patient, that I was to dismiss them, immediately. If it was Monday, I was to say "See Miss Enoch for an appointment next Wednesday." If it was Tuesday, I was to tell the patient to ask Miss Enoch for an appointment next Thursday. Dr. McCleary did not come in on Saturdays, but I came in, in case there was an emergency.

We clashed from the beginning. I could not limit a call to six minutes, and I could not treat my patients as he treated his. My patients were my friends, as well as my patients. I might be gruff with them, but I cared about them. He didn't consider me a very good business man, and said I would never become a millionaire, wasting so much time on each patient. I had given up thoughts of becoming a millionaire, after Sinc and I gave up our ambition to be a "rag man," when we were kids.

Sometimes, he wanted to talk about his life, and when we were through for the day, he would tell me about how he had reached his goal in life: to become wealthy and live in a wealthy area like the one where his father had worked so many years before.

He told me that when he was in Medical school he lived in a rooming house where there was an attractive young woman, who worked as a burlesque queen. He fell in love with her, and I suspect that he never stopped loving her, even after he married her, let her help support him, then divorced her after he became a doctor. He was not going to let love stand in the way of his goal. A burlesque queen would never fit into the lifestyle he planned for himself as a wealthy doctor.

It was when he spoke of her that his voice and his eyes softened, and it was at that time that I almost liked him. But, he would suddenly straighten, and his eyes would cloud over, as though he had not meant to share that part of his life with anyone, ever again. He never told me what ever happened to her, or if he ever saw her again, and I never asked.

Dr. McCleary's office was next door to Dr. Wiggers, who was Cincinnati's best known doctor. He treated many wealthy patients, and it was through one of Dr. Wigger's patients, that McCleary made his first step towards accomplishing his goal to become wealthy.

He already had an established practice when he met a Mrs. Potter, who had asthma. He told her that he too, had problems with breathing at times, and suggested that he move into her home in Walnut Hills, so that he could be on hand when she had difficulty breathing. She accepted, and he moved in with her. He had remained a bachelor after his divorce from the burlesque queen.

When Mrs. Potter died, she left the East Walnut Hills home to Dr. McCleary. Although she left money and other property to her relatives; they still tried to break the will, without success.

He now had an established practice, and a home in Walnut Hills. It was time to look around for a suitable wife to complete the circle. He was now in his late fifties. He married Myra, who was 45, the daughter of the Publisher of the Methodist publications.

When we met Dr. McCleary and Myra in Utah, he had told us that she had a small uterine tumor that could wait for removal until they returned from their planned trip around the world. The "tumor" turned out to be a pregnancy, which came as quite a shock, since they considered themselves too old for Myra to become a mother.

Years later, when I was practicing in Kanab, the daughter of the comptroller for Proctor & Gamble in Cincinnati, came to me for medical teatment, and told me that she had gone to finishing school with the daughter of Dr. McCleary and Myra. She said that McCleary had moved out of Walnut Hills, and had purchased a home in the exclusive section of Indian Hills, so that his daughter could ride horseback.

Despite their losses in the stock market, they found that they could still afford to spend the winter in Florida. I stayed in Cincinnati and took care of his practice. When they returned in April, I arranged to go to New York City for the summer of 1930, to take special training.

We decided that while I was in New York, Nita would return with Duke, to Navajo Lake, and run the lodge for the summer. This would help our financial situation while I was in school. In the fall, she would return to Cincinnati; I would have finished my special training in New York, and I would meet her in Cincinnati and again take care of Dr. McCleary's practice, while he and Myra went back to Florida for the winter.

When I left for New York, Dr. McCleary gave me a letter of introduction to Dr. Billy McLean, with whom I would be working in New York.

I rented a room in one of the old Brownstone mansions on 18th Street, on the third floor, in the back. I settled in and went to the clinic to report to Dr. McLean. I would be working at the New York Ophthalmic Hospital located at 23rd Street and Third Avenue.

When I met Dr. McLean, he asked me where I was from. When I told him Cincinnati, he asked if I knew Dr. McCleary. Before I could answer, he said,

"He is the most arrogant individual I have ever met." I left the letter of introduction in my pocket.

The clinic where I would be working was run for indigents. For twenty-five cents, a patient received a colored ticket, and the color of the ticket indicated which doctor he was to see. The waiting room held a large number of patients, and the room was crowded every day.

The two interns who were working at the clinic were Sam Morris, a Jewish doctor, who had been educated at McGill University in Montreal, and Robert Machado, a Cuban. They were at odds with each other all of the time. I was caught in the middle. They would both date during the weekend, and come in on Monday mornings, cross and out-of-sorts. As I got to know them better, they would ask me to cover for them. They would either pay me, or bring me a bottle of wine, so that they could be off on the weekend.

They had been doing twenty tonsillectomies a day since their internship began. New York had a contract to do tonsillectomies for indigent children, housed in various institutions.

When I first went to the clinic, I observed Dr. McLean and his assistant, Dr. DiAngelo. I learned that Dr. McLean had visited Bryce Canyon, Cedar Breaks, Kanab and the Grand Canyon, in 1929. He had taken color pictures (color photography was new) and they were some of the best I have ever seen. He had taken pictures of his children in front of the Middle School in Kanab, against a background of the coral cliffs behind the school.

He invited me to his home for dinner where he shared the pictures and his memories of Utah. I was grateful for the dinner and the evening spent with his family, especially since I missed my own.

Dr. DiAngelo invited me to his home in Bayville, Long Island, one Sunday. I had visited Bayville as a child, in 1902. We had spent the summer there.

My younger sister, Catherine, although she was very young when we were there, remembers getting her shoe caught between the cracks of the boardwalk crossing the Brooklyn Bridge, and losing it. When Mother asked her where her shoe was, she said she'd lost it. I don't remember it, but Catherine says I went back and found her shoe.

Bayville had changed in the intervening 27 years. The cliffs were the same; Connecticut was on the other side, but nothing else looked the same. There were so many boats, so many people, and the houses were built down to the water's edge.

Dr. DiAngelo took me fishing on Long Island Sound, where we trolled for bluefish and snappers. This consisted of trolling with a tin jig in the wake of the outboard motor. The hook was barbless. On the strike you yanked the fish out of the water, then taking hold of the hook at the eye, you flipped the fish into a bucket. I was not adept at this, so I missed the bucket with my first fish.

In picking up the fish from the bottom of the boat where it had fallen, I touched it on the side. It bit my finger so hard, and so unexpectedly, that I yelled. Of course, that was part of the game, learning why they are called snappers.

Dr. McLean assigned me a table between his table and Dr. DiAngelo's. I was kept busy doing examinations, refractions and various types of treatment. I had the opportunity to learn about cases rarely seen in a rural setting.

Since I was not working in the mornings, I went to Dr. Morris and Dr. Machado, and suggested that I help them perform the tonsillectomies, since I had experience. They were pleased to have my help, so we set up a system whereby the three of us took turns examining the patient, and doing the tests needed. The anesthetic was then given, and we would take turns performing the operation. We also took turns taking the patient to the recovery room, and to the ward. All of this is now done by someone else, but in the late twenties, the doctors followed through from the operating room to the recovery ward.

The technique they used was clean, and precise. The instrument used was called a *Braun,* a combination of the *Sluder,* with a snare attached. I had used both instruments, so it was not difficult for me to follow the method used by the two doctors.

We used a reflecting mirror while operating, with the light reflected into the patient's mouth and throat. The anesthetist used the ether suction machine. The scrub nurse was a personable Puerto Rican negress, whose feet were constantly tapping to some show tune that was popular at the time. Instruments were asked for by the position of the hand, so once in awhile we'd chime in with her, if everything was going all right. Toe-tapping and singing became a part of our tonsillectomies.

On Saturday mornings, we did what local operations we had: tonsils or deviated nasal septums. We averaged about eighty operations a week between us for the seven months I was there. This added to my experience. The Depression may have deprived some people of their choice of doctors, but the indigents received excellent care at a minimum fee.

In July of that year, the New York Ophthalmic Hospital was closed, so we were moved to Flower Hospital at 64th Street and York. By that time, I had run out of money. Nita was having financial problems at the lodge, and couldn't help me. I had to sell my camera to pay my room rent. When I had only a few dollars left I was about ready to give up on getting any more experience.

I had heard that my former dean at Ohio State, Dr. Burratt, was now in charge of Flower Hospital. I walked from 18th Street to 64th Street and York, hoping to find him in. I was in luck. Dr. Burratt gave me a hearty welcome, and asked me what he could do for me. I explained my circumstances, and my intention to give up and go home.

He told me I could move in with the two other interns, and continue with the clinic and operations, as usual. That solved my immediate problem, and I was grateful.

I stayed in New York until October, then returned to Cincinnati to practice while the McClearys went to Florida. Nita came back from Utah to Cincinnati to enroll Duke in school. The lodge was closed for the winter. The summer of 1930 had been slow at the lodge, because so few people had money to travel during the Depression.

In August of 1931, I left Cincinnati to go back to Navajo Lake and see about selling the lodge. I left Nita and Duke in Ohio.

There had been problems for Nita the summer of 1930, with Alvin Larson, an asthmatic, who also suffered from emphysema. He had been employed at the lodge, even during the building of it. Alvin was a farmer from Hurricane, who also did sheep-shearing. His father bought second mortgages, and tax-defunct properties.

When we left there, we had told Alvin he could work again the summer of 1930, but when Nita went back to open the lodge, she found that Alvin had put his entire family on salary! There was no way we could afford to pay the entire Larson family, consisting of Alvin, his wife, two girls and a boy. There simply was not enough income.

Nita told Alvin that he could work, but that his family would have to find work elsewhere. Alvin became angry, and Nita had to contend with his anger alone, since I was in New York. Alvin's health had improved at the lake, and he enjoyed the fishing.

We didn't know then that Alvin Larson had already made plans to take over the lodge. Without our knowledge, he bought Oscar Larson's mortgage on the lodge in the winter of 1929, right after we went to Cincinnati. He told Oscar that we were not going to come back and that if Oscar wanted to get his $2,000.00 back he, Alvin, would buy it. I do not know where he got the money. Perhaps this was Alvin's plan from the beginning, possibly with the help of his father. He now had us where he wanted, and promptly foreclosed.

I contacted an attorney in Cincinnati, a Mr. Clippinger. He told me there was a six-month redemption period on real estate in Utah. In the meantime, I had found a sale for the lodge. A Mr. Halverson, offered me $10,000.00. Since we had, what we believed was a six-month redemption period, we thought we could go out the following summer, and show Mr. Halverson the property, since the lodge was snowed in.

When we arrived in Utah that summer, with plans to close the deal on the real estate with Mr. Halverson, we found out that there was no redemption period on the lodge. I was told by both Alvin Larson's attorney, and the ones handling the court procedure, that the lodge was not considered real estate, but personal property, because it could be moved.

We had a lease from the government on the lots where the buildings were located, so they (the attorneys and Alvin Larson) said that it could be moved at any time, and that constituted *personal* property.

There were a number of possessions in the buildings at the lodge that I wanted back; my gun collection, some Indian and Pioneer plaques made by artist Evard Fairbanks, and some rare Seri Indian baskets. They said it was *personal* property and it had all been sold to a man named Eckerd from Provo. There was no redemption period on any of it.

Alvin Larson had done his homework, and the lodge that we had struggled to build, was now his. We lost our $10,000.00, which we could ill afford to lose; our personal possessions there, and three years of hard work. I was bitter.

Nat Goldman, who had driven me out from Ohio, was with me in Attorney Durham Morris' office in Cedar City, when I got the bad news. I felt like I had been kicked in the stomach. Nita had worked as hard as I had. She had been alone when she dealt with the Larsons, and I feel like the blow of losing the lodge to Alvin Larson, was the start of Nita's unhappiness, and her later decision to stay in Cincinnati and divorce me.

Nat tried to console me by pointing out the cost of running the lodge, and how I could make more money as a doctor than as a cowboy. I knew he was right, but it did not lessen the pain of losing the lodge, and later my wife for two years.

I knew that I would have to settle down and go back into medical practice. My parents had sacrificed to put me through medical school, but I no longer wanted to practice in the East. I had turned over my practice in Hurricane to Dr. McIntyre, so I had to look elsewhere.

Dr. Norris, who was now eighty-four, and practicing in Kanab, Utah, was tired and no longer wanted to practice. I had gone to Kanab to seek the advice of an older and more experienced doctor. He said, after our discussion, that he would be happy to have me set up a medical practice in Kanab. That was all I needed.

CHAPTER FIFTEEN
Kanab - A New Beginning

Nat and I stopped and talked to Whit Parry, who ran Parry Lodge in Kanab. At that time it was open all year. Whit told me that he had a cabin with two rooms in it that would be just right for me to set up my practice. I could live in one room; have my office in the other room, and eat my meals at the hotel, until I could afford larger quarters. Nita and Duke were in Cincinnati, so I only needed the one room.

We had been there little more than an hour when Dr. Stan Rees came in. He, too, was looking for a place to practice. When he asked if I had made a decision to stay, and I said "Yes," he decided to go to eastern Utah where he had a contract with the coal mines.

He later settled in Gunnison, Utah, and it is interesting that our careers from that time paralled somewhat. He later built a hospital in Gunnison, and when WWII started, he gave his hospital to the City of Gunnison; just as I would later give my hospital to the City of Kanab. He served in the Utah State Legislature at the time I was elected State Representative from Kane County. In 1964, the Utah State Medical Association awarded me the *Doctor of the Year* Award, and in 1965, Dr. Rees was given the same honor.

Nat Goldman liked Kanab right away. He said one of the reasons he liked it, was that it was the only place in the world where a Jew can be a Gentile, unless he's a Lamanite. The Lamanites were the Indians, according to Mormon belief.

The two of us walked around the town of Kanab looking over the stores, and found that neither of the two stores in town, had a pharmacist. They carried no drug supplies, which meant that I would have to supply and dispense my own drugs. There was no hospital, which meant I would have to make a lot of house calls.

My territory would cover the desolate area to the Colorado River; to Flagstaff, Arizona, 200 miles away, and to Richfield, Utah, which was another 130 miles to the north. There was a doctor in Panguitch, but there was no hospital there. The nearest hospitals were in Cedar City, more than eighty miles over the mountains, and in St. George, about the same distance, or even farther on the old road.

If I thought I was isolated in Hurricane, I was even more isolated in Kanab. I am told that at one time Kanab was considered the most isolated area in the country, and even today, in 1989, there are no trains, planes, or busses (other than tour busses) into the City of Kanab. The nearest commercial flights come into Page, Arizona, or St. George, Utah. Opening a practice in Kanab would be the biggest challenge I had faced in my life, but I was never one to back away from a challenge.

In those early days in Kanab, I could hear the sound of wood being chopped in the evening, and see the curl of smoke over the town, from the wood fires. Juniper, pine and oak were hauled from the mountainsides to provide fuel for the town. The sound of chopping would start again about five o'clock in the morning.

The Kanab townsite was about a mile square with fields and farms surrounding it. There was irrigation water in town for the gardens and orchards, and a culinary water supply that came through the pipelines and went into regular taps. Water was not yet piped into the houses, but there were taps outside the house, or by the barn.

When the farmers finished working in the fields for the day, they would turn their cows loose. Sometimes the kids would drive the cows up the lane to town, but sometimes, the cows were left to wander home on their own.

The cows were brought into town to be milked, then put in the barnyard for the night. The following morning they were milked again. When the men went to work in the fields they would drive the cows down the lane ahead of them, or let the school kids do it.

This arrangement stemmed from the early days when the town was centered near the water supply, and there was only irrigation water in the fields. This practice of turning the cows loose to wander down the lane in the morning, then to wander home in the evening, led to a lot of trouble for Whit Parry, and for the cows.

Before getting into that story, let me give you a little background on the Parry brothers, and their business. It was in 1927 that they brought their first load of tourists into Wylie's camp, which was on the north rim of the Grand Canyon. Del Robinson was working there at the time, as well as Whit Parry, who drove the bus. He was the youngest of the Parry brothers, and he said that at that time he could barely see over the wheel of the old second-hand, open-air bus they had purchased from the Yellowstone Transportation Company.

Those were rough, tough days for the passengers, as well as for the driver. The roads were in a constant state of repair somewhere along the route, and the steep grades on the mountains made travel nearly impossible. Many times the passengers would have to climb out of the old bus and push.

Ruby Syrett had a camp on the rim of Bryce Canyon, and there was also a private camp in the Zion Canyon. In 1929, the Union Pacific Railroad bought the transportation vehicle, and the permit from the Parry brothers for $150,000.00. The brothers then accepted jobs in transportation from the railroad.

About that time motion picture companies saw the possibilities of using the scenery in the parks, and before the Park Service banned them, some movies were shot in Zion and Bryce Canyons. Two of those early films featured Tom Mix, and Jack Holt.

After the sale of the transportation permit, Chaunce Parry took his share of money and bought the Jet Johnson home in Kanab, on the corner of Center and First East. He built cabins around the lovely old home, some with light housekeeping facilities, and added a dining room, using a wing of the house.

Whit Parry used his share of the money to open the *Cactus Club,* in the basement of the Grande Hotel, in Salt Lake City. He said that one night the club was filled with people dressed in evening clothes, with plenty of money to spend, and the next night, after the stock market crash of 1929, the place was empty. It was that abrupt.

Whit was forced to declare bankruptcy. He then came to Kanab to run Parry Lodge for Chaunce. It was then known as the Parry System Hotel, since

Chaunce had plans to open a chain of motels; some to be located in Flagstaff, and Richfield. The Great Depression changed his mind.

Whit knew how to run a hotel, and he knew how to make money. He was personable, and seemed to know how to keep his guests happy. He also had a temper, which he demonstrated on various occasions.

He planted a new lawn around the lodge that would have been protected by the picket fence around it; if Whit had kept the gate closed. But he didn't, and Mr. Spencer's cows were drawn to that nice new lawn of Whit's.

When Whit saw Mr. Spencer's cows contentedly munching on his new lawn; he was livid. When he saw Mr. Spencer riding home on his horse after working in the field all day, Whit would run out and threaten to pull him off his horse and beat him up, if Spencer didn't keep his cows off Whit's lawn.

The cows trampled the lawn on the way home from the field in the evening, and again on their way back to the field the following morning. Whit would chase them out each time, yelling at the cows and swearing at Mr. Spencer.

One Sunday morning, as I sat in my office at Parry Lodge, I heard Whit screaming outside. I looked out just in time to see four cows clattering through the yard, then I heard a blast from a shotgun. Whit had shot one of Spencer's cows in the backside. She jumped over the low picket fence and out onto the road. The cow later died.

Now Mr. Spencer was furious and wanted to have Whit arrested. The City Marshal could not decide on what offense to charge Whit with. Finally, Charlie Nash, the marshal, presented Whit with a summons to appear in court. Whit asked that I go along as a witness before the Justice of the Peace, Jake Crosby.

When we arrived, Whit was told by the judge that he had been charged with wantonly discharging firearms within the city limits. Whit protested, "Judge, that's wrong! I did not *wantonly* do it!"

The judge said, "Well, I know Whit, I know you didn't *want* to do it, but that's what you did."

Whit was exasperated. "Judge, you don't even know what wanton means! I tell you I did not shoot that cow wantonly. I shot it on purpose, like you would a thief who was robbing your home. That cow was trespassing and ruining my lawn. It had no business there, so I shot it, and I shot it deliberately. I did not do it wantonly!"

The judge insisted that he knew Whit didn't want to do it, but he really did do it, and he would have to be fined. The judge conferred with the county attorney (he was also the city attorney), who asked "How much shall we fine him?"

The judge said that he had lost three days work in the field because of the trial, and the county attorney, Willard Mackleprang, said that it cost him mileage to drive down from Glendale, and that ought to be worth twenty-five dollars for him.

The judge decided his time was also worth twenty-five dollars so they fined Whit fifty dollars. Whit protested, "Gosh, Jake, I don't have that kind of money!"

Willard owed me fifty dollars for a delivery. He actually owed me twenty-five dollars for the delivery, but since he figured *his* mileage was worth twenty-five dollars to drive *from* Glendale; I figured my mileage to Glendale to deliver a baby was also worth twenty-five dollars, so I spoke up. I told Whit that Mr.

Mackleprang owed me fifty dollars, so he could pay the fine; I would give Mackleprang a receipt for my bill an the delivery and the mileage, and Whit in turn, could give me a receipt for lodging and meals at the lodge. So that is how Whit's fine was paid.

I don't know why Whit was not required to pay Spencer for his cow. Only the judge and the attorney received any money. The cows continued their daily grazing on Whit's lawn, but after the fine Whit decided to resort to something besides shooting. He was busy painting one day when the cows trespassed again. He grabbed his bucket of paint and ran at the cows, grabbed one of them, and painted her bag and udders green.

Nothing was said, until they wandered onto his lawn again. This time he angrily threw a pitchfork at one of the unfortunate cows, and it stuck in her backside. Whit was horrified when he saw the terrified cow running through the lot, bawling in pain, with the pitchfork wagging in back of it.

Whit was re-arrested, and he asked for a change of venue to Orderville. It didn't help him. This time Whit was fined seventy-five dollars, and he had to pay on the spot. I wasn't there to help him out. Whit realized, too late, that he had made a mistake in asking for a change of venue to Orderville, because, as he said later, "They think more of their cows in Orderville, than they do of their kids!"

When Whit asked the judge what he could do about keeping the cows off his lawn, the judge in Orderville replied, "Just close the gate!" Apparently, the solution was so simple that it had never occurred to Whit.

During the time I was waiting for my medical supplies to be sent to Kanab, Nat Goldman and I did some sightseeing. When I took him to see Point Sublime, which I thought was the most beautiful place from which to see the Grand Canyon; I was pointing out the view of the river at the bottom of the canyon. In the meantime, two or three carloads of teachers arrived in back of us. They were oohing and aahing over the view. The only remark that Nat made when I pointed out the Colorado River was, "Let's get out of here before those school teachers leave." It was then I realized that Nat was nearsighted and he didn't even see the Grand Canyon, let alone the river.

We also drove to Las Vegas for four days. The changes that had taken place since Nita and I had gone there in 1925 were phenomenal. Boulder Dam had been built, so Nat and I took a tour through the dam, then drove to Cedar Breaks and Bryce Canyon.

When we arrived back in Kanab after our trip I found my medical supplies waiting for me. I set up my small office in the number one cabin, then sent out word to the surrounding communities that I was now available for medical practice.

One morning, about daylight, I was awakened by a loud knocking on my door. When I answered the door, there were two men, one of them holding a bloody towel around his head. When I examined the man, his *friend* told me what had happened. Thomas Esplin was the one with the bloody head; and Conner DeMille was the one who had given it to him, with a shovel!

They had argued over whose water turn it was, or who was taking too much water from whom. Thomas Esplin had become a little bit testy and called Conner DeMille a few names. He then told DeMille that he was going to go over there and knock hell out of him.

He dug his shovel into the earth to vault over the ditch to go after DeMille. Esplin was rather heavy, so his shovel sank into the soft earth, and he couldn't pull it out in time to whack DeMille first. As he bent over to try to pull the shovel out, DeMille whacked Esplin over the head with his shovel, knocking him out.

While I was sewing Esplin's head wound he said, "When I came to, I didn't mind so much that he was throwing water in my face, but instead of using his hand to throw the water; he was just shoveling the water over me! I didn't think that was very personal, and I didn't like it very much!"

The two men left my office together, like two old friends; DeMille driving the man whose head he had opened, back to Orderville, about thirty miles from Kanab. Neither man offered to pay me.

Fights over water were as serious in Kanab as they had been in Hurricane, in Alton, and in Glendale and Orderville. Tom Isom told me stories of shootings; some that took lives. A Mr. Seegmiller, was killed in Alton in the late 1800's, or early 1900's, over water. He answered a knock at the door, and when he opened the door, one of his neighbors blasted him, killing him instantly.

Wilford Greenhalgh, who carried a .22 calibre pistol that he called "an equalizer," shot over the head of Rell Little, in a dispute over water. Warren Olsen, frequently had disputes with Effie Carpenter in Glendale, over a few minutes of water usage.

Effie would always stand guard over the irrigation ditch, and when Warren would come at three o'clock to take his turn, Effie would insist it wasn't his time yet. Everyone always argued over whose clock was right. One day, the argument became quite heated. When Warren bent over the ditch to let the water run into his fields, Effie gave him a shove, and knocked him into the water.

Warren, sputtering and angry, climbed out of the ditch, soaking wet, and took out after Effie, who, skirt raised, was racing across the field to get away. He caught up to her, and throwing her over his shoulder, Warren marched back with the screaming and kicking Effie, and dumped her, unceremoniously, into the water.

There were so many fights that a town clock became the clock that everyone had to go by. A Water-Master, who was in charge of delegating times for water usage, packed a gun. I learned early, while I was still in Hurricane, that your neighbor does not turn the water into your field when his turn is up, and it is your turn. If you are not there and take it; you don't get it!

CHAPTER SIXTEEN
Cowboys, Indians and Wayfarers

There was not a lot of money to spend on entertainment during the Depression. There was no television, so people invented various forms of entertainment. Duff Pugh was good at stirring up a little excitement for the townfolk, and anyone else who happened to be in town. He promoted various fights, matching up a dozen or more men who were slight in stature, then a couple of larger men, and put them on a fight card.

One time he arranged a fight involving three Paiutes, who had fought in Las Vegas. The deal was that the three Indians would fight any two Anglos. The Indians came in three sizes, a big one, a little one, and a middle-sized one. Stanley Sampson, Sr., and Freddie Bullets were medium-sized to large, and Danny Bullets weighed about 120 pounds.

Tommy Logan, a lightweight fighter weighing about 135 pounds, had stopped in Kanab on his way to California. He had broken a bone in one of his hands, and had left Pennsylvania to come out West. He entered a few fights in Kanab and proved that he was a good fighter.

Tommy used the ropes a lot when he fought, and was a fast mover. He had a way of pushing his back tightly against the ropes, then propelling himself across the area, like a sling-shot. There was also a cowboy from Wyoming, Dan Lacey, who was a pretty good fighter.

Duff matched the three Paiutes against Lacey, and Logan. The night of the fight, while I was eating dinner at the lodge, two men came into the dining room. One was an attorney from Seattle, and the other one was a doctor. We were introduced, and when they found out I was a doctor, they asked me what one did for fun around Kanab. I told them about the fight Duff had scheduled, and invited them to go with me.

As we bought our tickets, they looked around the room. There were tall cowboys wearing white hats, high-heeled boots and Strauss blue jeans, and Paiute women with Pendleton blankets covering their shoulders; some with papooses in cradle boards. There was laughter, and bets being made on who was going to win. The Paiute women were as interested in seeing their men win, as the rest of the crowd was in betting on Lacey and Logan. The men said they had never seen anything so picturesque.

I was to be one of the judges that night, while Tone McDonald and Whit Parry were to be the referees. Logan and Lacy were in the corner, nearest to us; while Sampson and the two Bullets boys were located in the arena in the opposite corner.

When the gong sounded for the first round, Logan planned to whip across the arena (propelled by the rope) and knock out Danny Bullets, the smallest of the three, first. With Danny out of the way, there would be two against two.

Logan hit the ropes, and flew across the arena towards Danny. As Danny came up the side of the arena, Logan swung. The punch connected, but Danny had ducked enough so that the blow landed on the top of his head. It spun him over the top of the ropes so that he lit on his hands and feet, outside the arena, between the ropes and the front seats.

Danny stayed there, on his hands and knees, peeking through the bottom ropes. Logan stayed on the inside waiting for Danny, taunting him to come back in so he could beat him up. In the meantime, Lacey was standing in his corner in a classic *John L. Sullivan* pose, his hands out in front of him. Sampson came up in front of Lacey and sparred with him, forcing Lacey to keep his eyes up front.

Freddy Bullets, who weighed 160, danced up behind Lacey, giving him a blow to the back of the right ear. The crowd went wild. Lacey was out cold. When Danny, still outside the ropes, saw Lacey on the floor, he climbed back into the ring to help the other two Paiutes go after Logan.

Logan made a couple of little sashays, danced back and hit the ropes, then shot across the canvas with his head down. He wasn't looking at anybody in particular, but when he saw someone, he would swing. Tone, one of the referees, got in the way of one of Logan's punches, and doubled up like a jack-knife. He slid under the ropes and under the seats, on the other side of the ring. Just then the gong rang for the end of the first round.

The spectators were going crazy. Several people were trying to revive Lacey so he could get back into the fight, but no one was paying any attention to Tone. He was trying to signal Whit that he couldn't talk. The breath had been knocked out of him, but everyone was intent on getting Lacey back into the fight. The Paiute women were cheering, and talking in Paiute.

Whit was now the sole referee. Lacey couldn't be revived enough to fight, so that left Logan to fight the three Indians alone. Logan hit the ropes, flew across the ring, and hit Sampson squarely in the middle. This stopped Sampson for a few seconds, but the other two Pauites began hitting Logan with blows like jackhammers, and after Sampson shook his head, and got his breath back, he joined in. As good as Logan was, the three Paiutes were simply too much for one man to handle, so he threw in the towel - and the fight was over.

Billie Mackleprang, one of the spectators, was as much fun to watch as the boxers. He would shadow box, duck his head, come up with a blow to an imaginary opponent, and suffered along with the fighters in the ring. I doubt that he ever knew he was doing this, but he was a part of the fun, that the visitors from Seattle came back the following year to watch again.

This time they brought their wives, but we didn't have any fights scheduled. They said they felt like they were re-living a part of the Old West, and wanted to share the experience of the cowboys and Indians they had enjoyed so much the year before, with their wives.

Shortly after I started my practice in Kanab, May Black, who lived in Glendale and was the County Public Health Nurse, arranged well-baby clinics, pre-school clinics, and promoted DPT immunizations. We held clinics once a month in the communities surrounding Kanab; Alton, Orderville, Glendale, and Mt. Carmel.

One particular clinic was set up in the small church in Alton. The clinic consisted of two rooms; one heated by a small stove and used as an examining room, and the chapel, unheated and cold, served as the waiting room. It was after we finished at the clinic that I was asked, by Ruth Lamb and Ina Heaton, to check on Mrs. Roundy, who lived on the other side of the square. They told me that they were concerned, because she had been very ill.

Alton, which nestles in at about 7,000 feet in elevation, was extremely cold as we made our way through the snow to her house. The snow had been so heavy that year that I had to park my car on the outskirts of town, and walk to the clinic.

We stomped the snow from our boots, and called out before we entered the darkened, unheated house. Ina and Ruth stayed in the living room, while I knocked on the door, then entered Mrs. Roundy's bedroom. I pulled back the curtains to let in whatever light I could from the outside, then lit the kerosene lamp nearby. As I did so, I called to her, softly, but got no response.

Mrs. Roundy lay beneath several denim quilts, a flannel robe covering her flannel gown. She wore a night cap, and wisps of hair, un-combed, stuck out from the cap. She neither spoke, nor gave any indication that she was aware that anyone else was in the room.

The light from the lamp threw shadows across the walls, and even in the dim light I could see the livid color of Mrs. Roundy's face, and lips. Her temperature was 100 degrees, and her pulse was fast. Her chest was noisy, and the rales sounded like a death rattle.

I was sure she was dying, so as I came out of the bedroom I told Ina and Ruth, who were members of the Ladies Relief Society, that they should call the elders and prepare Mr. Roundy for burying.

I went home, depressed by the bad weather and the drive back to Kanab, and the fact there was nothing I could do for Mrs. Roundy. The elders and the ladies of the Relief Society would see that arrangements were made, and I would go back to care for the living.

Several days later, I met Ina Heaton in Kanab. I offered my condolences (assuming that Mrs. Roundy was dead and buried) and asked how the weather was in Alton. She laughed (a strange reaction, I thought), then told me that after I drove back to Kanab that she and Ruth had notified the Relief Society and the elders of the church that Mrs. Roundy was dying and that they should get ready for the funeral. They then notified the men so they could build her coffin.

Everyone gathered at Mrs. Roundy's house and built a fire in the fireplace and the kitchen stove. There was a piano in the living room, so the ladies used that to practice the hymns they planned to sing at Mrs. Roundy's funeral.

While the ladies sang in the parlor, the men built the coffin in the kitchen. Between the pounding of the hammers in the kitchen, and the piano playing and the singing in the parlor; no one heard Mrs. Roundy, as she suddenly pushed the door open and demanded to know what was going on.

Everyone was so startled to see the "dying woman" that they burst out with the truth; that they were practicing for her funeral, and the noise in the kitchen were the men, building her coffin.

No one had told me that Mrs. Roundy was addicted to Bromos. I realized then, that the livid color of her face, was the result of poisoning from too much Bromo-Seltzer. I am told that Sister Roundy was so shocked by the funeral preparations that she promptly stopped taking Bromos.

After one of my stories from the book appeared in *Southern Utah News* about the incident; a woman came into the newspaper office to say that when she was a young girl, she and her friends used to play in the old pine coffin, that was stored in a shed. I was not told whether the coffin was ever used for its intended purpose.

That same winter when the snow was still deep, and the weather was bitterly cold, I was called to Orderville to deliver Mary and Arlis Croft's baby. Mary's pains were infrequent, and I realized that I would be there most of the night. It was too far to drive back to Kanab in the snow, so Arlis suggested that I curl up at the foot of one of the beds where their two children were sleeping. The house was small and it held only the two beds, in addition to the other furniture. I accepted, gratefully.

The children were about two and four, and were already asleep. Because it was cold, I left on my brown cap with ear flaps, and my heavy brown overcoat. I curled up at the foot of the bed, and promptly fell asleep.

Apparently, I began to snore loudly, because the next thing I knew, the four year old reached down to see what was making that horrible noise. When he felt the fuzzy brown overcoat, and saw the brown cap with the ear flaps covering my head, he began to scream; "Daddy! There's a bear in my bed!"

On Tuesdays and Sundays, I would make a trip to Long Valley in the winter. In the summertime, I sometimes went fishing, and would drive through Mt. Carmel, Orderville, and Glendale. I told my patients that if they needed me, to hang up a white flag, and I would stop. There were only eleven telephones in the county, which made it difficult to reach me at times. It was easier for them to hang up a white flag, since I could often stop by earlier by getting this kind of a signal.

One Sunday night, when I was driving back to Kanab after having been in Glendale, I stopped at Jack Morrison's at the Mt. Carmel Y to exchange a leg of mutton, someone had given me on their bill, for some gas. He told me there was a man who was traveling on foot, and that he looked pretty tired. It was cold, so Jack suggested that I give the man a ride.

I had not driven far when I spotted the lone figure, trudging along, carrying a battered suitcase. His coat was thin, and worn; offering little protection against the cold night. I stopped and offered him a ride. When I asked him what he was doing our on a night like this, he told me that he was a preacher. He didn't belong to any particular denomination, but preached when he could get a small group together.

He told me that he depended on the Lord to provide food and shelter. Sometimes he took up a collection when he preached to a group, but that offered little financial support in the thirties.

I asked him where he had slept the previous night since he had come across from Zion. There were no restaurants, and no houses. He said that the park ranger had been very nice to him in Springdale, and had driven him to the end of the park, and given him permission to sleep in the last tunnel. He had matches, and had gathered firewood to build a fire outside the tunnel to keep warm.

In the morning, he left the tunnel, and walked towards Mt. Carmel. He had no breakfast, but when he reached the Jack Butler Road he passed some wagons by the side of the road. The men who owned the wagons had apparently taken their teams back into the woods to gather firewood. Beneath the seat of one of the wagons he found some lunches. He ate enough to sustain him, and left the rest for the men who would soon return.

I asked him if he felt the Lord had provided that meal for him, and he said that was the Lord's way. I laughed, and said that when the fellow whose lunch he had eaten came back and found it missing; I was sure he would not say that the Lord had provided lunch for some wayfarer, but was more likely to say, "Some sonofabitch stole my lunch!"

When I looked at his threadbare clothes, I told him that he was going to see a lot of hungry days, and that when he left Kanab and started across the Kaibab Forest on his way to Phoenix, that he had better have a way across that mountain road at nine thousand feet elevation; or Lord or no Lord, he would freeze to death.

I still had my two rooms at Parry Lodge, so I let him spend the night in one of my rooms. I bought dinner for him that night, and then bought breakfast for him the following morning. I had a call to make in Fredonia, so I drove him to the edge of Fredonia, gave him some money, and prayed that someone would give him a ride over the mountain. He seemed unafraid, and I could not help admiring someone with such overwhelming faith in the Almighty.

As I drove away, I looked in my rear view mirror, and saw the lone figure, with the battered suitcase, trudging along the highway towards the Kaibab.

CHAPTER SEVENTEEN
The Movie Industry Comes to Kanab

It took a little longer for the Depression to be felt by the westerners. They had sold some of their cattle, sheep and wool prior to the Depression in 1929.

In 1931, wool sold for six cents a pound, and you could buy a sheep for a dollar and a quarter. A full-grown range cow, to be used for beef, could be purchased for twenty-five dollars. Laborers were paid three dollars a day; skilled laborers (like a stone mason) were paid four dollars, and carpenters were paid up to seven dollars a day.

Lumber sold for twenty dollars a thousand, unplaned. Planed lumber (on one side) was twenty-five dollars a thousand. I don't remember the cost of gasoline, but it was low. So was the price of landland.

Many of the ranchers had over-extended themselves during the time the prices of wool and cattle were still high. They had BLM permits to graze their cattle on forest land, and some of them had leased private land for grazing. After the Depression hit, the ranchers found it difficult to meet their mortgage payments, leases and grazing rights, so some of them had to sell some of their stock at Depression prices.

Chaunce Parry, who was an amateur photographer, as well as a hotel man, came up with the idea of taking some of his pictures of southern Utah to Hollywood, to promote tourism. The roads were bad; people had little money, and cars were not very reliable. Chaunce reasoned that if he could promote the area to the motion picture industry, that it not only would bring business into southern Utah, but would also help Parry Lodge.

Chaunce was so successful that numerous motion pictures were later made in the area. *Drums Along the Mohawk; Green Grass of Wyoming; Flicka; Wild Bill Hicock; Daniel Boone; Desperados,* and many others were made in the area. The stars were housed at Parry Lodge.

It put Kanab on the map, and brought employment to the people living in the area. Some worked as extras and others worked as laborers. Nita, whom I had remarried, gave first aid, and I was called on from time to time to take care of some of the stars.

There was seldom anything serious; there were mostly minor things like removing the stinger of a bee from Diahann Carroll, or giving a shot of vitamin B1 to Yvonne DeCarlo. An English actor who was playing in an episode of *Daniel Boone*, with Fess Parker, broke his femur. He was sent to San Francisco to be treated, but returned within a week with a pin in the medullary canal, and wearing a cast. He finished the picture that way, even fighting a duel.

When Arlene Dahl was starring in *Bugles at Sundown,* she had a severe abdominal pain, and fainted, while on location. She had been flown in from Los Angeles a week after the movie company had started shooting. For a Civil War scene she was dressed in a gown that weighed close to forty pounds, and in the extreme heat, the fair-skinned star became ill and fainted. She was brought in from Cedar Mountain to Kanab, where I examined her.

I didn't know if it was a case of appendicitis, or Middle Schmertz disease. I knew that if it was appendicitis she would have to be flown back to Los Angeles as soon as possible, because the hospital had not yet been built in Kanab. If it was pain caused by an ovum follicle, time would cure it.

Time would cost the company money, with the possibility the picture would have to be delayed. The director, a small, nervous man, demanded that she return to finish the scenes. I insisted that she be given time off. Production was held up for three days, but after resting, Arlene went back and finished the picture.

She was, beyond a doubt, one of the most beautiful actresses I have ever seen. She was beautiful on the inside as well, with a sweet and undemanding disposition.

It was rumored that Arlene's female companion was her cousin, and that while Arlene was recovering in her cabin at Parry Lodge; her cousin was carrying on a love affair with Whit Parry.

Marlin Brown, publisher of Southern Utah News, was a teenager when Arlene Dahl and Joel McCrea starred in the *Outriders*. He was the double for Claude Jarman, the young actor who played the starring role in *The Yearling*, and the supporting actor in *The Outriders*. Marlin did some riding in the film, but sometimes, as he explained, he "simply sat around."

He was also in a dance scene with Burl Ives and about sixteen other dancers, in *The Green Grass of Wyoming*. The dance scene was filmed in the Mormon Ward Hall, and when Burl Ives showed up for the filming, he was accompanied by a huge black and white dog, possibly a Great Dane. He said that all of the kids loved Burl, who was wonderful with the kids. Burl sometimes showed up at Parry Lodge with two miniature dogs, one in each pocket.

Marlin said that everyone loved Joel McCrea, and the kids in Kanab would follow him down the street, idolizing him. Joel sometimes bought ice cream cones for them, making him a popular man to follow. Joel McCrea is known for his flawless manners, and gentlemanly behavior.

It was Marlin's father, Joseph Guernsey Brown, who raised vegetables for the movie *Buffalo Bill*, starring Joel McCrea and Maureen O'Hara. It was Marlin's job to cut off the tops from the one hundred and fifty gallon tins that were used by his father to plant corn, tomatoes and other vegetables that were then taken out to Johnson Canyon where the picture was being filmed. Marlin said that he doesn't recall seeing much of the garden in the movie.

Marlin's father died in 1966, shortly after Marlin returned to Kanab. Marlin had been living in Provo for nine years where he attended BYU, and worked on the university newspaper, *The Daily Universe*. When he returned to Kanab, he first worked for, then bought the local newspaper from Errol Brown, and has continued publishing *The Southern Utah News* ever since.

Anthony Quinn starred in *Bob, Son of Battle*, that was filmed near Panguitch Lake. The cast and crew were housed at Parry Lodge. The story was set in the Scottish moors, with stone bridges, sheep dogs, and long-haired sheep. We didn't get to mingle with the cast on that picture, but did go to watch some of the filming. I have always admired Quinn's acting, but didn't get to know him.

I don't recall the name of the western that was being shot at the time, but it was after the hospital was built in Kanab. A handsome actor who was playing the part of a cowboy was brought in to see me. A horse had thrown his head back, hitting the actor in the nose and breaking the cartilage from the bony portion of the nose. The nose was pushed to one side. I reached across the desk, and with the proper pressure and a little twist, pushed the nose back into place. There was no fuss, and no anesthetic. The handsome cowboy was Omar Shariff, before he became famous.

Later, when he and Gregory Peck were here on location, I treated Shariff for tonsilitis. When he had undergone a tonsilectomy years before, the surgeon had left in a part of one tonsil. It had become infected, so I treated him with a series of penicillin shots.

Gregory Peck was a Christian Scientist, so when a member of his family became ill with colds, he asked that they not be given any medication. Many of the stars were Christian Scientists and refused medication.

Duke, my oldest son, was a driver for the Teamsters Union during the time movies were being made in southern Utah. When Sidney Poitier was filming in the area, Duke drove him to and from the location in a pickup. On one occasion Duke climbed into the back of the truck to take a nap while he waited for Poitier. He had fallen asleep when he felt the it start to move. Poitier was driving. He looked over his shoulder and grinned, "Don't worry," he explained, "I have a chauffer's license. They didn't need me today so I am going back to town."

When they arrived at Parry Lodge, Poitier invited Duke to have lunch with him. Duke thought that Sue, his wife, would enjoy meeting Poitier, and asked permission to have her join them. Poitier graciously consented, so the three of them spent a pleasant visit over lunch.

Diahann Carroll came to visit Poitier while he was filming here. She had gone to Duke's Clothing Store to buy a pair of tennis shorts, but they were a little large in the legs. While she and Poitier were playing tennis; a bee got inside one of the legs of the shorts and stung her. Poitier brought her to my office where I removed the stinger, using dry ice as an anesthetic.

During the filming of *The Desperados,* with Randolph Scott and Ed Buchanan, Alvin Larson said I could use one of the cabins at Navajo Lake, so that Buchanan and Scott could fish. I am quite sure that it was only because they were movie stars that Alvin offered the use of a cabin, and not because he felt any pangs of conscience. I took him up on his offer, although I still felt bitterness over his crooked takeover of the lodge.

Buchanan and his wife had both been dentists in Oregon, but Buchanan had always had an interest in acting. His wife suggested that they go to Los Angeles, and he could act in amateur theatre. While she continued to work as a children's dentist; Ed sought parts in plays. It was in one of the plays that he was seen by someone from Columbia Pictures, and Ed Buchanan became a professional actor. He was down to earth, and likeable.

Randolph Scott was also personable, but Nita never forgave him for breaking her fishing pole. He never offered to replace it, so she held that against him. It cost me seventy-five dollars to pacify her. I bought her a seven foot, two inch flyrod, manufactured by Paul H. Young in Detroit. It weighed only three ounces, and was one of the finest available. It was a far better rod than the one Scott broke, but Nita still held it against him.

The men stayed there for one week, and were excited over the size of the trout we took out of Mammoth Creek. The lake was low and clear, so we fished with dry flies, from dusk to dark.

The actresses in *The Desperados* were Sally Eilers, Evelyn Keyes, and Claire Trevor. Most of the filming was done in the back lots of Kanab, with Charles Vidor directing. Harry Joe Brown was the producer, and Glenn Ford and Big Boy Williams played the male leads.

It was an informal group, and we had many good times together. Sally Eilers would call up Nita and tell her they were coming to our house for dinner that night. They always brought the food from the lodge, and prepared it. Trevor's mother and Vidor's mother were a part of the group, and they would make the salad. Big Boy Williams cooked his speciality, fried potatoes covered with cheese, in a large skillet. They would melt in your mouth! Either hamburger or steak would be put on the barbeque, to be served with the salad and potatoes.

We had a large barbeque at our apartment, which was a part of the old hospital. We also had a large stone fireplace, surrounded by a stone wall. When the old hospital was replaced by the current building, the fireplace was transported to the Heritage House, and is now in the back yard.

We hung lights in the trees, so it made a pleasant place for the cast to relax, away from the public eye. However; I have recently learned that Mardean Pugh, and her sister Lyall MacDonald, used to peek through the shrubbery when they were youngsters, and thought that the parties were pretty wild! Perhaps it was because after we ate, we would douse the lights, and sit around and talk. To young girls in a small Mormon town, that could seem pretty wild.

Glenn Ford was dating Eleanor Powell at the time, so he'd leave the group to go to the hospital to telephone her each night. They were later married, and then divorced around 1960. Charles Vidor and Evelyn Keyes were also married later.

During the filming of the *Wild Bill Hickock* series, Walter Brennan and another actor dropped by the house. I thought Brennan was seeking medical advice, but he said he just wanted to visit, and talk. He did, mostly about himself. I believe Gordon Elliot was starring in the early series.

When Frank Sinatra, Sammy Davis Junior, and Peter Lawford were in Kanab for *The Sergeants Three,* Sinatra leased Whit Parry's home, which was one of the nicest ones in Kanab. It is said that Sinatra spent $60,000 remodeling Whit's house to his taste; putting in cedar lined closets, and whatever else he wanted for his comfort. After Sinatra left, Whit had, not only the money from the lease, but $60,000 worth of improvements.

Karen Alvey, a beautiful blonde, who once worked for Whit, now lives in the home. She and her husband have race horses, and sleek and contented cats. It is said that the ghost of Whit Parry still comes back, and sometimes at night, one can hear him playing the piano in the home that once housed Sinatra.

During the thirties and forties, when the movie industry was filming in southern Utah, natives were paid an average of six dollars a day as extras. They also rented out teams, wagons, stock, horses, props, and locations, at a liberal price. Teamsters and special effects men were paid union wages.

Whit Parry got his share as well. In addition to the percentage of the money paid to the extras, he also lodged the crew at Parry Lodge. Because the extras were paid less in Kanab than they were paid in Hollywood, it made it attractive to the film industry. It was a mutually beneficial arrangement, for the people of Kanab, and for the movie industry.

Whit Parry had done the promoting, and deserved a percentage. Without the Parrys, the people in Kanab would not have been able to earn as much as they did, as extras, and by renting to the industry.

But, greed raised its ugly head. When the extras in Kanab (although they were making more money than they had ever made in their lives), found out the extras in Hollywood were making more money; they called a strike. They didn't take into consideration the difference in living costs between Kanab and Hollywood, so they *killed the goose that laid the golden egg,* by joining the Screen Extras Guild.

They also did not take into consideration that the movie industry had the expense of bringing the cast and crew to Kanab from Hollywood. I believe it was Eddie Small Productions that was filming here at the time of the strike. Artie Miller, a Hollywood cameraman whom I had begun to regard as a friend, told me that the film companies would not come back until after the extras in Kanab got out of the union.

I was the mayor of Kanab at the time, and was interested in what was best for Kanab. I met with the local members of the Screen Extras Guild, and explained the situation to them. I told them that it was not just the screen extras that would be deprived of wages, but that the entire town would suffer a loss of revenue if the film industry pulled out.

The union let the members withdraw; the first time a group was permitted to withdraw; but the damage had been done. Although some pictures were shot here after that, it was never the same as it was before the strike. Greed on the part of the people, drove the film industry to Europe, where they found the lower prices they had once enjoyed in Kanab.

Beside losing much of the film industry, Kanab lost their two main contacts: Whit Parry and Fay Hamblin. Whatever the film people needed, Whit or Fay could get it for them. There had been a good relationship between the film industry and Parry Lodge. Phyllis Stewart, who worked at the lodge, said that Robert Taylor used to telephone, without giving his name, and say "Save number nine cabin for me tonight, and tell Ethel (the bakery cook) to make two loaves of bread for me to take home tommorow night."

Louise Bell, who worked for about eight years for Whit, probably knew more about the comings and goings of the cast and crew than anyone, but she is not the talkative type. She later worked for me, and after Nita died, we saw each other occasionally. We are still friends today.

Ronald Reagan was here during the filming of the early episodes of *Death Valley Days,* and the location at Wahweap, where *The Greatest Story Ever Told,* with Charlton Heston, was filmed, now lies under Lake Powell.

One of the most colorful extras from Kanab was Silas Hicks, who just passed away this year (1989). Sy had a beautiful voice and could yodel like no one I have ever heard. Sy never trusted me, or any other doctor for that matter. He was convinced that I was Jewish, and he didn't like Jews.

He told a nephew that he would pay any bill, but a doctor bill. He was sure that if I gave him a shot, I would put water in the needle, and charge him for it. I always spoke to him, but he'd eye me suspiciously, then grunt, or ignore me.

In 1988, when Kathryn Vilips was in Kanab to edit my book; she went into the old deserted Sy Hicks house, hoping to write a story. Sy had been in a rest home for a year or more. On the kitchen table was an open can of beans, half-eaten, with a spoon sticking out of the can. A jacket hung on the back of the chair, along with a hat. It looked as though he had been called away for just a moment - and would return to finish the can of beans.

In the living room was a piano, and Della Johnson, who lives across the street from the house, and keeps an eye on it for the Hicks family, said that there was a mysterious woman who once rented a room in the house. She said that late at night, neighbors would hear the mystery lady and Sy, singing, accompanied by piano music.

No one seems to know who she was; where she came from, or where she went. Sy never married, and no one seems to know why. He told his nephew, George Mace, shortly before he died, that he wished now that he had married. When asked why, he said "Then I wouldn't be alone."

Sy was proud of the parts he played in the movies, and boasted that he had saved Buffalo Bill in the movie of the same name. When a film was being shot at Paria, sudden rainstorms caused flash-floods that sometimes trapped the cast and crew, and prevented their getting back to town. They called it their *Golden Hours,* because everyone was paid overtime. Sy was then hired to sit atop a lookout point, and when floodwaters threatened to block their way, he was instructed to start yodeling.

The Sy Hicks house had been the old Cole Hotel, later known as the McAllister Hotel after Elizabeth Adams McAllister, polygamous wife of W.J.F. McAllister, purchased the hotel. Zane Grey, Buffalo Bill, and other famous and infamous people, are supposed to have stayed in the hotel during its heyday. It was purchased in 1908, by George Hicks, to be used as a private home. After the death of his parents, Sy rented out rooms.

Even in its' run-down condition, the home and property, after restoration, would make a lovely art and culture center, with the grounds being used as a park. With the Heritage House close by, and the two historic houses belonging to Thayne and Jo Smith, and Vola Rider; it would enhance the entire area for tourists, and for our local people. There are numerous artists and writers living in the area, who would welcome such a center.

The Willows Gallery, owned and operated by Don and Melanie Pillmore, opened this year on Center Street in Kanab. The gallery has been a welcome addition to the town, along with the Variety Arts Council that is bringing the ballet and other attractions to the area. The Old Barn Theatre, behind Parry Lodge is re-opening this year, so things are looking up for Kanab, culture-wise.

Although most of the relationships between the movie industry and the Parrys were pleasant, John Ford had words with the Parrys over something, and took his pictures to Monument Valley. He vowed never to come back to Kanab, as long as the Parrys were here. No one ever said what the disagreement was, but it must have been serious, to provoke such a decision.

Dennis Judd, a descendant of several generations of Utah pioneers, is now the local contact for the film industry. When he was a freshman in high school, he worked as a bellhop for Whit at Parry Lodge. He learned much during the heyday of the filming industry through Whit. They became close friends, and Dennis, who is the owner of Denny's Wigwam in Kanab, tries to keep the legend of Whit Parry alive, through his advertising, and through the nightly western shows from March through November, behind his western store and museum.

Dennis provides Indians, wranglers, and transportation, and finds locations for various films. The last casting was for Sam Elliot's *The Quick and the Dead* filmed in Flagstaff. He also sent five Indians to Sonora, California recently to act in the film, *The Kid.*

Dennis, who has always had an interest in western history, has one of the finest stores and museums to be found in the Southwest. His wife, whom he met when he was on a mission, and she was serving in the Peace Corps, are two of the best *Ambassadors of Good Will* that southern Utah has to offer. Tour busses bring visitors from France, Germany, Japan, and other parts of the world, to Kanab, and it is at *Denny's Wigwam,* that they find the western regalia and handmade jewelry, that they take back to their country.

It is also at *Tribal Arts* in Kanab, that the gracious and knowledgeable Eula Bruce, along with her sister, make a visitor feel welcome while they are enjoying the museum quality collections from all over the world that Eula has displayed.

On the outskirts of Kanab, coming from Mt Carmel, Andrew Johnston has a most unusual museum, *Johnston's Primitive Arts,* with collections from China, local Indian collections, and collections from other parts of the world. Andrew, a descendant of Civil War General Sidney Albert Johnston, is also knowledgeable, and if one is fortunate enough to find the museum open, and Andrew in a talkative mood, most visitors will go away knowing much more than they did when they walked in.

From the exciting days of the filming in and around Kanab, to the slower-paced days of 1989, Kanab was, is, and will be, an exciting place to visit. It has not always been the easiest place for someone to live, especially if you are an "outsider," but it remains one of the most colorful spots on earth.

CHAPTER EIGHTEEN
Emma Jean's Appendix, and Other Surgeries

The weather in the wintertime was usually dry, with some snow and rain, but the winter of 1932-1933 was severe. Early in the fall, the bridge at Coal Hill, between Highway 89 and Zion Park was washed out by a small slide. The mail had to be taken out by cable. No cars could get across, making it difficult to get passengers from one side to the other.

The snow plow, driven by Johnny Glazier, consisted of a V-shaped plow, with side-walls of planks. Johnny would place rocks inside the box to weight down the plow. It was pulled by four horses, and on the narrow roads between Kanab and the surrounding towns; I sometimes came around a bend a little fast and would have to skid into the snowbank on the side of the road, to keep from hitting Johnny and the snow plow. Johnny would then un-hitch one of the teams and pull me out, and I would continue on my way.

Cedar Mountain, and the highway going over the Kaibab Forest, were usually closed during the winter due to heavy snows, but this year, the roads were closed early. We didn't have enough equipment to keep the roads open. Highway 89, since it was the route to Salt Lake City, was kept open most of the time, but due to the bridge wash-out we could not get to St. George or to Cedar City.

One night we attended a basket ball game in Orderville, followed by a dance. As I was leaving the dance, someone said that Bessie Brooksby's little girl had been ill for three or four days, and asked if I would check on her.

Bessie was a widow, whose husband, Alvin, had met with a tragic accident in Zion Canyon. They were on a picnic when a cable, used by the Wilkin's lumber people to carry logs to the bottom of the canyon, broke. There were several groups of people on an Easter outing, and someone unfastened the carrier on the cable, sending the carrier down, and decapitating Alvin Brooksby. I don't believe they ever found out who did it, but the person or persons who were the cause of this tragic accident, must have been haunted by the memory for the rest of their lives.

It was almost one o'clock in the morning when I arrived at the Brooksby home. Emma Jean, who was perhaps ten or twelve years old, was suffering from a painful and distended abdomen. She also had a high fever, symptoms of peritonitis, so my diagnosis was a ruptured appendix.

The hospital was not built yet, but Viola Adams, who was a nurse, was visiting in Kanab at the time. I drove back to Kanab, contacted Viola, and asked her if she would give the anesthetic the following morning. I told her we would have to operate on Emma Jean at home, since there was no way to get the girl to a hospital with the heavy snows and bridge wash-out.

I then called the dentist, Dr. Alfred Brooksby (an uncle to Emma Jean), to ask him if he could assist. I never went to bed, but gathered whatever surgical intruments I had, along with plenty of cotton and gauze. I was not really well equipped to do this type of surgery. We had rubber gloves, but no sterile surgical gowns.

We arrived at daybreak. There was no electricity in the home, and we could not use an open flame because of the anesthetic. There was a fire burning in the pot-bellied stove in the dining room, where we would have to do the surgery. The room was overheated and stifling - and dangerous, since we would be using ether.

We threw open the doors to cool the room, then boiled our gloves and the instruments. After boiling I placed the instruments in a Lysol solution in one large pan, and would rinse them in sterile water in another large pan.

The fire in the pot-bellied stove was put out, but the one in the kitchen was left burning.

The operating table was a large round oak dining table, which made it difficult for us to reach the patient. We had made pads for Emma Jean to lie on. I usually gave some of the anesthetic myself, but since Viola was experienced in giving the anesthesia; she took over. Dr. Brooksby was to assist me.

The vapor from ether breaks down into a formaldehyde, making it difficult to breathe, and to see. I don't think we gave much thought to an explosion other than opening the doors, but as I look back, we might easily have been blown up. I have heard it said that "God looks after fools and drunks." Perhaps, one should add, "...and country doctors!"

Dr. Brooksby had the other pair of sterile gloves. I prepared the abdomen by washing if off with a solution of Lysol, and as my scapel made the incision, and the blood came out, Dr. Brooksby fainted.

He got to his hands and knees and crawled out. To this day, in my mind's eye, I can see Dr. Brooksby crawling out through the dining room door, and into the kitchen to get some fresh air. There went my assistant, sterile gloves and all!

As I opened the abdomen and got down to the peritoneum, pus swelled up out of the wound. I had made a generous incision, and as I put my hand on the abdomen to express more pus; the ruptured appendix came up through the incision.

On that type of case, in those days, we usually did not remove the appendix. We'd just open up the abdomen, drain the abcess, put in a drain, and get the hell out of there!

When the enlarged appendix came up through the incision, showing a small perforation at the base where it hooked onto the cecum, I decided to remove the appendix. I took my scissors and clipped around where the appendix entered the cecum. I put a clamp on the appendix, and tied off the mesocolon, after splitting the mesocolon down to the perforation over the appendix. That left a hole in the gut where the appendix was removed, so I put in a drain, closed it neatly, after expressing what pus there was, and sutured the wound.

It was a clean operation, and one I am proud of. I had never performed one exactly like it before, or since, and I have long wanted to bring it to the attention of other doctors, because I feel it is a better way of performing an appendectomy than the method usually used.

At this point, the patient was quite dark, so I had Viola stop the anesthetic. After the patient was conscious, and breathing normally, we made a bed for her in the living room, and put her to bed.

Kezia Ann Stark Brooksby, a cousin of Emma Jean's mother, said that they will never forget the surgery. She lived across the street from Bessie Brooksby, and now lives in Fredonia.

The next morning I drove back to Orderville to check on Emma Jean. I was concerned because it had been an unusual surgery. When I arrived, Emma jean was sitting up in bed, surrounded by her dolls; each one wearing a band-aid, on incisions drawn on their bodies with merthiolate.

Emma Jean made a nice recovery, and later became a nurse. She lives today, in Oregon. When I celebrated my 90th birthday at the Heritage House, and my picture appeared in the *Southern Utah News,* Emma Jean wrote to me. It is always nice to hear from one of my patients forty or fifty years later. It is one of the joys of being a country doctor.

There seemed to be a run on appendectomies where the Brooksbys were concerned. The day after Emma Jean's surgery, one of the Brooksby girls in Fredonia, from one of the other Brooksby families, had an attack of appendicitis, that required surgery. This time my assistants were nurses, Roberta Jensen and her friend, who was a surgical nurse for Dr. Greer in Phoenix.

We had a little better set-up for the second girl. Although we did this operation on the dining room table, as we had on Emma Jean; the nurses had time to sterilize the sheets, and the appendix had not ruptured. She also recovered, without complications.

It was about this time that one of my obstetrical patients in Jacob Lake went into labor. There was so much snow they could not get her to Kanab, and I could not get to Jacob Lake.

She had been a nurse, and had a friend close by who was a practical nurse, so we talked her baby into the world by telephone. I hung onto the phone, giving instructions during the delivery. She got along nicely, which indicates that Mother Nature takes care of a lot of these cases.

It was while I still had my office at Parry Lodge that there was an automobile accident involving four young people. The two who were injured were riding in the rumble seat. Whit Parry, Billie Bowman, Peg Nelson and I were playing bridge at Billie's house when Erk Eddington came running across the street. He was yelling, "There's been an accident! She's been scalped, and her brains are hanging out!"

One girl, Alice Lewis, had been taken to my office at Parry Lodge, and as I entered the room she walked out of the bathroom. She was pulling the lower lid of one eye down, and said matter-of-factly, "Doc! I've cut my goddam eye out!" I yelled at her not to pull at the eye, but she pulled the lower lid off, right in front of me. We might have saved the eye if she had left it alone. I was angry because there was nothing we could do now to save her eye. It was an incredibly stupid thing for her to do.

I put a patch on her torn eye, and sent her home. The following morning, I removed the eye at Parry Lodge, since there was no hospital yet, in Kanab. I called Viola Adams to give the anesthetic. I first gave Alice morphine and atropine, then Viola gave the anesthetic. I had done EENT work in New York so I had the curved intrument for the enucleation, or removal of the eye.

The other girl, Velva Griffith, whose brains, Erk thought were hanging out, had almost been scalped, and what he thought were brains, was the exposed bone. I had to sew her scalp back on.

The two girls had been riding in the rumble seat of the car, and the two boys were in the front. The boys were unhurt. The kids, about eighteen or nineteen years of age, were speeding out of town when they missed a turn, and hit a culvert. They were a group of kids from Fredonia. I don't recall the names of the boys, although I think one of them was Wildcat Parker, a fighter.

Dart Judd's boy, from Fredonia, was in an accident in Moccasin in which a girl was killed. Judd's head went through the windshield and he was bleeding from the neck. I answered the call, and drove him into Kanab to the hospital and called Dr. Riley. When we laid him on his back and raised his chin to suture the neck; blood shot out and hit the ceiling. I almost fainted. We put in more than one hundred clamps in his neck. He lived, fortunately.

Another one of Dart Judd's boys was on his way home from high school one noonday. A friend of his was driving past and the Judd boy ran and jumped on the running board of the car, then jumped off. There was a car parked in front of Dart's home and he was running so fast that he could not stop in time, to avoid hitting the headlight of the parked car. It knocked the breath out of him, and he later became sick at his stomach. Dart called me and I took him into the hospital.

Dr. Riley and Dr. Sanella were then my partners, and I told them I thought the boy had a ruptured spleen. The doctors asked me how I knew, after we removed the spleen. He had gone into shock and was so sick that I was reminded of a case where I had missed diagnosing a ruptured spleen in a previous accident case, and the boy died.

That was the time a truck carrying CCC boys was sideswiped by another vehicle, and about eighteen boys were injured in the accident. One of the boys sat quietly in a corner, sick, but uncomplaining. It did not occur to me at the time that the boy was in shock. We had so many people from the accident lying in the hallway of the hospital that we were busy taking care of those who seemed to be the most badly injured. It was not until the others were taken care of that I realized the uncomplaining lad was worse off than the others. I had called Dr. McIntyre in Cedar City when the accident victims were first brought in, and when we took the young man into surgery, we found that the spleen was ruptured. He later died.

I was glad that Dr. Riley was there to assist me when Dart's boy was brought in. Dr. Riley was an excellent anatomist, and I would not have dared to go in and open up the Judd boy without Riley's help.

Nita and I were still separated, and later were divorced for two years, while I was at Parry Lodge. I had asked May Black and Grace Brinkerhoff, a nurse from Emery County, to attend the fights with me one night in Kanab. May lived in Glendale, and Grace was staying with May while she was visiting this area.

May lived across the street from the Ramseys. Bertha was expecting at any time, and when she saw my car at May's house, she sent someone to get me. She had begun labor, and her husband, Grant, was sitting on a chair massaging his feet. He said he was just thinking about going out to see if he could hire a car to take Bertha into Kanab, when I walked in.

I told him there wasn't time to hire a car, that we had to get her into Kanab, about thirty miles from Glendale. I ran across the street and told Grace and May what was happening and asked Grace to go along while I drove Bertha into town. It had started to rain, and the cows, who were on open range had wandered out onto the highway to lap up the water from the falling rain. Besides trying to keep the speeding car from planing on the slick roads; I had to drive around thirsty cows.

Just as we reached Three Lakes, Bertha let out a shriek. I told Grace to check and see what happened. We were in the front seat and Bertha was in the back. Grace reached over the back of the seat and checked under Bertha's dress and said, "The water broke."

It was sundown when we pulled up in front of midwife, Laura Broadbent's house. She and Pa Broadbent were sitting on the porch. I leaped out of the car and yelled at her to make preparations for a delivery. I scooped Bertha up in my arms and raced up the stairs of the porch. As I did so, I called over my shoulder to Grace to take the car and go to the Lodge to get my medical bag, and bring it back to the house.

I carried Bertha the seventy-five or one hundred feet to the porch, then into the house where Laura was trying to prepare a place for the delivery. She was so excited she couldn't find anything. Just as Grace burst into the room with my bag, Bertha Ramsey had her baby. I don't recall if it was Robert or Douglas, but I believe it was Bertha's last baby, and Douglas is the youngest. There was so much excitement that night, I don't even remember if Grace and I ever made it to the fights. I don't even remember if I took her back to Glendale that night.

My brother-in-law, Dick Knight, had a younger brother that was having difficulty finding a job during the Depression. My sister, Ann, wrote asking if Bill, the young man, could come out to Kanab. She hoped that we might be able to help him find a job.

Bill was a likeable young man and shortly after arrival went to work as a bartender for Milt's Bar on the Utah-Arizona border. He became Milt's first bartender. He also played the banjo at Milt's, then played with the local band for the Saturday night dances.

While Nita and I were divorced, the two small rooms at Parry's Lodge had been enough for me. Now that Bill would be living with me I had to find larger quarters. We found lodging at Grace and George Shield's house, where we had two bedrooms, and an extra room for my office. We had wonderful times there, since there was a piano in the house. Bill would play the banjo; I would play the piano, and anyone who wanted to join us could accompany us with the singing.

We had parties, and sometimes disturbed the neighbors with our good-natured antics, and loud music. Bill and I got along famously, and I enjoyed his company, since I did not have Nita and Duke with me. Perhaps these were some of the parties that were considered "wild" in this town.

Charlie Plumb, the cartoonist who drew the comic strip *Ella Cinders,* and his wife Rachel, used to come to our parties. Charlie would have a couple of drinks of whiskey, then head for the nearest bedroom to sleep, until the party was over.

Hoyt and Catherine Chamberlain, Dev and Billie Bowman, and Jim and Peg Nelson were also partying people that livened up our get-togethers. After Hoyt

Chamberlain died, Catherine (who is still a beauty) married John Martin. Before her marriage to Hoyt, Catherine was so shy that she rarely talked, but after her marriage her personality blossomed.

During one of the parties, we ran out of booze. Someone said they knew where we could get some moonshine. Carrie Johnson ran a small cafe on Center Street in Kanab, and was known to sell bootleg whiskey. I don't recall who went with me, but we went to the cafe and I said, "Carrie, we need some whiskey." She took the bottle from my hand, without answering. She went behind the counter, lifted her skirt, and filled our bottle from a gallon jug she had tied around her ample waist. She popped the cork into the bottle, handed it back to me and said, "That will be five dollars, please."

This was the same night that Norval Johnson, who was meaner than strychnine when he drank, tried to crash the party. Some of the men helped him out the door, and over the fence, after the girl giving the party refused to let Norval stay.

Jim Nelson, Peg, Dev and Billie Bowman and I, were at a dance in Fredonia one night, held in the attic above the Brooksby store. Norval was there, and Jim Nelson pointed out to me that Norval was wearing his Stetson while he was dancing. I was showing off for the girl I was dancing with, so I told Norval to remove his hat. Norval refused, and being made bolder by the moonshine whiskey I had had, I told him to take off his hat, or I would knock it off. Norval looked down at me and said, "Doc, you and me have a date right after this dance; I'll meet you in the alley."

I couldn't back out, so when the dance was over, I followed Norval down the stairs, and into the dark alley. I was hoping that someone would come to my rescue, and I was already regretting my foolhardy threat to knock his hat off.

About this time, Jim Nelson missed me and yelled, "Where's Doc?" The girl I had been dancing with said, "Oh, he's gone out to knock Norval's hat off!" Jim raced out the door, and from the top of the stairs, yelled, "Norval, you sonofabitch, if you lay one hand on Doc, I'll murder you!"

The next day, as I was crossing the street to my car; Norval drove up, got out of his car and started towards me. There was no one to come to my rescue this time, and I was scared! Norval was a big man, and I was less than five feet, six inches. I kept on walking across the street, when Norval met me half-way. "Doc," he said, "I like you. There's no need for us to fight!" With that, he thrust out his big paw, and shook my hand.

I was hunting pheasant one time near Panguitch, and met a deputy sheriff, who was also hunting. He said, after learning I was from Kanab, "You've got some pretty mean characters in your part of the country!" He then told me that he had arrested Denver Brandon and Norval Johnson for being drunk, and that on the way to jail, Norval took out his pocket-knife and cut up the upholstery in the vehicle.

Norval quieted down later in life, and I was happy that he never took me up on my foolish threat to knock his hat off.

Besides parties, there were school examinations, and clinics to attend. There were many children with enlarged tonsils, and sometimes, since there were no antibiotics yet; there were complications with mastoids, or otitis media. They often had enlarged adenoids, with mouth breathing, which subjected them to sinus infections and bronchitis. Without antibiotics, most doctors chose to remove the tonsils.

I asked Bill to assist me with some of these surgeries. I would teach him what to do, since I now had an ether suction machine, which made giving the anesthetic, an automatic procedure. I would induce the patient, then transfer to the ether suction. Bill would boil the instruments, and arrange them. By this time the patient would be induced, then he would take over the ether machine. Of course, I would be watching the patient too.

I had performed hundreds of tonsillectomies in New York, so I considered myself competent. We would perform two to four once a week, sometimes traveling to Glendale, Orderville, Mt. Carmel, or Fredonia.

When we went out of town, we would stay at the old Smith Hotel in Glendale, which was reassuring to the parents of the children who were to have surgery. They knew their children would have special care, if they needed it. Some EENT men used to come down from Salt Lake, when they wanted to go fishing, or visit the Grand Canyon. They would have someone line up a dozen or more tonsillectomies, ahead of time. The doctor would arrive; do the surgeries during the day, then take off for the Grand Canyon, or wherever it was he planned to go. If there were complications, the doctor was not available. I did not think that was fair to the patient, or to their parents.

Later on, after Nita and I remarried, and she came to Kanab to live, she assisted with the surgeries. One day, after having performed six or more tonsillectomies, two of my young patients let me know what they thought of me. Bill Spencer, after coming out from under the ether, raised up on his elbows and cried, "Doctor Aiken! You are a sonofabitch!" His sister, who had also had her tonsils removed got up on her elbows and said, "And I double it!"

In 1988, I went with a friend to buy apples from the Spencer orchards in Glendale, and Bill, a tall and very good looking man, reminded me of the incident; after he had carefully handpicked every apple in the large box, and sold it to my friend for only $5.00.

We also did mastoid operations in my office, then kept the patient overnight. We made a place for them in one of the beds, trying to make them as comfortable as possible under the circumstances. Today, with antibiotics there aren't the mastoid problems we once had.

There was one surgery, after the hospital was built, where the young Bundy boy, whose mother worked for the hospital, died, two days after surgery, of septicemia. He had a ruptured appendix, and when I went in, infection had already invaded the muscle below the appendix. There were no antibiotics, and his death from septicemia might have been prevented, if there had been.

CHAPTER NINETEEN
Airmail comes to Kanab

The first airmail stamps were issued on December 12, 1928, according to Theo McAllister, postmaster of Kanab. The two-cent stamp featuring the Wright Brothers, carried the mail across the U.S. and the five-cent Globe stamp carried the mail across the sea. Charles Lindbergh, before his famous solo ocean flight, flew the mail from the east to San Francisco.

It was in 1931, that the first airmail was flown into Kanab. Although there was a small strip where the present airport is located, the plane landed between Kanab and Johnson Canyon. There were no navigational aids then, so airplanes followed the railroad tracks, which meant they had to fly low enough to see them. When there were tunnels, the pilot flew over them, and picked up the railroad map on the other side.

Two National Guard planes flew alongside the first airmail plane as escorts, since there were no railroads to follow. The National Guard planes landed on the small airstrip outside of Kanab. The pilot of the first airmail plane into Kanab was the father of the present senator from Utah, Jake Garn.

Wesley McAllister, who still lives in the house he was born in more than 80 years ago; son of Angeline Brown McAllister, and W.J. F. McAllister, said that he was on the Kaibab at the time the first plane flew in, and that all he remembers is that the plane dove off into the creek, and the men had to pull it out before the plane could take off.

When I was still in Hurricane, a pilot, whose name I don't recall, became lost in the rain on a mail flight from Los Angeles to Salt Lake City. I don't think he landed in Cedar City, but he crashed into Cedar Mountain and was killed, sometime in 1928. It may have been the first mail flight from Los Angeles to Salt Lake City.

Before 1931, the mail was brought into Kanab by bus. Julius Dalley was the postmaster, and the postoffice was located where the present Zion Bank is now situated.

On January 10, 1969, pilot Arland Brooksby, mayor of Fredonia for eight years, was killed in a plane crash outside of Kanab, along with Cody Jake, Tribal Chairman for the Kaibab Paiute Tribe, Bud Button, Head of the Arizona/Utah Port of Entry, and Eldon Johnson, cattle inspector and marshal of Fredonia.

The four men were returning from a flight to Kingman, Arizona on government business, concerning advancing lands and properties for the city of Fredonia, according to Arland's wife, Kezia Ann Stark Brooksby. Arland was the brother of Lyle Brooksby, who is the veterinarian in Kanab.

Kezia Ann said that no official investigation, nor autopsies were ever conducted, nor any cause officially established for the crash. However, Theo McAllister, who is a pilot, and used to fly with Arland, said that he believed that the plane, a V Tail Bonanza that Arland was piloting, and had recently purchased, had a faster stall rate than the old Cessna Arland had flown for years. Theo believes that it simply stalled when the speed was too slow, and the altitude was too low for Arland to pull out of the stall. Families of the victims who were waiting at the airport to greet the incoming plane witnessed the tragic accident.

I don't recall which Brooksby it was who was given a poison mushroom by a friend as a *joke*. Brooksby often picked mushrooms with the new Forest Supervisor in Fredonia, and one day when Brooksby was gone, his friend delivered a plate of wild mushrooms to him. On top of the good mushrooms, was a different mushroom, that Brooksby had always believed to be poisonous. But, he reasoned, the Forest Supervisor might know something that he didn't, so he thought it must be alright to eat.

Brooksby cooked the large mushroom, and almost before he had eaten it all, he began to vomit, and suffer severe abdominal pain. His wife called me, as he sat on the floor in the bathroom vomiting. I rushed to Fredonia and gave him a shot of atropine. He lived, and surprisingly, remained friends with the prankster.

Men in southern Utah often played pranks, on me as well, that could have led to serious injury, or death. In Hurricane, one of the Winters boys, Dan, from Springdale, slapped a horse before I was on all the way, and I was thrown and hurt my back. He slapped his thigh and *hee-hawed* at his clever sense of humor.

One of the more interesting people in the area was Paul Hamblin, who was a cowboy singer. He was always well-dressed; perhaps even fancy in his dress. Paul worked part-time as a guide on the horseback trails at Grand Canyon. He met Beverly, a girl from a wealthy family in Boston, on one of the rides. They fell in love, and later when Bill developed leukemia, Beverly talked him into seeking treatment in Boston.

After treatment, Paul and Beverly were married and moved back to Utah. They were living at the Cave Lakes Ranch, when their child who was about a year and a half years old, fell into the fireplace from his high-chair, and was hideously burned.

Since there was no telephone, Paul's brother Mark rode horseback into Kanab to get me. It almost killed the horse.

I raced back, taking what I thought I might need for a case like that. I took some atropine and a tracheotomy kit, in case fire had gotten into the throat causing an edema of the larynx that could shut off the child's breathing.

When we arrived I bathed the baby's face, removing the ashes and irrigating the eyes. We used cold packs to keep the skin moist, and unguentine ointment on the skin.

It took three months for the burns to heal, and in the end, the child was left with a scar on the mouth. He later developed muscular dystrophy, and died before the age of thirteen. Beverly had been told that muscular dystrophy, which had been in her family, could not be transmitted through her; that it was passed through the male line. Tragically, this was not true in Beverly's case.

That summer, Dr. Lou Feid, a brother-in-law to Bill, asked me if I planned to return to the east to practice, or if I planned to stay in Kanab. He urged me to stay in Kanab and find some way to build a hospital, that was so desperately needed in the area, despite the objections of Dunc McDonald.

Charlie and Rachel Plumb came out with their family from California that summer. They liked the area so much that they leased the Cave Lakes Ranch, and built a summer cabin on it for their summer home.

Along with Lou, and Dr. *Snake* Kennedy, who was the physician for the Cincinnati Reds, we all had a summer of partying. Jack Butler, the lion hunter-guide, and his wife, suggested that a group of us get together for a horseback trip. He put a camp up at Two springs on the mountain at Quakie. Jack furnished the tents, horses and saddles. The rest of us bought a week's supply of grub, hired an old cowboy cook, and got half a beef and hung it in camp.

There were about twelve of us in the group. We rode the rim of the Grand Canyon to Powell's Plateau, and back. At night we sat around the campfire and sang, and exchanged stories. It was the camaraderie, on trips such as this, the people who were my friends, and the magnificent colors of southern Utah, and all that it had to offer in the way of fishing and hunting, that made it difficult to even consider going back to the east to practice.

Nita was still in Cincinnati with Duke, and I missed them. I wrote to Nita and told her I wanted to stay in the west. I asked her to join me. Her response was that she was tired of pioneering, and did not want to come back. It went on this way for a couple of years; Nita in Cincinnati, and me in Kanab. She felt abandoned, and later filed for divorce.

In 1933, I wrote to Nita and asked her to let Duke come back to Utah for the summer. He loved it. There were horses to ride, and fish to catch. He wanted to stay in the west, so when Nita came to take him back to Cincinnati to put him in school, I asked her to stay. I told her that I hoped to build a hospital and I needed her help.

She didn't come back that year, but the following year we were remarried in October in Parowan by a Justice of the Peace. Duke sat in the car after I met their train, and was unhappy that he could not be a part of the short marriage ceremony. He did admit later, that he had peeked in the window, while we were being remarried. We remained together for the rest of her life, until I lost her to a stroke, forty years later.

Conditions were better for us financially, in Kanab, than they had been in Hurricane. Early in 1935 we were busy with the building of the hospital. From that time on Nita worked with me, and we were able to spend more time together. Nita loved entertaining, and being involved. Her illness, and my frequent house calls miles away, had prevented this in Hurricane.

CHAPTER TWENTY
The Building of the Hospital

It was the day after Christmas in 1934, that I made the decision to go ahead and build the hospital. I had a confinement case in Orderville the day before Christmas. After the delivery I returned to Kanab to dress for a dance at the Ward Hall. While we were dancing, Guy Chamberlain, from the Chamberlain Hotel, came with a message that May Black was on the phone. When I answered the telephone, May said that I had better get back to Orderville right away, because my confinement case, Nellie Covington, was hemorrhaging.

Snow was piled at the side of the road up to the doors of my little Ford, and it was still snowing. Since it was so far from the hospital I had to resort to using packing to stop Nellie's bleeding; a procedure I did not use very often. It stopped the bleeding and I was able to remove the packing the next day. Nellie recovered without complications.

In the meantime, my car had frozen up. It was two o'clock in the morning and bitterly cold when I finally left the Covington's. I stopped at the Mt Carmel Y, but their water was frozen. There was nothing for me to do but try to make it over the mountain, and pray that I could make it back to Kanab.

Before I reached the top of the Sands, my old Ford started to steam, melting the plug that was in the head of the engine. I thought that all the car needed was some water, so I got out my obstetrical bag with the copper boiler that I used for sterilizing instruments to melt snow in it.

I built a small fire on the road, in front of the car, with dead twigs pulled out from the junipers on the side of the road. I didn't know then that the plug had melted, until the water went in one end and out the other. I put the boiler away, and knew then that I would have to concentrate on keeping the fire going, to keep from freezing to death. The rest of the night was spent trudging through snow-drifts in my heavy overcoat, and four-buckle brogans, looking for dry wood.

It was Christmas Eve on Mount Lonesome (actually called the Sands by the natives) and here I was, a country doctor, carrying wood through deep snow, trying to keep the fire from going out. It suddenly dawned on me that I was practicing medicine the same way. I told myself "There is somebody who has a little fire (a nice hospital in St. George or in Cedar City) and *I* am carrying patients over there to keep *their* fire going!"

My decision was made. I was going to build a hospital! I didn't know how, nor where I was going to get the money, but I was spending much of my time traveling great distances, in all kinds of weather, to see my patients, and they were not getting the care they deserved. Without a hospital close by, and with the roads often closed by snow, it was sometimes impossible to get them to St. George or to Cedar City. This put their lives in jeopardy.

No one came over the mountain that night, but as I shivered over my small fire, I was warmed by my decision to build a hospital. I spent what remained of the night making plans for what later became *The George Aiken Kane County Hospital* in Kanab, Utah.

The next morning the postman, Hugh Swapp, came by and said that he would stop in Orderville and tell Bill Heaton that I needed help. Bill came out, picked me up, pulled my car into Kanab with a chain. He repaired it after I took him to breakfast. I never knew when I left Kanab on one of these trips, when I would return.

I contacted the City and County and told them of my plans to build a hospital. Dunc MacDonald, County Commmisioner, said "We don't need a hospital; you need a hospital! We've done without a hospital for seventy years, and we don't need one now!"

I have found that it is difficult to make changes in Kanab, even today. I remembered how Charles Petty, in Hurricane, had tried to intimidate me, so I persisted. I argued that I could not do my best work for the people in the area, without a hospital. I explained that practicing medicine out of a black bag, and dispensing my own medicine was a poor way to practice medicine. I told them I had more knowledge than that, and the good that I could do for the people was limited by not having a hospital, just as their vision was limited.

Despite what I considered a logical argument for a hospital, I was turned down, by both the City and the County. I was discouraged, but determined. I had chosen to stay in the West to practice medicine, and I was going to do it properly; with a hospital.

Every time I would be on the road on my way to a house call, I was busy mulling over my plans for a hospital. The summer of 1934, I told Charlie Plumb about them. Charlie had a brother-in-law who was an architect. I gave Charlie a tentative floor plan, which he gave to his brother-in-law. He drew up rough plans for the hospital from mine. People who began to hear about our plans became enthusiastic, which gave me the incentive to go ahead.

During that time, I received a letter from my father who wrote that the government was starting to do something about the unemployment situation. Franklin Delano Roosevelt was in office, and the government had established the WPA (Works Projects Administration).

Many people in the Kanab area had little money since the price was down on wool, cattle and produce. Most of my patients paid me by trading, but there was just so much coal, so many horses, and so much food I could use. There were several thousand dollars outstanding in unpaid medical bills.

After I had the plan for the hospital pretty well formulated in my mind, I had no lot to build on, and no money. LaVar Pratt came up with a plan after I had operated on him, to pay me for the operation by trading his lot on the north side of Kanab, in exchange for the surgery.

The lot was on a talus slope with a rock mountain in the background. It faced south and was a good spot for a hospital. LaVar wanted to go to California and needed sixty-five dollars in cash. He said that if I would give him one hundred and fifty dollars in credit, and sixty-five dollars in cash, I could have the lot for the hospital. This sounded fair to me, so we made the deal.

I then contacted the people who owed me money and asked if they would be willing to trade labor, lumber or produce, and help build the hospital. Everyone was happy to make the trade. Some even offered to build up credit for the future, by helping ahead of time.

Wages for unskilled labor in 1935 were three dollars a day, and skilled laborers, like a stone worker or rough lumber man, were paid four dollars a day. Carpenters were paid seven dollars a day, and a man and his team were paid six dollars.

We made an agreement that half the wage would be paid in cash, and the other half would be applied to credit their account. It was agreed that if a patient was hospitalized, they would pay the cost of the hospital room, which amounted to three dollars a day.

Nurses were paid seventy-five dollars a month, plus room and board, and a cook made sixty-five dollars a month. After I received the letter from my father telling me about the WPA, I contacted Franklin Heaton, who was in charge of the local WPA, and the unemployed.

Franklin had some men who were hauling dirt to a place a few blocks from where the hospital was being built. He agreed to let the men work with us.

On January 2, 1935, we started work on the hospital. The sun was shining brightly when twenty men with their shovels arrived to begin digging the basement. Dave Rider and his brother were there with their teams. The men began by taking off the sod and rolling it up, and as the teams drove up, the men would throw the dirt into the wagon.

The wagons were just two-by-fours on a running gear, with one-foot sideboards, and a tailgate. The trouble was, when the wagon was full, and the drivers clopped their teams off down the road about four blocks, twenty men leaned on their shovels and talked. Sometimes they sat on top of the piles of sod they had rolled up, and waited for the wagons to come back.

When the men on the wagons got to the place where they were to dump the dirt, they merely took off the sideboards and the tailgate, and the dirt would fall off the sides. To complete the job they would take one end of the two-by-fours that made up the floor of the wagon, tip it, and let the rest of the dirt fall off. They would then put the two-by-fours back on the bed of the wagon, replace the sideboards and tailgate, put the seat on top of that, then return for another load of dirt.

A neighbor, Maggie Cram. who had been watching the men and their method of working, called me and said, "Look, I don't know if you are paying these men, but if you are; you are getting hooked. There are twenty men over there, sitting most of the time, doing nothing!"

I told Maggie they were WPA workers so they were not costing me anything. It did not last very long. Within a few days Franklin came back and said that he had learned that since the WPA was a Federal program, the workers were not allowed to work on a project that benefited only certain people. It seemed to me that a hospital benefited everyone, but I did not argue. I was grateful for whatever help I had received.

Later on, we hired those same men with their teams when they were not working for the WPA. A plow and grader were brought in to dig the basement with horsepower. The sides of the walls still had to be dug by hand, then the dirt shoveled into the center where it could be reached by the scrapers, and removed.

Indian artifacts were uncovered while the basement was being dug: charcoal and bits of pottery. On the northeast corner of the basement, we ran into a large spring, and each morning the basement would be filled with water. We finally had to dig a channel through the basement into an outlet onto the street. This was a temporary solution, so to overcome the problem permanently, we put a drain tile in the walls of the basement, and drained the spring water into a large cistern in the northeast corner where the ramp was located.

Tom Robinson, a wily old character, who had previously tried to claim the overflow from the *city* reservoir, unsuccessfully, now latched onto the idea that he would claim the overflow from *our* spring water. According to his plans we would be required to furnish him water through all eternity. I told him to get the hell out of there, and we stopped the overflow, dug a cesspool, then later ran the water into the sewer line. I have never been able to understand the greed that is so much a part of the character of too many men.

We had been advised to use structural steel to reinforce the concrete in the building, but that was expensive, and we didn't have that much money. A friend, in Virgin, who worked in the oil fields, told me that I could buy black steel cable from the oil rigs for one cent a foot. I bought a mile of the cable which we then wrapped under the windows four or five times, and around the basement as reinforcement for the concrete. It was a good solution, and did not cost much.

It was mid-summer before the basement was completed. We had planned to go down nine feet, but we hit solid rock at eight feet, so the hosiptal was built on that sold ledge of rock.

One of the places where we used to perform operations before the hospital was built, was in the Croft Hotel in Orderville. Ed Croft had the hotel which was used all year, but in the summer time he also ran the sawmill at Swain's Creek on Cedar Mountain. When he heard about the hospital being built he told us he would supply us with all the lumber we needed, in exchange for medical credit. There were several couples working for the sawmill, and they sometimes needed medical attention for pregnancies, and an occasional accident.

Lumber sold for twenty dollars a thousand for plain sawed lumber, unsized, and lumber sized on one side was twenty-five dollars a thousand feet. Sized on both sides lumber sold for thirty dollars.

John Chamberlain, who hauled cattle to Salt Lake City, provided us with cement at the regular price, without freight charges. Cement sold for one dollar a sack.

Albert Anderson was our Head Honcho. He was as concerned about getting the hospital built as we were. He could do anything, work with a shovel, do cement work, and was a good all-around foreman. We were lucky to have him.

There was one side-walk foreman, a tall, lanky fellow who stood on the sidelines, picking his teeth, as he watched the workers. He had a negative attitude and would tell the workers that they would never get a hospital built, that they couldn't build it that way, that we'd never have a hospital. I believe the heckler was Nate Adams.

We had decided that the hospital would be a western colonial structure, to fit in with the scenery, but the lot was at the slope of the red cliffs, so we had to cut down on the back of the lot, move the dirt out toward the front, and build a stone wall so we would have the large level lot needed for the building.

We hired Boyd McAllister to do the rock work, for four dollars a day. He hadn't done any rock work before, but he owed us some money and wanted to do the work. We paid him two dollars a day in cash, and added the two dollars credit to his account. Boyd started in the back corner where the garage was, and worked towards the front. As the wall progressed one could see how Boyd matured as a stone mason.

Delbert Riggs didn't owe us any money, nor did Owen Johnson, but they both wanted to help. Delbert built the retaining wall in front of the building along the street. As he and Owen were hauling the stone and building the wall, he would joke with the women he passed by. Delbert told them that Doc Aiken had promised to deliver the first baby born in the hospital free of charge, and that in the year it would take to build the hospital, they could plan accordingly. I knew nothing of the alleged promise.

After the side walls were built, we acquired the Henderson property adjacent to ours, and built the walls on the west. In planning for the hospital, we had included an apartment for ourselves, plus a large recreation room with a fireplace. The X-ray room was downstairs, with a ramp going to the basement to wheel the patients to and from X-ray. There was neither the room nor the money to install an elevator.

I wanted to include the red stone of Utah in the architecture of the building, so I went to Casey Jones, the best stone and brick man in the area. When I explained the type of building I wanted, Casey told me that it wasn't possible, that I had to lay the stone in courses. I had watched Casey dress stone for his work and knew that it would take too long, and that we could not afford the time nor the expense of doing it his way.

My idea was to build a board wall, put cement against that, then lay random sizes of stone into any way they fell. Casey predicted that the wall would fall down. Charlie Nash ended up doing the stone work, following my instructions, and fortunately, the wall stayed intact.

Casey later worked for me as a carpenter, and built up a lot of credit, which he never used.

Long after the hospital was completed, I would operate on someone, thinking I would be collecting a fee; I would get one of the old credits I had given out to people who helped build the hospital.

By September, we were putting up the sidewalls and roof. Charlie Hepworth made the shake shingles up in the canyon. On Halloween, we threw a party. One room had a floor in it, so we used that room for dancing. Curtains had been put up to make it look a little nicer. We had to climb down to the basement on a ladder, which was spooky, but it only added to the spirit of the occasion. Everyone was invited. Their hospital was becoming a reality, and there was much laughter and sharing of memories.

The hospital had reached a stage of development where we could now take pictures of it with our box camera, along with plans, and see if we could arrange for a loan in Salt Lake City. We didn't know anyone there, nor how we were going to do it, but we had come this far, and we were not going to stop now.

Mr. Anderson helped us get the meausrements we needed; we then drew plans on brown wrapping paper, and with our box camera beside us, and our hearts full of hope, we set off for Salt Lake City, more than three hundred miles away.

We went straight to the FHA, and met with Grant MacFarlane. He had spent summers on a ranch at Scutumpah with the Robinsons, so he knew our area. MacFarlane said he would like to help us but he couldn't loan us any money on the building. He suggested we see Junius Romney of State Building and Loan.

He said to tell Romney that the government would guarantee the equipment, the beds, the furnace, and the medical equipment; but that was all they could do. They would loan us all we needed for medical equipment, but the loan would have to be repaid within five years. That meant that we could not borrow the amount we needed because we could not hope to repay the loan within five years.

Romney at State Building and Loan said they could loan us nine thousand dollars, five thousand over the amount guaranteed by the government. This meant we could only purchase four hospital beds, and two beds for the nurses, plus the medical equipment we needed. This left no money to pay for labor. We had gone over every cost with Henry Sholzen, and had gotten bids while we were in Salt Lake on the materials needed to complete the hospital.

We suggested to Mr. Romney that he loan us twelve thousand dollars, instead of nine thousand. We told him there was no way to repay the loan if we could only purchase four hospital beds. Four beds, at three dollars a day, would only give us twelve dollars a day, and we would still have salaries to pay, and food to buy. With twelve thousand dollars we could purchase five extra beds, giving us a chance to make enough money to repay the loan.

Romney refused. He said that we had figured things out so far, and that he was sure that we could figure out the rest of it. So, we settled for the nine thousand dollar loan, to be repaid at the rate of $225.00 a month. It made it difficult to make ends meet, and we were in arrears with our payment about half the time. We got to know Mr. Sproul, who came each month to collect, very well.

That fall, while making a house call to Long Valley one Sunday, a little girl ran out to my car and called, "Oh, Doc Aiken; I saw you in the funnies today!" I replied, "No kidding?"

She ran inside the house and brought out the funny paper section and handed it to me. Charlie Plumb, who attended our parties when he was in Kanab, and who drew the comic strip *Ella Cinders* had featured Kanab - and me - in the comic strip that Sunday. *It went like this: Ella Cinders had the hiccups and someone (in the strip) told her that the only one who could cure her would be Doc Aiken in Kanab, so they would have to fly her to Kanab.*

On the way to the airport they were accosted by the Hamblin Brothers, robbers, and along the way there were other narrow escapes before they finally made it to the airplane. Then, as the plane flew over Kanab, the engine conked out, and Ella Cinders had to parachute out of the plane.

Later in the day, someone found Ella wandering around in the yard of Parry Lodge. She was brought to my office (in the comic strip) and I asked what the problem was. I was told that she had a bad case of the hiccups and had been sent to Kanab because it was believed that I was the only one who could cure her. "Well" I replied, "That's simple! What she needs - is a real good scare!"

CHAPTER TWENTY-ONE
One Silver Dollar - and a Hacksaw Blade

While the hospital was under construction, but not yet ready for occupancy, in 1935; I received a call that there had been a shooting at Buck Lowery's place near the Navajo Bridge, at the lower end of House Rock Valley. I was the only doctor within a one hundred mile radius.

Nita and I had to drive over ninety miles of narrow dirt road to reach the scene of the shooting. We grabbed what we felt would be needed, and I drove as fast as the road, and my old car, would allow.

When we arrived, we found that George, the attendant at the service station, had been shot, and was having difficulty breathing. Two men had attempted to rob him, after filling their car's tank with gas.

The lights had been out in the station when the men entered. One of them pulled a gun. George grabbed a long-handled flashlight and attempted to hit the robber. Whether the gun discharged accidentally when George swung the flash light, or whether the young man meant to shoot, was never known. The two men, and a frightened hitchhiker, jumped into the car and sped off towards Fredonia.

George, holding his stomach, staggered to the pumps to lock them, then collapsed. Peaches Beard was across the street at Navajo Lodge and heard the gunshot, and the sound of the car speeding away. He ran outside just in time to see George collapse.

He half carried, half dragged George to the lodge and laid him on the couch, then yelled for his son Dave to drive to the nearest telephone, forty-five miles away to call me. Dave then contacted the sheriff in Fredonia, and the sheriff in Kanab, to tell them that the bandits were headed in that direction. It was the only direction they could take, other than turning around and heading back towards Flagstaff.

As Nita and I were speeding towards Navajo Bridge, and before we reached Fredonia, we were stopped by Sheriff George Swapp of Kanab. We told him the bandits were headed in this direction, and that we had to get to the bridge to take care of the attendant who had been shot. We had no idea what condition he was in.

He waved us on, and when we reached Fredonia, Dickie Lewis, the deputy sheriff, was already rounding up a posse. The men in the posse were standing under the street light, the light reflecting off their gun barrels. We saw the men at about the same time that an approaching car saw them, the car making a quick turn and heading back towards the mountain on the old Ryan Road.

The fleeing bandits were now in front of us, seeking an escape route. The hair on the back of my neck stood up, but I couldn't stop now. I had no choice but to keep driving towards the bridge; a man's life was at stake, and I was the only doctor around.

Nita begged me not to drive so fast, and reminded me that I might catch up with the fleeing men. She asked what I would do if I caught up to them. I told her that I didn't know, but that I had a tire iron in the car, and I would try to disable the man, by hitting him across the wrist if he approached the car. It didn't occur to me that George had been shot, while attempting to do something similar.

We could not be positive that the car ahead of us was the bandit's car, but the fact that the car had turned around suddenly when the men saw the posse, left little doubt in our minds. When the car reached the foot of the mountain where Ryan Road turns off, the car spun around and headed towards the mountain.

When we reached the cut-off at LeFevre, a fellow named Chuck, who worked for the Arizona Highway Department, jumped off the ledge and stopped us. We told him we thought the bandit's car had turned off Ryan Road, and that if he wanted to catch them, that would be the place to go.

The idea didn't appeal to him, so he said "Move over; I'll drive you to the bridge. That way you will be protected." So, our *protector* drove Nita and I to the bridge.

When we arrived, and I examined George, I could see that the shot went down through the abdomen. Things didn't look too good for him. Since the hospital was not ready for occupancy in Kanab we had no choice but to drive him to Flagstaff. We drove him first to Tuba City, but he was refused treatment. It was a government Indian Hospital and we were told they could not treat white people.

Whether we could have saved George's life had a hospital been close by, I do not know. I could not help but think how I had fought to get our own hospital started, against the wishes of Dunc McDonald, County Commissioner in Kanab. His words came back to me now, "We don't need a hospital. You need a hospital. We've done without a hospital for seventy years, and we don't need one now!" George died, three days later, in Flagstaff, of peritonitis.

It is never easy to lose a patient, no matter what the cause. It is even worse when you realize they might have been saved with a medical facility close by. We were both saddened as we drove back to Kanab. We stopped and told the sheriff that the bandits had probably gone out Ryan Road. The next morning the sheriff and his posse drove out towards Big Saddle.

The posse spotted the car in the distance, pulled off to the side of the road. There was no sign of life. As the posse came nearer, the bandits, apparently aroused from a deep sleep, jumped out of the car and ran. One of the men in the posse raised his rifle and fired, hitting one of the men in the arm. The other two young men ran through the Quakies, and into the Grand Canyon. The injured man ran into the woods, but was later picked up that afternoon.

The posse contacted Jack Butler, the lion hunter, to see if he would go down into the canyon and track the young men. He refused, saying, "Let's just sit here and wait. They'll come back this afternoon because there is no water down there, and there is no other way out.

And he was right. They came out that evening, thirsty and exhausted, from lack of sleep and food, and gave themselves up. The two young bandits were brothers, named White. The posse took the three of them to Buck Lowery's where they turned the hitchiker loose, since he was innocent of any wrong doing.

Two weeks later, after being jailed in Flagstaff, the two brothers broke out. They had somehow acquired a hacksaw blade. After the breakout, the man who distributed oil to Navajo Bridge warned Peaches Beard that the bandits might come looking for the men responsible for their capture.

A road block was set up by Peaches and some men in the posse. They took turns watching the narrow road that led from Flagstaff to Navajo Bridge. Buck Lowery and his son, Dave, would sit for hours on watch until someone else would take over.

A tourist who was driving through, was curious about the excitement, and asked why the men were armed with rifles, and hand guns. When told the story, he said he had seen two young men at The Gap, trying to trade a spare tire for some gasoline. When he described the men, Peaches were sure they were the White Brothers headed in the direction of Navajo Bridge. Everyone was nervous.

Buck Lowery, who was a deputy sheriff, decided to drive to Cedar Ridge, thirty miles away, to see if he could intercept the bandits. His son, Dave, went with him. Before leaving, Buck instructed Peaches and the other men guarding the bridge that if he and Dave missed the men, and if Buck was honking the horn as he drove back, that would be a signal that the bandits were in front of them and that the posse was to shoot at the car in front.

As Buck and Dave drove up the road near The Gap, they saw a car coming towards them. Buck stopped his car and got out, waving for the oncoming car to stop. Instead, the driver drove towards Buck, then swerved, barely missing him, according to Buck.

As Buck fell, he turned and shot through the back of the fleeing car. The bullet went through the back of the seat, and into the passenger.

Dave, who was at the side of the road, did not realize the passenger had been shot. He aimed his revolver at the bandit closest to him, and pulled the trigger. The already wounded boy was killed, when the shot from Dave's revolver tore away the side of his head.

The car went into the ditch and stopped. The driver, too, had been wounded. He was tied up and placed in the back of Buck's car. Dave climbed into the bandit's car, with the dead boy beside him, and headed back to Navajo Bridge.

As the two cars made their way back to the bridge, Buck began honking his horn. In the excitement, he had forgotten that this was the signal to start shooting at the car in front. Following Buck's instructions, the posse leveled their guns at the bandit's car. Dave suddenly remembered that he was driving the car in front. He leaped out of the car and started waving his black hat, and shouting, "Don't shoot! Don't shoot! It's me, Dave!"

The surviving brother was sent back to Flagstaff, where he was tried for armed robbery, and was sentenced to fifteen years. It was rumored that he threatened to come back after the men responsible for his brother's death. He had lost his brother in what had begun as a holdup, during the Depression of the thirties, when there was little money around, for any of us.

Before taking the wounded bandit and his dead brother back to Flagstaff, they were searched. The searchers found, that between the two brothers, all they had between them was one silver dollar - and a hacksaw blade.

That was more than fifty years ago. The surviving brother could still be living today. If he is, his rumored threat was never carried out. There was tragedy enough, in the past.

Peaches Beard still lives in Kanab, and runs a motel here. According to Herman Haskie, Buck Lowery was drowned years ago, while trying to catch bull frogs for bait. His son, Dave, was lost and presumed dead, when his submarine was torpedoed during WWII.

My wife, Juanita is gone, so I guess that only Peaches and I are still living. It comes back to me sometimes, when I sit before the fireplace on a lonely night, the tragedy of it all; the death of George; the trigger-happy posse; and the two young brothers who had between them, only one silver dollar - and a hacksaw blade.

Clarence Mortimer Aiken
Born: January 21, 1874
Married: Sept. 10, 1889

Margaret Bain
Born: August 31, 1873
Thurso, Scotland

Grandfather Thomas Aiken
School teacher around Indian Hill, Ohio

Medical School
Columbus, Ohio - 1920s

My Favorite Girls

Nita

Nita

Nita and Louise

Doctor Aiken making house calls in the snow

Winter scene - Kanab, Utah - 1932

Navajo Lake

Navajo Lake - 1930

Bob Perrin

Toroweap - The Saturday Evening Post returned the photo
saying they did not accept "trick photography"

Jack Butler, the Lion Hunter, and his wife Mary. Her dog is Saugatoon, but I don't know the name of Jack's dog.

Gloria and Si Fleur and Donna (Sue) Aiken

George Russell Aiken, M.D.
Brisbane, Australia

Utah State Representative Dr. George Aiken

Dad and Mother Aiken

Hunting and Fishing in Color Country

Dr. George Aiken

Duke Aiken

Dr. Aiken with Duke and Bob

Kanab, Utah

Nita with Bob and Duke

Dr. Aiken with Bob

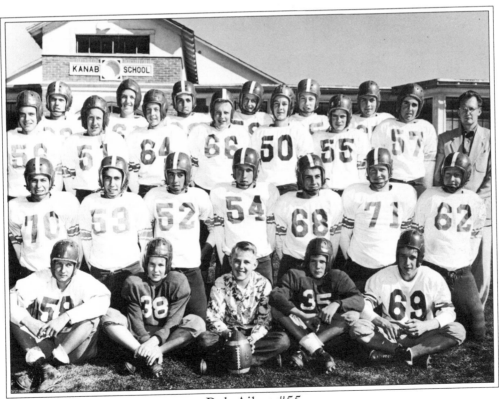

Bob Aiken #55

CHAPTER TWENTY-TWO
The Hospital Opens in March, 1936

It took us fourteen months to complete the hospital. We started in January 1935, and completed it in March, of 1936. The hospital then became the center of all our medical activities. Since we also lived in the hospital, we were on duty twenty-four hours a day.

Five cases came in on opening day. We had only four beds, so we had to borrow one of the nurse's bed's in the basement. We figured there would be only one nurse sleeping at a time anyway.

The next day, I was in the hallway when Iva Maxwell walked in. She hadn't noticed the steps at the front, so she climbed over the wall. She asked if what Delbert had told all the women was true, that I would deliver the first baby free. This came as a surprise, since Delbert had neglected to tell me, but I said that I would.

I asked if she was in labor. She said she wasn't in labor yet, but that she would have her husband, Horace, take her for a ride on Johnson Road, and she might start early. My own wife was expecting our youngest son, Bob, and I learned later that some of the women thought she would be the first to deliver in the new hospital.

Iva's plan worked. Johnson Road was a pretty rough road in those days (and still is, in some parts), so that night she was brought into the hospital in labor. We delivered a healthy young boy the following morning.

As I was filling out the birth certificate, I suggested that since this was the first baby delivered in the hospital, and since I delivered it free of charge; I would like to give the baby his first name. Iva objected, saying that she and her husband wanted to name the baby Jim, after Horace's father. He had no grandchildren named for him, so they wanted to honor him by naming the new baby James.

Undaunted, I suggested that I give the baby his middle name, and she relented. The middle name I chose was Freeborn, so the first baby born in the new hospital was named James Freeborn Maxwell. He was embarrassed when we had to go to the school to examine the students and I would say, "Oh! You're James Freeborn, aren't you?" It bothered him when he was growing up, but I think he has finally gotten used to his middle name, more than fifty years later.

Once we had the hospital operating, we had to buy additional beds. This used up any cash that could be used for making our monthly mortgage payment. We were always pressed for cash, so when Florian Johnson, in charge of welfare at the time, told us about a fund that would pay for tonsilectomies for the children, we were relieved. We would be paid $22.50 per tonsilectomy, and if we could do ten a month, that would give us $225.00 to apply towards our mortgage.

We performed tonsilectomies in Mt. Carmel, Orderville, Glendale, and other towns in the area. Nita would give the anesthetic, and I would do the surgery. One time, in Alton, as we waited for one little fellow to recover from the anesthesia, we were sitting on the bed when Nita saw bedbugs dashing out across the bedspread! She just about had a fit!

When we had our first deliveries in the new hospital, we thought we might save money by having the mothers furnish layettes for the newborn babies. The mother had to have a layette for the baby when she took it home anyway, so why not have her bring the layette to the hospital and use it there. Well, that policy did not work for very long! We found that some layettes had bedbugs in the baby clothes, so we had to make it a policy that no bed clothing was allowed to come into the hospital. It seemed to be a common thing in the area, to have a lot of bedbugs. Maybe the people did not know how to get rid of them; I don't know.

One little fellow we treated had a broken humerus, and when he was brought in to have his splint removed (an aluminum splint padded with felt), his mother said, "It must be getting better; it sure does itch!" When the splint was removed and laid on the counter, bedbugs came scurrying out. Miss Hahn, our nurse, grabbed the splint, and popped it into the autoclave.

There were a number of pnuemonia cases the winter of '36. One boy, Royden Hepworth, whose right lung was solid with pus, had to have his lung irrigated and drained. We had to remove a section of the rib due to the empyema, then put in a drain that he wore for months.

We found that we had a lot of new experiences ahead of us. Since running the hospital was a commitment for total care, we had to take care of patients that we might have sent to someone else. We became very much involved, and sometimes a little bit over our heads, as far as our medical training was concerned.

One day, I was working in my yard, when I saw Karl MacDonald leave his house, which was across the street from us. He was on his way to Fredonia to see his girl friend. Meantime, Gordon McAllister was at Milt's Bar across the Utah border, in Arizona, celebrating. I don't know whether it was Gordon's wife Margaret's first husband's birthday, or the date of his death, but they were obviously doing a little too much drinking.

About the time Karl was on his way to Fredonia, Gordon (who was an epileptic) decided he was tired of toasting Ol' Joe, and left the party and headed for Kanab. Just as Karl reached the Utah-Arizona border he saw Gordon's car stop, then go into reverse and start up the side of the hill, backwards, then flip over.

Karl stopped his car and raced to Gordon's car, which was upside down. Gordon was lying against the inside top of the car and was making gurgling sounds. He tried to pry the door open, without success, so he ran back to his own car and turned around and headed back to Kanab to get me.

By the time Karl and I got back to Gordon's car, Gordon was convulsing. Between the two of us, we managed to pry the door open and get him out on the ground. After awhile, Gordon managed to get to his feet and walk around a little bit. He was bleeding from a large gash in the forehead, so I knew we'd have to get him back to the hospital and sew it up. He placed an arm around our necks, and we helped him down the hill and into Karl's car.

Just then, the rest of the party drove up; and Margaret, who had lost her last husband in an accident, promptly fainted when she saw Gordon and the wrecked car. I yelled to the others to take care of Margaret, and Karl and I raced to the hospital with Gordon.

While I was in the operating room stitching Gordon's forehead, Beaulah Frost, the nurse on duty, rushed into the room and said, "Doctor, I think you better come and see Margaret; I think she's a lot worse off than Gordon! She looks to me like she's dead!"

But I knew Margaret, so I said, "Oh Beaulah, she's had little spells like this before. It's just a little hysteria. Go down in the kitchen and get a pitcher of ice water, and throw that on her. That will bring her out of it!"

Poor unsuspecting Beaulah went into the kitchen, got the pitcher of ice water, came back to where Margaret was lying on the gurney, and raised the pitcher to throw the water in her face. Suddenly, Margaret bounced up off the gurney and yelled, "Don't you throw that water on me, you sonofabitch!."

Lyle Chamberlain built a dance floor at Hidden Lake in 1928. Things were pretty lively there on Saturday nights. Young people came from twenty to twenty-five miles away, to attend the dances. Some of the men like to have a little shot of home-brewed *Joy Juice*, or the Virginia Dare wine sold by ZCMI, as a stomach tonic. A few shots of that, and a person had the jitters for a week, along with sleepless nights.

Vanilla extract was another popular substitute for liquor. If you talked to one of the guys who had been drinking vanilla, you would swear he had been eating fruitcake.

One night, Berdel Haycock had had a pretty good load of *fruit juice,* and was one of the last people to leave the dance. He was driving back to Kanab alone, when he went through the guard rail of the wooden bridge across Muddy Creek at Mt. Carmel. As his car plunged off the bridge, the rear axle caught on one of the supporting timbers. Berdel found himself looking down into the face of eternity, and the bottom of old Muddy.

When the musicians, who were the last ones to leave the dance, saw Berdel's car teetering on the edge of the bridge, they piled out of their car to see if they could help. Some of them raced back to Orderville to get someone to bring one of the large Croft's lumber trucks, and log chains.

Austin Pugh, the sax player, saw that he couldn't be much help in getting the car out, so while the others went for help, Austin got out his sax and began playing *Nearer My God To Thee.*

Berdel's car was pulled to safety, but there were some frightening moments while he waited to be rescued, and Austin's choice of music didn't help to alleviate his fear.

Berdel later married Ada Watson in the thirties. Shortly after they were married, Ada became pregnant and complained of a pain in her side. She had gone into the bathroom early one morning and fainted. I was called, and when I arrived, she was lying on the bathroom floor in shock.

When I brought her around, she said that she had missed one period about two weeks before, and now she was spotting blood. Her abdomen was rigid and painful, signs of an internal hemorrhage. I called the hospital and told them to get the operating room ready, because I was positive that Ada had a ruptured ectopic pregnancy.

She was unconscious again by the time we reached the hospital. We could not get a pulse on her. After a quick prep, I had Nita give her a light ether anesthetic. When I opened her abdomen, I found it filled with blood. The first thing I did was grab the bleeder and tie it off.

I knew that Ada needed blood quickly, but in the thirties, we did not have blood or plasma stored for transfusions. There were no blood banks either. I told Marelda, the lab girl, to bring me the large glass stick funnel and to put some magnesium citrate in it. I then scooped Ada's own blood from her abdomen, with both my hands, putting it into the funnel. We then hooked the tube from the funnel to the saline drip we already had in her arm. I don't know how much blood we gave her, but her pulse came back, and she survived.

We tied off the tubes and removed the fertilized ovum and placenta. Ada told me later that when she told people the story they'd say, "That's crazy! They can't do things like that!"

I met Berdel and Ada at his sister's Golden Wedding anniversary celebration not long ago, and we had a few laughs about the good ol' days during prohibition.

One of the first times we used sulfa, was when Helena McAllister had a baby. About the third day after her delivery, she developed a slightly elevated temperature. Hearing that sulfa was good for infections, I decided to give her some. She went into shock. One of the nurses came to me early one morning and said she could not get a pulse on Helena. I found her unconscious.

The only answer I could think of at the time was to give her blood. There was no blood typing then, let alone cross-matching. I didn't have any blood donors, so I stated calling her former high school classmates. We couldn't find anyone whose blood matched hers. That was on a Sunday morning. I sent word to her parents in Toquerville and told them that Helena was in bad shape and needed blood.

Her father, Walt, rushed to the hospital. He was *pure chicken* when it came to hospitals, but his blood matched, so we set up a procedure where the donor and the recipient were on adjacent tables. We drew the blood out of the donor, lubricating the syringes with magnesium citrate to keep the blood from coagulating, into a syringe, turned the valve, then put the blood into the recipient.

We then had to turn the valve and draw more blood from the donor, then give some more to the recipient. I don't remember the capacity of the syringe, maybe 25cc or 50cc at the most, but we repeated the process four or five times, until the patient had enough blood to overcome the shock. Helena subsequently recovered, but I was extremely cautious in the future about using sulfa.

I was a member of the Lions Club at the time, and one of our service projects had to do with blood donors. All of those who were available to donate blood were typed, so whenever we needed blood after that, we had someone to call on.

One of our patients in September of 1951, was Sharee Lewis, a beautiful and talented girl, whom I had delivered eighteen years before, with the help of midwife Laura Broadbent. Sharee was on her way back to Kanab from Salt Lake City on a bus, when it stopped in Panguitch. She met some of the local boys who were home on leave, and they talked her into driving back to Kanab with them.

As they drove down into Black Rock Canyon, the driver missed the turn; the car leaped fifty feet across the creek and hit a stone wall on the other side. Two of the boys, Pvt. Vance Meeks and DeLyn Farnsworth, were killed. Vance, 22, son of Kane County Sheriff Mason Meeks and the late Lenore

Avarett Meeks, died on Sunday, September 9, 1951 at 9:15 a.m. DeLyn was killed outright. Seaman Billy Mackleprang, suffered multiple fractures of the hips and pelvis, broken cheek bones, and two broken bones in the foot; in addition to severe lacerations and shock. Despite this, he managed to crawl up the twenty foot embankment, to seek help. Sharee was knocked unconscious, and in the end, would spend the rest of her life in a wheel chair.

Sharee was unconscious for more than a month, and was kept alive with intravenous feedings. We had several neurologists come to Kanab to examine her, and see if they could give me some idea of what we could do to bring her out of it. In spite of everything we did, she ended up with spastic hands and legs, making it difficult for her to walk.

Prior to the accident, Sharee was active in drama and played the organ, so about a year after the accident, she began playing the organ again, but found it difficult. She had lost many of her friends during her long recuperation, and finally lapsed to the point where she couldn't take care of herself. After her mother remarried, Sharee was put in a nursing home in Provo.

Lorin Broadbent, her mother's brother, who lives in Fredonia, Arizona, said that when he last saw Sharee in 1988, she was in a wheelchair; but she was in good spirits, and was on her way to have her hair done.

Asked if she still played the organ, Lorin said she could no longer play. Cousins who live in the area, sometimes come to visit her. Marlin Brown, Publisher of Southern Utah News, said that Sharee took organ lessons from his mother. He has not seen her for years, but said she was a beautiful girl.

Verla Lewis, in Kanab, Sharee's mother's sister, said that Sheree's mother died on January 4, 1987, in Provo. Sharee, who was born in 1935, is now 54. Verla did not remember the address of the nursing home, but said that it is the Crestview Convalescent Home in Provo, if old friends would like to contact Sharee. She is unable to write, but would welcome cards or letters from friends from the past. Marlin said that he believes Billy Mackleprang now resides in Las Vegas.

1953 was also the year another lovely Kanab girl, Alta Kay Heaton, was chosen Miss Kane County, after she presented a court scene from George Bernard Shaw's *St. Joan,* where Joan of Arc denounces her accusers.

At the same time, across the hall from Sharee, was a patient we called Captain Hornblower. His real name was Borntrager. He and his wife, Vi, had flown out from Chicago to take a trip down the Colorado River with Art Green's boys. This was before the dam was built at Glen Canyon, and the river had many dangerous and exciting rapids.

Art's boys used to stash big tanks of gasoline along the river; then as they came down the river with various parties, they could stop and gas up their boats.

On the trip downriver with the Borntragers, before they reached Lee's Ferry, the party stopped to fill the tanks with gas. Earl Johnson told Borntrager to put the end of the hose over his (Borntrager's) mouth and blow on it, to blow the gasoline that was in the line back into the tank, as Johnson released the valve.

Most of the gas had been taken from the tank, but apparently while they were doing that, pressure had been built up by the sun beating down on the tank. When Johnson released the valve, gasoline shot into Borntrager's mouth, lungs, and abdomen.

It was evening when it happened, so they made the trip down to Lee's Ferry during the night, a trip that was difficult enough during the day. When they reached the ferry, they still had another hundred miles, by car, to bring Borntrager to the hospital.

Borntrager was critically ill. I don't know how he lived through the night. We put him on oxygen, then put him on negative pressure to help eliminate the gas. It gave a reverse peristalsis, instead of vomiting. The gas was taken out, and it provided some relief.

It was a month before we could get anything into his intestines, and before he had any movement of his gut. He developed a severe bronchitis, along with central pnuemonia.

Three weeks after Borntrager was hospitalized, he started running a high temperature. One day, after a severe coughing spell, a large abcess in his lung broke; and he coughed up a lot of pus. He then developed empyema between the lungs and the pleura, which we drained.

He was hospitalized for six weeks before he was well enough to fly back to Chicago. His wife stayed with him the entire time, helping to nurse him back to health.

The Borntragers came back to visit us every three or four years for the next twenty years.

About 1936 or 1937, Hank and Ruth Bahen opened a men's store in Kanab, At one of the Saturday night dances at the Three Lakes Dance Pavillion, Hank was dancing with my wife, and was bragging about the size of the fish at Fish Lake. Nita said that if he and his wife would come to dinner the following night, she would serve them a five-pound baked trout from Navajo Lake.

It was two in the morning when we left the dance. On the way home, Nita told me I had to catch a five pound brook–trout before dinner the next evening. That meant I would have to drive to Navajo Lake, sixty-five miles away, that night.

I dropped Nita off at home so she could get some sleep, and I changed into fishing clothes and took off for the lake. After I had driven only forty miles up the road to McDonald's ranch, I had to pull over to the side of the road and sleep. The five-pounders would have to wait.

It was almost daylight when I woke up. I knew that the best time to fish Navajo Lake was between four and six in the morning, and between eight and nine in the evening. The lake was shallow and those big fish were smart.

It was daylight when I reached the lake. I picked up a boat at Bierdmans' and started to row across the lake to Breathing Spring. Findlay Bunting and Lloyd Pugh were already there fishing, just out from the spring. Oscar Brooksby and two other groups were in the cove at the spring, so all of the best fishing holes were already taken.

This was in August, and I knew from past experience, that there would be stone rollers and helgermite flies hatching on the reeds around the lake.

I had tied a few flies, using a #4 japanned hook, some light green for the body, and a dozen short, light tan hairs from near the tail of a deer. I had these tied on black silk, with no varnish or preservatives added. They were so poorly made, that after a dozen casts, the flies would fall apart.

There was a light mist rising from the lake, and it was smooth and calm. As I rowed, I would ocaasionally see a fin or the tip of a tail stick up above the surface of the water. Sometimes, I would see the snout of a trout as he gently took a nymph, as it floated to the surface from the weeds below.

I anchored my boat out away from the spring, some distance from Findlay and Lloyd. After tying on one of my homemade flies, I did a few false casts. As I was extending the line, and the fly touched the water, a big trout smacked at it. Although he made quite a noise and splash, I missed him. This alerted the other fishermen, who called out, "Well, you got here just in time. Sounds like they are starting to bite." The fishermen pulled up their lines, re-baited with worms, and became very attentive.

I cast my homemade fly out, let it settle, then slowly began the retrieve. There was not an actual strike; those trout seemed to inhale the fly, and as the line straightened out, I set the hook.

This technique may seem difficult to anyone used to fishing a stream where you get a tick, or a solid strike. The first fish was a two-pounder, the next one a three-pounder, and finally I hooked the five-pounder I needed for the dinner Nita promised the Bahens.

As I was pulling up anchor, Oscar Brooksby called over to ask what I was using for bait. I told him about my homemade flies. He rowed over, took one look at my poorly made flies and refused to believe me. I offered him the few I had left, but he refused. I didn't blame him. Compared to the fly-tying job he did, mine were terrible. But, they did catch fish! The other fishermen had been using worms, and fishing low in the water, but the fish were feeding close to the surface that particular day.

Findlay and Lloyd had left their families at the Duck Creek Campground to set up the tents for the Swapp family reunion. They left their wives to do the work, while they took off to go fishing. They invited me to go back with them, to help them win a bet, using my fish. They had made a bet with Parv Church, on who could catch the biggest fish. Parv had gone to Mammoth Creek to fish. I gave them the two and three pound fish; then after having coffee with them, drove back to Kanab with the five-pounder.

CHAPTER TWENTY-THREE
The Death of Vern Glazier

The morning of April 5, 1938, Dave Pugh called me to come down to Vern Glazier's to investigate what he thought was a suicide. When I met Dave at the gate to Vern's home, he said he believed it was a suicide because the auditor of the Conoco Oil Company had been down there the day before, going over Vern's books. Vern's wife, Viola, had found Vern, in the basement of the storage shed behind their home, dead of a gunshot wound.

We went into the house and Viola explained what had happened. The two of them had been reading until about 9:30 p.m. the night before. Vern had gotten up, as he always did, to go out on the back porch to roll a cigarette and smoke. Viola did not like for him to smoke in the house, and out of courtesy to Viola, Vern respected her wishes.

He told her that he was going out to get his rifle in the basement of the storage shed, and put it in his truck. He had a gasoline delivery to make to Jacob Lake the following morning; and it was customary for the men in Kanab to carry a rifle with them, especially when they were going in to the Kaibab Forest.

When Vern had not returned to the house by midnight, Viola sent their daughter to the basment to see what was keeping him so long. The door to the basement was partially open, but when the girl called to Vern, there was no answer, so she told her mother he was not there.

Viola was worried, and when Vern had not returned by three that morning, she called Dev Bowman, whom Vern frequently played pinochle with, to see if he was there. Dev said he had not seen him.

It happened to be the night of the Lions Club 49's party, and there had been much horseplay and shooting the day before, so if Viola had heard a shot, she would not have thought anything about it. When daylight came, and Viola saw that Vern's truck was still parked outside, she went to see if Vern had taken his gun from the storage shed. When she tried to push the door open to the basement, she found that Vern had fallen against the door.

Dave and I entered the basement and found Vern lying on his right side, with his shoulder against the door. There was a hand-rolled cigarette, partially smoked, and on his hand was a bent match. The gun had been in a scabbard, lying on one of those shelves like the pioneers hung from the ceiling to store flour and grain.

We tried to imagine how Vern had lit the match and walked down the stairs, using the light of the match to locate the rifle on the shelf. I first thought that the gun went off when he pulled it toward him, but a later examination of the course of the bullet disproved that. The bullet had entered the lower rib cage from the back, coming upward and out just below, and to the left of the nipple. I couldn't see how he could get in that position to have a bullet make that course.

Re-tracing his steps, and putting his rifle in his scabbard under the left arm with a match in his left hand, then turning to go to the door, we concluded that the rifle must have slipped from the scabbard, hit the cement floor, and discharged. When we searched the ceiling, we found scattered fragments of a bullet that had entered the ceiling. This was the evidence for the conclusion we made.

Vern had loaned the gun to someone, and when they returned it to Vern, a bullet had been left in the chamber. It was a repeating rifle and the magazine with the other shells had been removed, but one had been missed.

There was a coroner's inquest at the courthouse. I called Dev Bowman and Jack Butler to testify about the rifle discharging in that manner. Dev said that he and Jack Butler had been hunting one time with Vern, when one of them shot a flying hawk in the wing. To put the hawk out of its misery, Jack caught it and killed it, by crushing its head on a rock with the butt of that particular rifle. When he did that, the gun discharged, scaring the men next to Jack. I used that as evidence to support the events we had reconstructed. It was shown that the rifle was sensitive to jolts, and discharged easily.

Dave Pugh still held out for the suicide theory, because of the audit. Lester Little said that I said it was an accidental shooting because I liked Viola, and wanted her to collect double indemnity on Vern's insurance. This is common in a small town; it makes a shooting more interesting, if the townspeople can make the story a bit scandalous, but I felt the evidence was conclusive. So, the death certificate was signed *Accidental death, due to gunshot wound.*

Not long ago, while I was at the hospital for tests, Marelda Black and I talked about the old days. She was in charge of the lab at the hospital, but she had worked for us in the original hospital as a cook, nurse, laudress or whatever we needed. She took additional training over the years and was an invaluable help to us. She is still living in Kanab today.

As we reminisced, she said, "Remember when I was on the night shift, and Norman Atherly drove up in back of the hospital in a huge ore truck, and called out for help; he had a man in the cab who had been in an accident.."

Marelda had called me (our apartment was still in one wing of the hospital) and we both ran out to help Atherly lift the man, who was quite large, out of the truck cab and onto the gurney. I don't recall his name but he was from Roosevelt, Utah, and had driven to Texas to buy a second-hand oil rig. The truck he was driving was overloaded, and as he came down LeFevre Ridge, the truck's brakes failed, causing him to lose control. On the wild ride down the ridge, the truck hit the side of the cut, and caused the truck to overturn.

Atherly was on his way home from Fredonia, and could not get past the wreckage. He found the man unconscious, with a large laceration on the left side of his head; starting at the top of the head, slicing through the outer plate of the parietal bone of the skull, and down through the ear canal to the neck, making a big flap. We could not see, at first, that his ear had been severed from his head.

After we cleaned away the clotted blood, and checked the bleeders, we found the ear canal and the ear, attached to the flap of skin that was lying on his shoulder. We used a local anesthetic around the scalp wound, but no other anesthetic.

The patient was, by then, conscious, and conversed with us, answering our questions. Despite the fact we worked on him until dawn, he never once complained, or objected to anything we did to him. He was unable to move, but could talk with us.

He was hospitalized for a week, and was sent home. A month later, he complained of a sharp pain in his neck while he was driving to Salt Lake City with his parents, to see a doctor. He told us later that something suddenly snapped in his neck; he was conscious, but could remember nothing between the time of the accident and the trip to Salt Lake. His parents drove him back to Kanab to thank us for taking care of him.

Marelda also reminded me of the night we had seventeen or eighteen CC boys in from the Pipe Spring camp, who had been in an accident. Our hospital was already full when the injured boys were brought in. We had only nine beds in the hospital, so we had to make beds of blankets on the floor in the hall, in the lab, and in the office.

When Ormand and Ada Cram were brought in, after a wreck on the mountain, we patched them up, and put them in the two beds in our guest room.

The CC boys had injuries ranging from broken ribs and collar bones, to ruptured spleens and neck injuries. The doctor from the CC camp was summoned, and he helped us do the footwork, and identifications.

It was about seven the next morning before things quieted down and the CC doctor returned to camp, and I went to bed. I had been asleep only a short time when one of the officers returned with another one of the boys who had been hurt in the accident. He had not been missed in the confusion and had returned to the camp and gone to the dispensary. He had been hit in the face with a piece of glass, severing the nose upward. The nose hung from a flap from his forehead and he breathed from the two holes in front of his face. Fortunately, I had experience in nose operations so we were able to attach the nose, sew him up, and the operation was successful.

It was in this wreck, that I wrote of earlier, where the young man sat in a corner, uncomplaining, and we did not know he was suffering from a ruptured spleen. He died, after surgery.

Still reminiscing, Marelda said, "Speaking of noses, do you remember Rose Clark's little boy who got kicked in the face by a horse?" The horse's hoof had caught part of his upper lip, peeling the boy's nose upward, leaving the nose hanging by a flap, and two holes in the middle of his face. This turned out to be a more delicate operation than we performed on the young man from the CC camp, but it too, turned out well. That was more than forty years ago, and I have not seen him since the operation.

"...and then there was Fern Esplin," Marelda said, "I remember you had to do a lot of work on him." Fern had driven his truck to the gravel pit on the Mt. Carmel hill, and when he backed his truck up near the gravel bank, a wall of gravel collapsed, crushing Fern downward. Fern's back was broken in two places, the fourth and fifth dorsal in the dorsal region, and the first and second vertebrae in the lumbar region. His sternum was also broken.

As he was sitting and holding himself up, with both arms as crutches, it looked as if his chin was down on his chest. The gravel, as it fell and spread, forced his face against the I beam in the back of the truck, peeling the right side of his face back past the ear, fracturing and displacing the cheekbone on that side.

I gave Vern demerol for pain, took x-rays, then put him on the extension table for suturing. We tried to get the cheekbone in place, then sutured the big flap that included his ear. That sounds pretty bad, but Fern said the worst pain was my taking his cigarettes away from him. He had a cigarette cough from having smoked so long, and he insisted that he had to have his hand-rolled cigarettes so he could cough up the stuff in his throat. I finally gave in, and gave him back his cigarettes, after a few days.

Fern had had several operations for a perforated ulcer of the stomach, and a few years later, after he suffered a severe hemorrhage, I had to send him to Salt Lake City for surgery.

Still later, while loading a horses into his truck, and standing on top of the cab pulling on the reins to get the horse to jump in the truck, the horse reared up on his hind legs, striking Fern with his front hooves, and knocking him from the top of the cab, fracturing Vern's femur.

After I X-rayed his leg, I could see that it was so comminuted that I knew I could not hold it with a cast, so I sent him to Salt Lake for a specialist's care. For years after that, his main complaint was pain in that leg, and his cough. He was still using his hand-rolled cigarettes to cure his cigarette cough.

Fern died, not long ago, without ever giving up his cigarettes. He always told me he hoped he'd die before I did, because if I died first, he would have no one to take care of him. I miss Fern; we had a lot of good times together.

I remember the night Burns Riggs and Doc McDonald were brought into the hospital. After the two of them had been hitting the bottle a bit, they decided to take a ride through Zion park. They apparently tried to cut across one of the turns in the road, and ran into a rock wall. Burns was thrown through the windshield. A large portion of his head was shaved off, taking the ear with it. This type of wound very often leaves a large attached flap. Doc sustained some bruises, but only minor wounds from the glass. Whoever helped bring them back to Kanab, tried to check the bleeding from the side of Burn's head, using a towel as a compress.

When they were brought into the hospital, Cecelia Pickett was the nurse on duty. She had dated Burns a couple of times. She put the men into the operating room, then called me. She began to clean up the mess, and when she unwrapped the towel from Burns' head, and saw the raw side of his head with no skin and no ear; she fainted.

When I came in and examined Burns, I could see the flap of skin attached to his neck. I cleaned off the clot, placed the flap with the ear in place at the side of his head, then sutured the ear in place. Eventually, when it healed, the ear was a bit smaller, but it looked good.

Doc recovered from the accident without any problems. Several years later, his car collided with a carload of Paiute Indians near Cave Lakes Ranch, killing eight indians, and nearly ending his own life. He suffered both physical and emotional problems after that, and was never the same. Later on, while driving home in a severe rain storm from the Glen Canyon dam where he was working, he collided with another car. McDonald was killed in the accident, and the Canadian couple in the other car were injured, but survived.

In the summer of 1938, I was asked to run for mayor of Kanab by Fuller Broadbent. I was nominated on the Democrat ticket, and won my first term in 1940-41, and was then re-elected for another term in 1942-43.

It was in late November of 1942, when some men brought Lafe Robinson into the hospital with a badly broken leg. Lafe had been operating the county grader on Johnson Road, when the blade struck a rock. The grader was tipped, throwing Lafe off the grader, and down the side of the road into the sandy borrow pit.

As Lafe hit the side of the pit, his left leg snapped just above the ankle. He suffered a compound fracture, with both the tibia and fibula tearing through the skin on the side of the leg. Lafe's weight, and the height from which he was thrown, forced the bone down into the sand. His foot, with the shoe and sock on, was pushed about halfway up the medial side of the lower leg. That was the way he was brought in. The stump that protruded through the skin, was covered with weeds and sand.

After examining him, I told Lafe that the most simple, least expensive, and least painful way was to amputate. He refused, and demanded that I save his leg. When we removed his shoes and socks, I could see that he still had circulation in his leg, so we began the clean-up process on the stump. After thoroughly cleansing the leg inside and out, I used a long strap cast to lay the leg in, from his buttocks down the lower leg, and up around his foot. By simple traction on his foot and knee, the lower bones were approximated. The wound was enlarged and debrided, then irrigated with a saline solution. Rubber drains were inserted into the wound, leaving a large window in the cast for dressing.

Lafe's knee was semi-flexed, and we hung his lower leg in a sling, which enabled him to turn from side to side. The wound drained well, but he soon got some swelling in his ankle and foot.

After a few days, Lafe lost his appetite and he told his children that the only thing he wanted to eat was a trout. It was out of season, but that was the only excuse I needed to go fishing. I figured the game warden and the Lord would forgive me under the circumstances.

I drove to Mammoth Creek, about sixty-five miles away, and turned into the meadow at the white bridge. There was an inch of snow along the stream, and the water was crystal clear. It was lower than it was in the summer. The place was quiet, with no sheep, horses or cows in the pasture, as there were in the summertime.

I tied on a nine-foot tapered leader with a 4X tippet and a #12 grey hackle fly. As I approached the stream, I could see fish leaving the shallows for the deeper pools. I was wondering if they would like a dry fly. After making a few false casts, I dropped the fly into the stream near the bank. When I had landed three good trout, it proved to my satisfaction, that trout will take a dry fly in the winter; even when no hatch is visible.

I had to be back at the office at three o'clock, so I left, after catching the three trout. I took them back to the hospital to have them cooked for Lafe. He enjoyed them, so it was worth the risk to see him so happy.

He eventually left the hospital, but always complained about his ankle swelling and being stiff, so he refused to pay his bill. I remember that I charged him seventy-five dollars for the three weeks hospitalization, and the doctor bill. The county had no industrial insurance at the time, but grudgingly paid the bill out of a special fund. To top it off, Lafe threatened to sue me, but I went into the Navy as a doctor, and by the time I returned from my tour of duty, Lafe had passed away.

CHAPTER TWENTY-FOUR
The War Years - WWII

By this time (1942), we were in the war years, and many of the men around Kanab were leaving for the higher wages the war industry was paying. In our agricultural and stock growing community, the prices seemed to remain low, but the wages were getting higher.

After the usual January review of the past year's work, my secretary, Kay Heaton, told me that I was paying out-of-pocket more than $600.00 a month, to support the hospital. Few people had insurance, and there were no independent funds, or welfare, to collect from at that time. There were numerous automobile accident victims who had no insurance. This made our losses heavy, because we never turned anyone away for lack of money.

I figured we could stand a loss of $300.00 a month, since we lived in a wing of the hospital. I came up with a plan that I presented to Dunc McDonald and Lloyd Pugh, County Commissioners. I told them that if the City could provide $300.00 a month, and I contributed $300.00 a month; we could keep the hospital open.

I should have realized that Dunc McDonald had opposed building the hospital in the first place. Dunc made the statement that they could not "subsidize a business that was failing because of poor management. He said "You know, we can't subsidize the grocer or garage business." He did not take into account that the grocer and the garage business did not provide merchandise and services without being paid.

I pointed out that we had been running the hospital as a public necessity and convenience. Again, Dunc repeated what he said when I first wanted to build the hospital, "We got along without a hospital for seventy years. You're the one who needs it; we don't."

Kanab has always been a difficult place for one to make changes. It was then, and it is now. Someone recently made the statement that they live in a cocoon, and that they don't want that cocoon disturbed. It makes it difficult for the outsider, who is progressive.

We were doing without, and working long hours to provide medical care for the area with little monetary return, and Dunc refused to even discuss the situation. The patients needed us and wanted us, but we could not survive without some kind of support, and we could not get it from Kane County.

"Then do you admit that the hospital is mine, and that I have no obligation to the public?" I asked. When Dunc answered "Yes," I said, "Then tommorow the key goes in the door to lock it up, and I will join the Navy as a doctor."

I don't think he believed me, but I did just that. I had tried to enlist in WWI while I was in medical school in Columbus, but I was told that doctors were needed at home, so I was deferred to stay in school. Now, in WWII, doctors were again needed, and this time I had years of experience to offer the Navy. Mr. Tietjen, County Commission Clerk, told me I was too old, and that I would not be accepted. I told him I would leave that up to the Navy. I was forty-seven, but I felt my age was an asset because of my experience, and the Navy thought so too.

We locked the hospital door and left for Salt Lake. I had mixed feelings about leaving, but I could not go on without some kind of help. In Salt Lake City, I was told to go to San Francisco, where I could be given the commission I rated. We drove to San Francisco, and after passing the physical and other exams, I was given the rank of a Lieutenant Commander in the Navy. This was on February 28, 1943. I was given orders to report to Bremerton, Washington, on March 4.

When I got back to Kanab, and took some papers to Teitjen, he expressed surprise that I had been commissioned by the Navy. Now, he said, they did not mind my leaving, but said that the county would like to buy the hospital. I could not help reminding him that Dunc McDonald said they didn't need one!

I still owed $15,000 to State Building & Loan, so I told the County they could buy the hospital for what I owed. This meant we were actually giving the hospital to the County.

We had been in the hospital for seven years; March 1936 to March 1943, and it had been an enriching experience. It was interesting to learn that after I left, the county commissioners (who never *needed* a hospital); hired a doctor, paid all of the hospital expenses for him, and for the duration of the war, paid him a salary of $500.00 a month, plus whatever he could collect.

I left Kanab on March 3, 1943, and headed for Bremerton. Duke was attending high school in St. George, so when Nita closed the hospital, she and our youngest son, Bob, moved to St. George to be with Duke. Duke wanted to join the Army Air Corps, but I insisted that he finish high school first.

After I left for Bremerton, Bob was injured when the tongue of a trailer fell on him. One of his legs was fractured, and Dr. Reichman of St. George, set it for him.

When I checked into the Navy Yard in Bremerton, the Officer of the Day, Fred Lindholm, asked where I planned to stay. I didn't want to live in the officer's quarters because I felt there might be too much drinking going on. He said that he and his wife had a large home and that I could board with them if I liked. I accepted, gladly. It was a large room, with windows overlooking the bay that was connected to the Straits of San Juan DeFuca.

One Sunday afternoon, as I sat writing a letter to Nita, I looked out of the window and saw a school of small fish jumping out of the water. Immediately afterward, I saw a large fish jump up in the middle of the school. Suddenly, I had an attack of fishing fever. I had brought a fly rod in my suitcase, along with a few spinners and flies; so I turned the letter over to finish later, and dashed downstairs to see if I could find someone with a boat that I could borrow.

A neighbor, Bob McCorkle, said that he had a boat in his garage, but said that boats were not allowed in the bay because of the marine arsenal that was there. There were gun emplacements and balloon stations all along the bay, so it was a restricted area.

I argued that I was an American, up there to fight for my country, and I did not think that going out into the bay to catch a few salmon would have an adverse effect on the war. After a few more arguments about rights and restrictions, Bob agreed not only to let me use the boat, but to go with me.

The school of candle fish were still in the bay by the time we had the boat in the water. I had an eight-foot bamboo fly rod with a nine-foot leader, with a 3X tip. I looped on a willow leaf spinner, that resembled a shiny minnow.

Bob rowed around the school of fish, and when we were on the opposite side, I trolled the spinner under the fish. A large salmon hit it and came out of the water like a rainbow. Then he dove and stayed down, fighting like a brook trout, strong and dogged.

I knew from past experience just how much tension to apply, so I just kept the pressure on. I could feel a release after a few minutes, and I knew he was on his way up and out. As he came out, I released a little line; then when he came down, I again applied pressure. He didn't go deep again, so we tried a figure-eight manuever with the pressure from the rod, to tire him out.

When the salmon rolled on his side alongside the boat, I knew if it flopped, it would break the leader. I asked Bob to row toward shore, where we both got out. I had Bob get behind the fish to push it up on the beach, while I pulled it in. Sure enough, when the fish touched shore, it flopped and broke the leader, but Bob was behind him, and threw him up on shore.

We were being watched by nearby residents, and before long, we heard boats being rolled down to the beach from the garages. Thirteen salmon were caught that Sunday evening. One old fellow wandered down to the beach and told us, "You can't catch salmon with that kind of an outfit!" We laughed, and proudly hoisted our ten pound silver salmon.

The next day, the sheriff came out and notified all the residents and boat owners that there would be no more boats on the bay; so that ended my salmon fishing.

After Fred told me that the small beach house two doors away was for sale, I contacted the real estate agent and bought it. Since it was wartime, I had to give the occupants three months notice, so they could find another place to live. In the meantime, I rented the real estate man's house on Hood's Canal.

When school let out in St. George, Nita, Duke and Bob drove to Washington. We all enjoyed the water and the cottage. Duke had joined the Air Corps, and I had duty at the Navy Yard Dispensary.

Nita was anxious to move into the cottage I bought on the bay. It was occupied by an Army officer and his wife who had been given the customary three-months notice, but who refused to leave.

In August, I received my orders to report to San Francisco, for overseas duty. Duke received his orders to report to Pullman, Washington, the same day. Nita didn't know how to drive, and Bob was too young, so with Duke and me leaving, it was imperative that we move into our cottage.

The Adjutant and his wife, who were occupying our house, were out when we arrived on a Saturday afternoon. We simply moved their belongings out, and our belongings in. When they returned, and found us happily ensconced in our cottage; the adjutant was livid.

He threatened to sue us. He knew he had no basis for a suit, so after much discussion we told them they could stay that weekend, but then they would have to leave. I mixed drinks, and we invited them to join us for dinner. On Monday, Nita called his Commanding Officer and he was told they would have to move; which they did, reluctantly.

Duke's train, and the train that I was to take to San Francisco, left at about the same time from Seattle, so Nita and Bob rode over on the ferry to see us off. Saying goodbye was a sad affair for the family. Nita had the car, but did not know how to drive. It was wartime, and both her husband and her son were going off to war; and like other wives and mothers, who saw their loved ones off to war, Nita knew it could be the last goodbye.

One good thing was that she and Bob had wonderful neighbors; the Lindholms, the Nordsbys, and the McCorkles. They were all Navy people and knew how lonesome she would be, so they helped her a great deal. Nita and Bob lived in the beach house for the next two years.

When I reached San Francisco, I found that I was assigned to *Mobile Hospital #9,* in Brisbane, Austrailia. We were in San Francisco for a month, before we sailed in September, on an army transport, the *Sea Pike.* We arrived in Brisbane in October, 1943. In Brisbane, I was attached to the S.O.Q. (Sick Officer's Quarters). The executive called me in and said, "I see you list yourself as a *General Practioner.* What the hell does *he* do?" I smiled, and answered, "He picks up the scraps the *Specialists* leave and puts them back together!"

I was twenty years older than most of the doctors there, so that was why I was assigned to the S.O.Q.. I also delivered a few babies for wives of the men who had married Australian girls. Mostly, I depended on the sixty-odd specialists we had for diagnosis and treatment.

In January and February of 1944, following the invasion of Tarawa, the Exec of our hospital asked for volunteers for surgical teams to be placed on the LSTs. While I had no degree in surgery I had enough experience to handle the job, so I volunteered. I was flown to New Guinea in April, along with seven or eight other doctors. Among them were Ralph Har, Bill Oldham, and a fellow named Miller.

The Head of the Amphibius Force doctors was Dr. Tom Ross, who was a graduate of Ohio State Medical School, where I had taken my medical training. However; Tom had graduated years after I did.

In the *Battle of Tarawa,* the Marines were invading the island in rubber rafts when the Japanese surprised them, killing and wounding many of them while they were still in the water.

It is the Navy doctor's job to take care of the Marines when the casualties are in the water, and the job of the Army doctors to take care of the casualties on land. In the Tarawa invasion, where most of the casualties were in the water, there was only one Navy doctor for eight LSTs, so many of the wounded were being picked up by ships with only a Pharmacist's Mate on board.

Because of the shortage of doctors, casualties were heavy. Some of the wounded had to be laid on the tank floor, and treated there. In many cases, it was five days before the wounded could reach a hospital.

After that experience, the Navy decided to send at least one surgical team for each invasion; a team consisting of a surgeon and his assistant, a First Lieutenant, ten corpsmen, and a Chief Pharmacist's Mate, on each LST.

On the ship carrying the surgical team, an opening was cut in the bulkhead wall, so the wounded could be taken onto the tank deck and passed through the opening to the passageway that was connected to the crew's quarters. We could house eighty-five patients, and we had a small operating room and sterilizing room.

It was early in April of 1944, that we were flown to Morsby, then to Lae, in New Guinea, and assigned to various surgical teams. I was assigned to *LST 395* and our first invasion was Hollandia, New Guinea.

There was a large enemy airfield at Hollandia, with what was rumored to be, three or four hundred Japanese planes. We were the second wave of the invasion, going in about three o'clock in the morning on April 21. I went up to the conning tower and talked to Admiral Carter, who was in charge of the flotilla of about twenty LSTs.

Occasionally, we would see flashes of light and rockets. The Admiral said he knew that a fight was going on, but he couldn't understand what was happening. When we got closer to the harbor, we could see what had taken place.

The first wave of landing craft had come ashore on what looked like an ideal beach, where they unloaded their trucks, ammunition, guns and Marines. The Japanese had also used that beach to unload supplies and ammunition and had established a large ammunition dump there.

What our men did not know was that there was a shallow lagoon between the beach and the mainland, and that they had no way to get off the beach, and into the interior of the island. The Japanese had used big-wheeled carts and shallow draft scows to transport their supplies and ammunition to the mainland, where there was a road that led to the airfield about twenty-five miles away.

During the first night when the men were stuck on the beach, *Washing Machine Charlie* (GI term for a small Japanese plane) flew over the stranded men and dropped three small bombs; one at the far end of the beach, one in the middle, and one where the beach hooked on to the mainland at the foot of a large red sandstone ledge that reminded me of the red bluffs of Utah.

The middle bomb hit the Japanese ammunition dump and all hell broke loose. I talked to an Army doctor from St. Louis the next morning, who said he had spent the night wading around the bay, dodging rockets.

The doctor said that the first explosion was so powerful, the concussion blew their hospital and all the equipment into the bay. The Japanese ammunition and flares landed on our ammunition carriers, and they too, blew up.

This was the disorganized firing and rockets, the Admiral and I had seen in the distance the night before. There was no place for the men to go, but into the water. Nearly everyone, who was still alive, were wading in the water when we came in, that second morning. The landing craft for that first group had discharged their loads of men and equipment, then backed off and gone back for another load.

We had heard *scuttlebutt* that we might be attacked by Japanese planes, since they had such a large airfield close by. However, we found out later that our *Fifth Air Force* had braved a warning about a severe storm, and flew in and attacked the Japanese airfield at daylight, on Easter Sunday.

Many of the enemy planes were still in their revetments, and the rest were just getting onto the airfield when our pilots from the Fifth came flying over. According to reports, there were close to two hundred planes annihilated. We heard that our planes had run into very bad weather on the way home from the attack, and some of the planes were lost. Pilots bailed out, and some were rescued.

We knew that many of our men were saved because our brave pilots put our safety before theirs, even though they knew they would encounter a severe storm. There have always been men in all branches of the Service who put the lives of their fellow-men ahead of their own.

Later, we drove to the airfield and saw the shattered Japanese planes. General Douglas MacArthur subsequently built his headquarters there.

We had some trouble on our own LST in the early morning of that invasion. An Army Captain of an *ack-ack company* went beserk. He had some of our officers pretty well scared. When I talked with him, he begged me not to put him in a straight jacket, which made me suspect he had been in one before.

We placed him in isolation in one of the cabins, but had to restrain him by hand-cuffing his right hand to the headboard, and his left leg to the foot of the bed. A few days later, we discharged him to the army hospital in Finchhaven.

That same morning, an Army chaplain tried to jump overboard from our ship but was caught by the shirttail by one of the sailors. My assistant, who thought he was a physchologist, asked the chaplain a lot of questions and learned that the chaplain had had an affair with an Aussie girl and was trying to end his life. We left him at Finchhaven, along with the captain who went beserk.

Later on, after the invasion of Hollandia, we left about eighty-five burn and accident cases at Finchhaven, and I asked about the Army chaplain. The nurses said that he had died the Sunday before. He told them when they went off duty that afternoon that he would be dead before they came back on duty. He died that night. The post-mortem showed that he had died of a hemorrhage into the brain.

Going back to our invasion story, our Skipper tried to find a way from the bay into the shallow lagoon. When he found that it was too shallow we discharged the Army, with their supplies, on the beach south of the first landing beach.

That night a few Japanese planes flew overhead dropping magnesium flares over the bay. We felt pretty well exposed when those brilliant flares were descending over us, but we suffered only minor damage from the few bombs that were dropped.

The wind beached our LST, and a Navy tug was trying to drag us off the beach when we were brought our first casualty at dusk. He was a young Filipino boy who had fallen on one of the long metal spikes that were driven into the ground, and used to fasten barbed wire. The spike had pierced the muscle in the left side of the lumbar region, making the abdomen extremely tender.

The boys had our operating room set up with sterile drapes under the steam and water pipes, and on the side walls. We opened up the abdomen, after giving him a spinal anesthetic. We found no blood, except for a large hemotoma under the peritoneum, but no perforation.

We closed and dressed the wound after debriding, putting in sulfa powder, and a drain. He was discharged to the army hospital at Finchhaven in April of 1944.

It was in January of 1945, that someone called to me as I went past the galley on our ship. I was on LST 12 at this time. The young man said, "Dr. Aiken, don't you recognize me?" I admitted that I did not, and asked him to refresh my memory. He was the young Filipino that I had operated on in April of 1944. he said that his home was on the mountainside above the Lingayen Gulf, where we were then, invading.

When our team was transferred to *LST 475*, and I was climbing up the *Jacob's Ladder,* the Officer of the Deck looked down at me, called to the Captain that an officer was coming aboard, and as I pulled myself onto the deck he exclaimed, "What are you doing here? You're older than God!"

After introductions, I was asked if I played bridge. I was told there were a couple of sharpies aboard and they needed someone who could beat them. We played bridge that night, and lost. The next day, we were transferred to *LST 912.*

We were involved in the invasions of Wajke, Biak, Morati, and Sansapore. By that time, the invasions were pretty well organized. The Fifth Air Force would fly in at, or before, daybreak, bombing targets and dropping napalm bombs to burn vegetation and clear the underbrush.

Sometimes, the LST's, loaded with rockets would bombard the area to be invaded, and the destroyers or destroyer escorts would shell the shore to protect the LST's loaded with men and equipment. The landing site would be chosen after aerial photos were studied, and after the *frog men* went into the water to check for obstructions or mines.

The first thing off the LST's would usually be the diesel-powered road-making equipment, with the blade up, to be used for protection. It would be driven down the ramp, and once it was ashore, it was used to build roads for the men, jeeps and trucks that followed.

This routine was followed at Biak. The Army landed, got their jeeps and took off down the road to the airport at about four o'clock in the afternoon. Their route lay under a long ridge. We were told that there were several thousand Japanese soldiers living in the caves along the ridge that ran through the middle of the island.

The Japanese soldiers waited until our men were in their jeeps, and the soldiers marching towards the airport. The did not open fire until our men had almost reached the airport, thereby almost annihilating our army.

The Japanese had a hospital and supply station in the caves. Shells from our destroyers could not penetrate the natural defenses, and it was only through the use of flame-throwers, used close-up, that our men could do the job. They had to sneak up to the entrance of a cave, turn on the flame-thrower, and when the oxygen in the cave was depleted, the Japanese would either come out and surrender, or stay in the caves for good.

It is interesting, that many years later, there were cases that came to light of Japanese soldiers who lived in the caves and didn't know who won the war. They went into the Japanese Imperial Army as young men, and returned as middle-aged men, to their startled, but happy families.

After so many of our men were killed and wounded at Biak, we returned with a full load of army patients to Finchhaven. One of them had been shot through the back, fracturing the spine. He had been put in a full body cast, but had breathing difficulties, and died shortly before we reached Finchhaven.

One GI had his chin shot off, and had to be given water and medication by spoon, night and day, during the entire trip. Another soldier had a bullet hole through both buttocks, and when I asked him how he could get a wound like that, he grinned and said, "Did you ever try to hide in a wheel track?"

He was a small Mexican-American, who spoke broken-English, but everyone had praise for him. He was part of a group that carried parts of the field machine-gun, and on signal, each man had his part to perform in assembling the gun. This young man was *low man on the totem pole,* carrying the equipment to clean the gun. When the Japanese opened fire from their cover on the ridge, everyone in the group was killed or disabled.

This brave young Mexican-American took over and assembled the gun alone. He turned the gun on the attackers, giving his buddies who were not already dead, a chance to survive. I don't know his name, or where he came from, but he was a Hero. Whether he was ever officially recognized as one, I do not know, but he should have been.

After Biak, we took Morati, then delivered a company of SeaBees to Sansapore, on the west end of New Guinea. The SeaBees job was to lay steel matting for a runway in the jungle, from which our Air Force could bomb Borneo. Then came the Leyte Gulf invasion, in the Phillipines, in October.

When we landed the First Cavalry at Tacloben, I tried to find my old friend, Dr. Roy Eklund, but was told that he had been hospitalized for a severe case of dysentery.

We made another landing at Yellow Beach, in Leyte Gulf, after a trip to Hollandia. While we were unloading at Yellow Beach, a Japanese bomber flew over us at a high altitude. Our beauforts and 20 mm anti-aircraft guns opened fire, as well as the destroyers and anyone else in the gulf who had a gun, making a floor of flak about ten thousand feet, but he was above that.

I was sitting behind a sailor from Heber City, Utah, named Henline, when we saw approximately twelve small Japanese planes flying down the valley at a low level. Before we could swing our guns around after the alert was given, the planes were dropping small bombs, trying to ignite the ammunition and stores of gasoline we had on the beach. I don't think we got off a shot, until after they were past, but when they turned and came back, we were ready for them.

I saw one plane descend in a dive towards us, so I grabbed Henline and pointed. He swung his gun around and opened fire. The wing of the plane began to crumple, as the plane started to fall. We got a lot of static from a Merchant ship that was in our line of fire, but happily, there were no casualties reported. I believe that all of the *Kamakazi* planes were shot down, and from the shouting and back-slapping, you would have thought we had won the war. This was our first Kamakazi attack.

There were ten LST's on that invasion. Our radar could not pick up the small planes as they flew down the valley. A big bomber would lead them down the coast in back of the mountain, then act as a decoy, while the small planes flew down the valley to drop their bombs and dive into the ships lying in the gulf, trying to destroy as many of us as possible.

As we were backing out into the gulf to go back to Hollandia, three Kamakazis dove for a cargo vessel. The middle plane dove straight down through the hatch into the center of the ship. There was a thunderous explosion before flames and a great cloud of smoke rose up into the sky, making a giant smoke ring. The other two planes veered off, but were brought down by our gunners.

I had the only surgical team when we invaded Puerta Princessa, on the island of Palawan, south of the Philipines in the South China Sea. One night, the skipper sent a messenger to my cabin to say that one of the LST's was sending over a patient with appendicitis.

When I went up on deck to await the arrival of my patient, the sea was like a millpond. A full moon hung low over the ships lying in the gulf, making it one of the most beautiful nights in my memory. Not far away, and clearly visible, was the hospital ship, all lit up like a saloon.

I asked the skipper why he didn't send the appendix case to the hospital ship. I was sure the young man would have preferred having female nurses taking care of him, instead of sailors. The skipper said he could not jeopardize the convoy, nor the hospital ship, by breaking radio silence.

The LST came alongside with the patient on a stretcher. He was lifted over the rail, and after examining him to verify the diagnosis, he was taken to our operating room and given a spinal anesthetic. The next day, the young man was walking around the ship.

The amphibious forces were perfecting their technique of invasion. By the time of Puerta Princessa, there was a new type of ship, a landing dock in which ten to twenty LCI's could be dry-docked, and carried to the point of invasion. The dock was then filled with water, the rear doors of the dock opened, and the LCI's floated out. They then circled the large dock like ducklings around a mother duck. The LCI's were loaded with rockets that were fired in groups, and they were later used at Lingayen Gulf.

The Army landed at Puerta Princess, without opposition. That evening, I went to the army hospital that had been set up during the day to see if there were any casualties to take back with us. There were only three patients that the hospital personnel said that they would keep. They had been practicing for two years, and this was the first time they had been able to practice in enemy territory.

The Lingayen invasion on January 9, was next. It was a large operation, with several hundred ships involved in the invasion. This was also the closest we ever got to Japan.

We were passing near Manila, about four o'clock in the morning. The night was dark, with just a slim sickle of a moon showing. The wind was blowing off-shore, so the smoke machines we were using, blew the smoke away from the land side where our group of LST's were, over the rest of the convoy.

I had been up on the conning tower talking to the captain, and had just returned to my post on the fantail where I stayed when we were on alert. Suddenly, without warning, a plane hit the deck and the gun tub near us, spilling out burning gasoline. The guards who were on the stern immediately floated the area with carbon diozide, extinguising the flames almost before the plane fell into the ocean.

I ran to the upper deck where I heard a man groaning. He had been knocked out of the ready-box and I thought the plane might have hit the rear anti-aircraft gun. I called out, but there was no answer, so I crawled over the side of the tub. Shells had been opened when the plane hit, spilling gun-powder all over the deck and into the tub.

The four men, manning the gun, were crushed and killed, instantly. I had goose-pimples all over my body, terrified that the powder I was walking on, would ignite at any moment. I wondered if any of the firing fuses were about to go off; my mind flashing back to Nita and to my two sons.

We had a burial service at sea that morning, for the men who were killed. Each of the four men were sewn into a canvas bag, then the bottom of the bags were weighted with shells, and placed on canvas cots; side by side.

An Army chaplain conducted the services, as directed by the Navy. After the ceremony, at a signal from the chaplain, the stretchers were tipped, and the bodies slipped into the sea. Latitude and longitude were taken, so as to note the spot where they were buried. Our ship took its place at the side of the convoy line, and proceeded slowly. As the other ships passed, their crews lined up at attention, and saluted. There were tears in the eyes of many of us. We had lost four men, and we couldn't help wonder if we too, might find our final resting place in the sea.

We sailed into Lingayen Gulf, the night of January 8, 1945. The big guns first began to soften up the enemy positions, and everything was being fired. Suddenly, on a pre-arranged signal, it all stopped. It was early morning when we tried to put our load ashore, but the wind broached us, as it did other LST's, so we received orders to land on the north shore, and that proved to be lucky for us.

After the Japanese had routed MacArthur out of the Philipines, they placed our big Navy guns in trenches on the north slope above the gulf, thinking that we would land on the south. From their location, they could not hit us on the north shore, but would shoot over us with a short fuse, causing only small shell fragments to fall on us. We had only one man hit in the back with a shell fragment. He was sent to an attack hospital cargo transport for care.

On Easter morning, April 1, 1945, we were at Ligaspi Peninsula. There was a beautiful, deep harbor surrounded by sloping hills with palms. One vivid memory I have, is of the bombs hitting in the edge of the water, and sending up a big spray, creating an exquisite rainbow.

Ligaspi volcano was still active, with plumes of white smoke rising from it. The landing for us was uneventful, but the Army fought a long and bitter fight in the mountains, behind the town of Ligaspi.

We were at Biak to pick up some Aussies to take to Borneo, when I got my orders to return home. I flew to Takloben, 1300 miles to the west, then took an Army ship home, three weeks later. Nita was there to meet me when we docked at San Pedro, California.

My orders were to return to Bremerton, Washington, where I was discharged on December 31, 1945. Duke had gotten out of the Air Corps in October. We sold our cottage in Bremerton, and moved to Provo, Utah, where Bob attended public school, and Duke went to college at Brigham Young University.

I then went to the Polyclinic in New York for a six-month post-graduate refresher course: three months of general medicine, and three months of eye, ears, nose and throat. At the end of the six months, Nita, Bob and Duke drove back East to join me. They spent one week with Nita's sister, Louise, and her husband, Morris, in Washington, D.C., and then drove to New York.

For one wonderful week, we simply relaxed and enjoyed ourselves. We took in Broadway shows, like *Showboat,* and *Annie Get Your Gun;* then went to movies that had been shot in Kanab and the surrounding area, while we were away. One of the movies was *Smokey,* and it gave us added pleasure to recognize the scenery and some of the cowboys, and even some of the livestock.

CHAPTER TWENTY-FIVE
Back in Kanab

We left New York and drove back to Utah, planning to set up an EENT practice. We went to Cedar City, but had always seemed to meet opposition there. I was, by now, fairly well known in southern Utah and thought of re-locating someplace other than Kanab. The hospital we had struggled to build, with the help of our patients and our friends, now belonged to Kane County.

While we were in Cedar City, Fen Covington called me and asked me to come back to Kanab to practice. He had been released from the service ahead of me and had just leased the hospital from Kane County. He said he would handle the medical work and OB, and I could do the EENT work, as well as do some surgery.

As we drove up Center Street in Kanab, I saw a "For Sale" sign in front of Pruda Hamblin's house. We stopped, talked to Pruda, and gave her a deposit for earnest money.

It took a few months to close the deal, but we eventually moved into the house. It was situated on a large lot, so when Duke graduated from the University of Utah, and married Sue Major, Nita and I gave them half the lot as a wedding gift. They built Aiken Lodge on it.

Duke later decided that the house Nita and I lived in on the lot, was where the Lodge should have a swimming pool, so our large home was moved onto Main Street, where it stands today. It is now occupied by my youngest son, Bob, and his second wife, Lenore and her son. Duke and Sue kept the property, and the lodge. It still stands in Kanab today, but it was sold when it became too confining.

I rented an office in the Bybee Building and set up my medical practice. Shortly after I set up practice, Fen left and went to Idaho, so I again had the whole practice to myself.

In 1948, I was again elected mayor of Kanab for a two-year period. The airport had been built outside of Kanab, but had not been paid for entirely. I asked Elmer Jackson if he had enough money to pay the contractor. He said he had talked to Mr. Crandall at the Salina State Bank (we did not yet have a bank in Kanab), and Crandall had assured him that the bank would loan the City of Kanab the money.

As soon as I could, I spoke with Crandall. He told me the same thing he told Elmer, that they would loan all they could loan *legally*, which was $19,000.00. That left a balance of $12,500.00.

I was concerned about raising the rest of the money, because it was illegal to borrow any more. When I talked to Odel Watson and Hoyt Chamberlain, the two Commissioners representing the Kanab side of the County, they told me they had a fund consisting of B&C road money that had not been used since the war. This was money that had to be used for roads that connected to the main highway. We reasoned that using this money on the entrance to the airport, and roads to the hanger, would be legal.

At the next Commissioner's meeting, Hoyt and Odel out-voted Hans Chamberlain, and the money was loaned to the city to finish paying for the airport. Mr. Tietjen, clerk for the County Commissioners, and I, handled it this way: I signed a note to the county for $12,500.00, and the city was assessed a small fee for the use of the money. It was arranged that Mr. Tietjen would deduct $2,500.00 each year for five years from the tax money that was given to the city by the county. That would pay back the loan of $12,500.00.

When LeGrand Heaton replaced Hans at the next election, he promptly went to Salt Lake to the Attorney General, with the story about our loan from the county. The Attorney General came to Kanab to investigate.

At a meeting in the courthouse one night, the attorney general questioned Elmer, Hoyt Chamberlain, Odel Watson, and me, about how we got the $12,500.00 from the county. At the conclusion of the meeting he said that since there was no legal way for us to borrow the money, it was likewise illegal to pay it back! With that, he gave up, and went back to Salt Lake. It had not turned out the way LeGrand thought it would, nor the way we thought it would.

When I talked to the county clerk in 1978, he said the county had received $2,000.00 of the loan before we were told it was illegal to repay it, so in 1977 the county had written off the balance as a bad debt. We were honest in our intent, but technically illegal in our plan to pay off the city debt.

In the early fifties, another excitement developed in Kane County: The uranium boom. Nearly everyone had a hot rock in one hand, and a geiger counter in the other.

Many strangers were filing claims at the courthouse, and among them were a few rough characters, ones you would not want to get acquainted with.

Holland was a fellow who lived in a trailer behind the Purple Sage Motel, which was run by Zirker and his wife, Illene. Wilson, Gripes, and Rasmussen roomed in the old Kanab Hotel. While they didn't seem friendly to each other it was said that they all came from Bull Valley, near Viejo, a small town northwest of St. George.

Some of the local stockmen were upset at the trespassing of prospectors on their property, so when Orval Robinson saw a car parked at the side of the road near his ranch, he stopped and checked the registration certificate in the vehicle. It belonged to Holland.

Orval looked around and saw two sets of footprints leading away from the car. Two men had apparently climbed through the fence and walked north, toward a rough break in the hills. This was about four o'clock in the afternoon.

Orval went on to his ranch, and when he drove back on his way to pick up his wife at the city offices, where she was the city clerk, the car was gone. It was then five o'clock.

The next day, Orval stopped again on his way to the ranch, to look around. The two sets of prints he had seen the day before were still clearly visible in the soft sand, but in checking further, he found that only one set of footprints led back to the car. This aroused his curiosity.

He followed the two sets of footprints that led to the head of a wash. One set of prints had gone into the wash, while the other set circled it. As he stood, wondering which set of prints to follow, he suddenly froze! In the wash was a dead man, and a gieger counter, still clicking, where the victim had dropped it when he was shot.

The man had been shot five times with a .45 calibre pistol. The killer then returned to the car, using a different route. Empty shells from the automatic lay in the wash. The body was that of Wilson.

Orval notified Merril Johnson of the Highway Patrol, and Mason Meeks, the county sheriff, who investigated the killing. About four hundred yards away from the place where the car had been parked, at the head of the wash, they found Wilson's body, and the empty shells.

When I examined the body of Wilson at the site of the murder, and again at the morgue, I observed that there was a bloody froth from his mouth, so I concluded that he had been shot in the back first, and that the other four shots had been fired, as he lay dying. There was little blood from the later shots.

We removed a slug from under his skin, and it matched the empty shells near the body, at the scene of the murder; shells from a .45 calibre automatic. The shells and slugs were not admitted as evidence!

On the basis of what was known, Holland was arrested and jailed, on suspicion of murder. Zirker, who ran the motel also became a suspect when it was revealed that he and Wilson had a fist fight over a uranium claim, and Zirker, subsequently, had asked the sheriff for a permit to carry a gun.

Kane County was not prepared to handle a murder trial. Our County Attorney was not even an attorney, and our sheriff was a rancher and a cowhand. There was no professional investigation to gather evidence, and organize the prosecution.

As a result, Ken Chamberlain, from the District Attorney's office came down from Richfield, to help Willard Mackleprang, Kane County Attorney, to prosecute the case against Holland.

It was a jury trial, conducted by the district court judge, from Richfield. The courtroom was packed. Ellis Pickett, was the defense attorney for Holland.

To establish a motive for the murder of LeRoy Wilson, it was brought out that Holland bought some uranium claims from Wilson for $3,000.00, and had begun to promote the sale of those claims, when Holland's check to Wilson, bounced. Since he had already sold some of the stock, Holland was in a spot. That was put forward as the reason Holland allegedly killed Wilson.

Defense Attorney Ellis Pickett objected to the inference, and Judge Sevy ruled in his favor. So, the motive was thrown out.

The time of the murder was pretty well established, as Ronald Mace testified that he had directed Holland and Wilson to the road that went west from the airport. He testified that he knew it was close to four o'clock in the afternoon because his wife was just leaving a meeting of the Relief Society. It was also the time he took his water turn for the irrigation.

That is the way things stood when the court recessed on Friday afternoon. On Monday morning, Ellis Pickett called on Zirker to testify. Zirker said that Holland could not have been the killer; because on the day of the murder, Zirker and his wife, along with Holland and a girl friend, had been together at a party that afternoon. The four of them had eaten dinner at Parry Lodge, and then had driven to Orderville to attend a dance for the rest of the evening. The story established an alibi for both Holland, and Zirker.

Attorney Pickett then moved for an acquittal; for lack of evidence. No gun, no witnesses to the murder, and no motive, according to Pickett. The case was dropped and Holland was set free.

The next day, Tom Indian came into my office. While I was preparing some medication for him he asked me if the man who shot Wilson was still in jail. I said, "No, Tom, he was acquitted; set free. There was no evidence that he did it."

Tom Indian was astonished and said, "You mean that two men walk out there, and only one man comes back, and that man did not shoot the other man!" He shook his head, thought for a moment, then said, "White man's laws are sure funny!"

I had one more four-year term after that, as mayor of Kanab, starting in about 1954. The city grew slowly. We worked hard for an improved water system, and put in our first well. Up until that time all city water came from springs. We also put in a new lighting system; a new sewer system, and storage tanks for water.

In 1958, when the Utah State Medical Association planned to introduce a basic science bill in the legislature, they were anxious to have a doctor in the House of Representatives, to help get the bill passed. That is how I came to be nominated for the House on the Democrat ticket. I was elected, and found the experience an exciting and learning process. The bill was introduced, and passed.

There was a Democrat majority in the Legislature that year, with a Republican governor. Kane County had always been considered *cow country,* and strongly Republican, but my voting record must have been approved by the residents of the county, because I served for three terms in the Legislature.

I did not always vote as a Democrat, nor did the representative from Washington County. One year when the House of Representatives was through with their bills for the session, and they were already sent to the Senate the representative from Washington County and I were each presented with half a toilet seat. We were told that the seats were for *two half-assed Democrats,* because we voted Republican so often.

Since the State has gone to the one-man, one-vote situation with a multi-countygrouping, instead of districting by counties, it is hard for us to have a representative completely dedicated to Kane County.

In 1959, when I went to serve in the Legislature, I called the secretary of the Utah State Medical Association and told him I needed help.We were getting a big influx of people connected with the construction of Glen Canyon Dam, and the bridge across the Colorado River. The secretary told me about two young doctors who were then living in Park City, who might be interested in providing the extra medical help needed.

Dr. Richard Reilly came down first. He saw about forty patients his first day, so he put in a hurried call to his partner, Dr. Joseph Sanella, who also moved to Kanab.

When I returned from the legislative session, we opened a clinic together, on a three-way split. It worked out well for me, since it gave me extra time in the winter for vacations. They also had training that I had not had, and they proved to be invaluable in our practice.

One of the nicest things one doctor can say about another, was told to my editor, by Dr. Sanella. He said, "When I came to Kanab, I was hungry. I had been in practice for a year in Park City, and I had a family to support. In retrospect, I realize that I was sometimes a little testy, but Dr. Aiken said, 'Look, you'll find that if you get out and do the very best, get out there and practice medicine; the money will take care of itself'"

I was touched by this, especially since Sanella said that he has given other young doctors this same advice. He said that when they have come back to thank him for the advice, he tells them, "Don't thank me, thank Dr. Aiken."

He also said, "I will remember Dr. Aiken as one of the real heros of medicine, a man of integrity and guts..." and told the story of the parents who knocked me to the ground when they lost their child. Dr. Sanella said, "He got up, brushed himself off, and went back to the practice of medicine."

I owe both Dr. Sanella and Dr. Reilly a lot. They were there with knowledge in surgery that was not being taught when I was in school. They lifted the burden from my shoulders, and let me get away for my trips to Mexico, with Nita and Louise.

Before Dr. Sanella and Dr. Reilly came to Kanab, several doctors (one or two at a time) moved into town, stayed a few months, and then left. One of these young doctors, was a Dr. Fulstow. In 1960, he opened a practice at the head of the stairs in the same building we occupied. After his nurse called me one time to revive him from a over-dose of sleeping pills, I lost confidence in him. He also made some errors in diagnosis, which were quite obvious.

He had a friend in Colorado, whom he had met while interning in a TB hospital in Denver. The friend came to visit him in Kanab, and Fulstow drove with him to show him the Grand Canyon. As they were returning to Kanab about midnight, and about ten miles east of Fredonia on Highway 89, they had a one-car accident.

Slim Latham, sheriff of Fredonia, called me. When I arrived on the scene, Fulstow was dead, and his friend was paralyzed in the upper extremities. Fulstow's neck had been broken, and he had a possible skull fracture. Neither of them were wearing seat belts, which were new at that time.

Someone arrived with stretchers, and Fulstow's friend was taken to the hospital for X-rays, then transferred elsewhere for further treatment. I don't know what ever happened to him, after he left Kanab.

In 1964, I received the *Robbins Award* from the Utah State Medical Association, for outstanding community service as a physician.

On June 18, 1968, I was called from my office to the community swimming pool where a six-year-old boy, Burke Beesley, had tried to dive from the wall at the side of the pool, and struck his thigh on the edge of the pool; fracturing his right femur.

He was carried to the swimming pool office where the attendants placed him on a plank and secured his leg, so he could be transported to the Kane County Hospital. X-rays showed a comminuted fracture at the middle of the right femur.

I had previously had several fractures of this kind in younger children, so I applied a cast, and called Dr. Ed Evans, an orthopedic surgeon at the Intermountain Clinic. He said it would be alright to go ahead with the cast; so we encased both legs, including the feet, in a plaster cast.

First, each leg and foot was encased in a stockinette; then an elastic bandage was applied around both the ankles, and the feet. A bar was placed between his knees, and a plaster cast was applied from the feet to the perineum.

The patient was then suspended from an overhead bar, so his hips did not touch the bed. This allowed the patient considerable movement. Burke did not require much medication for his pain. Liquid aspirin was all we used to control his pain and restlessness.

At the end of three weeks, x-rays showed good approximation, but I told our nurse, Rosalie Esplin, "I think I detect a faint odor. We'd better take off the cast and take a look."

Upon removal of the cast, we found a slough of skin over both feet, and both Achilles tendons. We applied an Elase dressing, and the next day removed the skin that had been sloughed. I had the parents come in, and I showed them the extent of the slough. I told them that the best treatment would be to do a skin graft, which I could do; or, if they preferred, they could take him to Children's Hospital in Salt Lake City.

They chose to take Burke to Salt Lake, and after skin grafts were done at Children's Hospital in July of 1968, someone at the hospital told the parents that that was no way to treat a fracture of that kind. On the basis of that comment, Beesely then brought suit against me for $200,000.00.

John Snow was the attorney for the Utah State Medical Association, and for my insurance company. Oscar McConkle, Jr. was the attorney for the Beesleys. The jury trial was held in Kanab, so it was hard to pick a jury that was not prejudiced in my favor. I had practiced in Kanab, built the hospital, and had taken care of most of the residents in the entire area since 1931.

Another thing in my favor was that young Burke had gotten out of the hospital, and was running around the courtroom, and up and down the stairs during the trial. I was surprised that his parents would bring him to the trial. The jury could see that the boy was not in pain, and suffered no particular disability.

My attorney said, "Well, that's good. He is our best witness for the defense."

In the beginning, I told John that since the Beesleys had undergone extra expense and anxiety, that we should offer to settle out of court. I judged that $10,000.00 should cover any expense he had incurred, or would incur, with a little extra for the anxiety.

John thought that was a fair offer, so we called Oscar and Beesley in, for a compromise, the morning the trial began. When we made the offer, both Beesley and the attorney laughed, and said they were going after the full amount. So, the trial began.

I had practiced medicine since 1921, and in that time had treated numerous fractures, quite a few of them, fractures of the femur. I used, as reference, a book by *Key & Cromwell* on fractures.

In his questions to me, John brought out that I had followed the text, and that I had consulted with Dr. Evans, orthopedic surgeon, and that at no time, was there shown to be negligence on my part. Attorney Oscar McConkle had to go along with that, since Burke was running around, refuting his arguments.

McConkle called in a Dr. Hess, to testify against me. He was a Salt Lake City surgeon, of international repute. He told of his unlimited experience in London, Paris, New York, and at Children's Hospital in Salt Lake. He gave quite a dissertation on the ideal way to treat a fracture of that type. In a boy, Burke's age, Hess said that he would not have done the treatment as I did. Then he sat down.

Judge Ferdinand Erickson, from Richfield, whom I had known for many years, leaned over toward Hess and said, "Listen, Doc."

Dr. Hess looked startled and asked, "Are you talking to me?" I don't think he had ever been called "Doc" in all his medical career.

Judge Ericson said, "Yes, you!" and then continued with a lecture that went something like this: "Do you know what a country doctor like Dr. Aiken does? He's alone, with no one to consult within a hundred miles! He may drive fifty to a hundred miles to deliver a baby, or to take care of a patient. He never has the ideal situation in his work, that you do in the city. But, he delivers babies; takes out tonsils, and takes care of all kinds of sickness among men, women, and children; and that includes surgery of all kinds, as well as setting fractures!"

Judge Erickson gave better testimony for me than either of the attorneys, although John brought out that there was no basis for a suit.

The jury was dismissed to deliberate on the verdict, so we all went downstairs, and outdoors. While we were outside, someone asked Judge Erickson how long the jury would be out, and he answered that he thought it would take about fifteen minutes, with an acquittal.

After about fifteen minutes, as Judge Erickson had predicted, the jury came back, with a verdict of *no cause for action.*

Between 1970-1974, I had a four year term as City Councilman. During that time, June McAllister, who lived in the old Bowman Chamberlain home, died. The home had been designated by the Utah State Historical Society, as an historical site. Adonis Robinson, and Harvey Judd, who were instrumental in getting that designation, came to a Council meeting after June's death, and suggested that the City buy the home. The price was $25,000.00.

The Council was lukewarm about the idea, because they thought that it should be used as an office building. They wanted to build a new office building for the City and the County. Another objection was that they were afraid that it might raise our taxes.

I was in favor of buying the home, so at a public meeting, I urged the city to buy the home with the concept of development as a living history. The City had $75,000.00 in savings that had accumulated over the years. $25,000.00 of that amount could be used to purchase the home, assuring the residents that their taxes would not be raised.

The decision to buy the home was finally made, and I was given the job of overseeing the restoration of what is now known, internationally, as the *Kanab Heritage House.* I was recently looking at the *before* and *after* pictures, and am proud of the years we have dedicated to improving the house and property. Visitors from all over the world come to share in this part of southern Utah history.

CHAPTER TWENTY-SIX
Mexico

Nita and I, nearly always with another couple, made many vacation trips to Mexico. Our first trip there was with Floyd and Iva Maddox, old friends of ours. Floyd, who was originally from New Mexico, wandered into southern Utah looking for a cattle ranch. He and Fay Hamblin got together and operated a combined spread for years. It was during that time that Floyd met Iva, and they were married.

Floyd had an old friend, Jack Miner, from Tombstone, Arizona, who had a mine in the State of Sonora, in Old Mexico. Jack had built a small concrete cabin in the fishing village of Libertad. Jack had given permission for Floyd to use the cabin if he ever went down there. Things were quiet at the hospital at the time, so Floyd invited Nita and I to go down and take a look. That was our first trip to Libertad, in 1960.

We didn't know what shape the cabin would be in, so we packed sleeping bags, a tent, and other supplies into a pickup. The roads were pretty slippery getting through Flagstaff, on account of the snow and ice.

We drove to Tucson, then headed for the Mexican town of Pitiquito. From there the direction to Libertad was generally southwest, but the road was almost non-existent. It took us twelve hours to travel the seventy-five miles to Libertad.

We used the old cabin on that first trip. The winds were cold so the cabin was roomier and more comfortable than our tent. There were several couples there fishing, including Augustine and his wife, Maria, who had run the old hotel during WWII.

The fishermen fished at night, and mended their nets during the daytime. It was a colorful setting, and had I been an artist, instead of a doctor, I would have enjoyed capturing the Mexican fishermen on canvas.

We did not have a boat on that first trip so we did our fishing from the shore, casting for kelp bass and sea trout. We enjoyed the long, lonely beaches, and walked miles gathering seashells along the shoreline. After a storm we gathered dozens of the glass balls the fishermen used to float their fishing nets.

About one hundred feet in front of our cabin, Frankie, a small Mexican, had his dugout. When he would hear the door to the cabin squeak, his head would pop up over the bank, like a gopher. Outside the entrance to his dugout he had built a small enclosure of brick and turtle shells, about three feet square, and used that for his small garden where he planted tomatoes.

Above the tomato plants he had placed branches of brush to form a protective covering for his plants. The entrance faced our cabin, so oftentimes when we looked out, Frankie's backside was sticking out while he was watering or weeding his miniature garden. The Mexicans are an industrious people and happily make do with whatever they have, without ever voicing a complaint. They are warm and generous, sharing what little they have, with those they consider their friends.

One morning, Frankie knocked on the door and offered us a plate full of chunks of fish that had been broiled over wood coals. It was delicious. Frank said that is was *checo tortuava*, the cheek of the white sea bass. It is a large fish, weighing between forty and fifty pounds, with a soft muscle under the eye and a hard plate on its head. It was the most delicious fish I have ever eaten, and if I had to choose one last meal on this earth, it would be checo tortuava.

At night, bands of coyotes would come down from the hills and gather on the beach where the fishermen were cleaning, or had cleaned their fish. When the coyotes were on the beach, Augustine's large black dog, Negro, stayed at home.

One day the fishermen caught a coyote with a snare, and to have a bit of fun they dressed the poor coyote in pants and a shirt, tied a can to its' tail, and turned it loose. The coyote went through a lot of antics trying to get rid of the clothes, then took off with the can banging behind him.

One day, while we were walking up and down the shoreline casting into the seaweed beds and rocks, we caught some small kelp bass. Iva, Floyd's wife, was fishing in a small bay and was catching one sea trout after another. We were fishing on either side of her, without any luck. There was a deep trough in the floor of the bay where she was fishing the length of it. We were fishing across it, but she was the one catching the fish.

I got tired of hearing her shout everytime she caught a fish, so I began to look for a spot of my own. Afterall, I pride myself on being a pretty good fisherman, and I could not stand having a woman show me up, and laugh about it.

I walked up the beach to a large bluff where I could look down into a large blue hole, just off the point of the bluff. I could reach the hole by using a spinning reel, so I put on a one-ounce feather jig, and cast out beyond the hole, letting the bait sink as it came across. It did not take long before almost every cast brought in a fish.

After I had caught about fifteen fish, and my bruised male ego was starting to heal, I climbed partly up a hill where I could see Floyd, Iva and Nita, about a quarter of a mile down the beach, still fishing where Iva was catching so many fish.

I began to holler for them to come, but the only answer I got, was some howling from the coyotes. So, I found two long sticks on the beach to string my catch on, and cockily started back down the beach, to show off my catch.

A Mr. Herrera had an ice house nearby, where all the fishermen stored their catch. He came around twice a week and picked up their fish. We cleaned our catch, then used ice from Mr. Herrera's ice house to store them in our refrigerator, to take back to Kanab.

It was interesting to watch the large fish hawks sit on the bank, or in the Joshua trees, then dive into the surf and come up with a fish in their claws. They would carry their catch back to their nests in the cactus trees. Some of the nests must have housed several generations of hawks, judging from the layers of nesting material, and the heighth of the nests.

We dug small butter clams from the gravel of the beach, and Iva, who was a stickler for cleanliness, would scrub every clam like it was a kid on his first day at school. After Iva's scrubbing, we put the clams in sea water and added cornmeal, to clean them out. The cornmeal went in one end and out the other, cleaning out the sand in the process. We'd steam them, and dunk them in butter, and all the cares of medical practice vanished in the crisp air and good food.

We ran out of booze after the first week, so one morning at five o'clock, I left for Caborcas, eighty miles away, to replenish our supply. I bought the booze, and some lemons, and by the time I drove back over the road that was little more than a trail, it was evening.

The place where we were staying was almost primitive, however; there was a small, un-surfaced landing strip that had been used during WWII by patrols looking for drug violators. There was also a small, abandoned hotel. We enjoyed ourselves so much, and the fishing and clamming were so good, that we decided, despite the inconveniences and bad roads, to come back the following year.

The next time we came down, we had purchased a fourteen-foot fiberglass boat, the *Blue Goose,* and an eighteen-horsepower Evinrude motor. We built a rack on our truck to carry the boat, then loaded sheets of plywood, along with some two-by-fours, cots sleeping bags, food and utensils. Floyd brought along an extra tank of gasoline and oil.

It was February when we made our second trip, and that time we drove to Santa Ana, Mexico through Nogales. The road from Santa Ana to Pitiquito was extremely rough, with a road bed made of crushed rock. There were no bridges over the streams, so when we came to a dry stream bed we had to leave the road, go down a steep embankment, then cross the wash and struggle up the embankment on the other side to get back on the road. During flooding the streams are impassable.

We camped along the road near Pitiquito, and arrived in Libertad the following day. We found that the road through Santa Ana was no better than the road we had taken the previous year.

When we un-loaded the boat, some paint was knocked off in a few places, so we could see through the bottom. This frightened the superstitious fishermen because they could see the water through the boat, and they refused to ride in the Blue Goose.

We built small tables and shelves for the cabin with the lumber we had brought with us. Little had changed in the year that we were back in Kanab.

A band of Seri Indians, a fish-eating tribe, with a permanent settlement at Tiburon, had followed the fish migration up the coast, and were camped near our cabin. Their living quarters consisted of a crude shelter made of tumbleweeds, brush and turtle shells piled against a bank. They crawled in and out through a hole in the brush. They used animal skins, and old quilts or blankets for their bedding.

Two of the young Seri girls, who appeared to be about sixteen years of age, caught our attention. One was especially lovely, with a most attractive face and figure. She had painted some light beaded lines over her cheeks. Her sister was darker, and not quite as pretty, but she too had a good figure and excellent posture.

We watched them as they crossed the road to a well near Augustine's house, to get a bucket of water. They attached the bucket to a rope, then dropped it into the well and filled it. The prettiest of the Seri girls got down on her knees, while the other girl placed a circle of cedar bark on her head, to serve as a cushion. She then lifted the bucket of water, set it on the kneeling girl's head, and helped her to her feet.

The girls held their head high as they ambled past our cabin, and returned to their camp. What a difference between the posture of the Seri girls, and the posture of some of our young people today!

Later in the morning, some of the women and the children left the camp and walked off through the brush. When they returned in the afternoon, they were carrying what appeared to be large bird nests on their heads. We learned later that they were stacks of small mesquite twigs for their cook fires.

We had a water well too, and it wasn't covered. Shortly after the two girls passed our cabin, we heard a dog howling. A small mongrel had been following the girls when Negro, Augustine's dog, came on the scene. The frightened dog, much smaller than Negro, turned and ran. He was looking over his shoulder to see where Negro was, and fell into the well.

When we located the source of the howling, I dropped a bucket on a rope down to the terrified dog. He was pawing the side of the well, trying to get a foot-hold, and every time he would manage to get his front feet in the bucket, and I would start to lift, he would fall out.

Floyd, being an old cowhand, ran to his truck and came back with a lasso. He then dropped the lasso over the dog's head and pulled him out. The dog, shivering from fright, and the water in the well, shook himself off, then ran off in the direction of the Seri camp. After that, we got our water from Augustine's well.

When the two Seri girls, who spoke a little English, learned that I was a doctor; they came to me and asked if I would come to their camp to see two ladies, who were sick. I usually did not carry my medical bag with me when I was on vacation, but this time I had brought it along.

Floyd carried the bag for me when we went to the Seri camp. He set the bag down at the entrance of the brush shelter and I crawled on my hands and knees inside to see my patients, who were lying on a bed of blankets and animal skins.

One of the women had pnuemonia, accompanied by a high fever. I had some penicillin with me, so I gave her an injection. The other patient had suffered a stroke, and was paralyzed on one side. She was not doing well, so I gave her an injection. I thought it might help her psychologically. I left some aspirin and instructions with the two girls, and told them I would check back in the morning.

We had another patient the next morning. An old man had broken his hip when he stepped into a hole during the night. The poor old gentleman was so cold that I took a suit of heavy underwear that I used on hunting trips, and with the help of Floyd, got him into the underwear, to help keep him warm.

We took the wooden case the outboard motor had come in, and made a splint out of it, to go around his pelvis and leg. I gave the old man demerol for pain, then tried to make him comfortable by propping his back up. He had a pile of mesquite twigs and ironwood sticks that burned with a lot of heat, and a little smoke, to warm his shelter.

The nearest hospital was in Hermosillo, about eighty miles inland from the Seri settlement at Tiburon, and we were fifty miles from Tiburon! So, transporting the patient to Hermosillo seemed out of the question.

The sea was too rough to put the boat on. We had not been fishing because of a storm that made the Sea of Cortez too dangerous for boats. A strong wind was blowing, that made it bitterly cold. All I could do, for the time being, was to try to make the old man as comfortable as possible.

Floyd and I made house calls to our two women patients, two and three times a day. The woman with the pnuemonia, after injections of penicillin, began to show improvement. The woman with the stroke, although she was still paralyzed, began to feel better. Her appetite improved, and she smiled shyly when we talked with her. Even the old gentleman with the broken hip seemed to be fairly comfortable.

The Seris, grateful for the care we were giving to their people, showed us where to dig for clams, and showed us how to dig for fresh water on the beach. In the many years we traveled to Mexico we found that away from the border towns, they are an honest and generous people.

We caught a few fish from the shoreline, despite the storm. We dug for clams, and we had fresh water. The coyotes continued to howl each night, and we were getting restless, waiting for the weather to clear.

At the end of the first week, the wind died down, and we began to see signs of spring. The small fish were starting their migration northward, so we launched the Blue Goose, anxious to get back to our fishing.

The two gasoline cans were filled with old gas, so we decided to take a short trip to burn up the old gas. We could then fill the cans with new gasoline. We were all in the boat and set to go when Frankie, who did not appear to share the superstitions of the other fishermen, came running down to the boat, and climbed in behind the wheel. He was a cheeky, likeable rascal, so we all just laughed and let him handle the boat.

We put on trolling gear and caught a few cabrilla, but by the time we were five miles up the coastline one can of gasoline had been used up. We turned around, after putting in the rest of the gasoline, and headed back, still trolling. It was a short time later that we ran out of gas. We had to row ashore, pull the boat up on the beach, and walk home. It was a long walk in the soft sand, and by the time we reached the cabin, it was dark.

The next day, we loaded our gear into Floyd's truck, and drove up the beach to pick up our boat. Augustine went with us this time, and Frankie stayed home. I had some spinning gear and tried to fish from the shore, but we caught nothing.

After we filled the gas tank Nita and I took off for the cabin in the boat. Floyd, Iva and Augustine drove back to camp in the truck.

We were almost home when we saw a plane approaching the un-surfaced landing strip. I recognized the type of plane, a Bonanza, but I could not read the identifying numerals. We had told our son, Duke, and his friend, Mack Frost, both of whom worked for Kaibab Lumber mill in Fredonia, Arizona, to fly down and see us if they could. Duke had been a pilot in WWII.

We could see that the plane was in trouble. It would level off just above the runway, then zoom up and make another landing attempt. On the next approach it would do the same thing. We were getting nervous and I told Nita that if it was Duke, I hoped they would go back to Nogales and take a car down, or simply turn around and go back home.

The plane made another approach, and was coming in low and fast. By this time we were in the bay, directly at the end of the runway. We saw the plane hit the runway, but instead of coasting to a stop it made a big ground loop, then nose-dived into the ground.

I nearly capsized the boat trying to get to the shore. After the boat hit the beach I tried to pull it out of the water. Floyd and Iva came racing up in the truck. They, too, thought it was Mack and Duke, since we had all been expecting them to fly down.

When they reached the crash site, ahead of us, Augustine identified the occupants of the plane as Mr. and Mrs. Moon from Nogales. They were both dead. There were two other passengers who were alive, both of them girls about thirteen years of age. One girl had been flipped out of the plane when her seat belt and harness broke, and she was unhurt. The other girl was still in the cabin of the plane and had a broken arm and jawbone.

Augustine stayed with the plane, while Floyd and Iva drove down to the beach to get us. The run across the beach had left both of us exhausted. I stopped at the cabin to pick up my black bag, then raced back to the crash site. By that time, a group of Seris had gathered around the plane.

We could not tell who had been piloting the plane, since it had dual controls, and we were told that Moon had been teaching his wife to fly. Mr. Moon, a building contractor had suffered a coronary attack some time before the crash, and had only recently been released from the hospital. They had a cabin at Libertad, as did Moon's brother, a Dr. Moon. The girl with the broken arm was the daughter of Dr. Moon, and the other girl was the daughter of the Moons' who had been killed in the crash.

We set up cots to put the bodies on. It was amazing to see so many nice things appear out there in that faraway place. Maria, Augustine's wife, brought white sheets, colored ribbons and candles, and set up a night-watch to ward off any marauding coyotes.

The Seri Indians formed a large circle around the two cots, put the white sheets on the bodies, and placed candles at the head of each cot. They were very quiet and religious about the deaths of the Americans.

According to local law, if a person dies in Mexico, and the body is not removed within twenty-four hours, it will be interred, and cannot be removed for five years.

We tried to think of a way to get word to a mortuary in Nogales, Arizona, and to find a local doctor to pronounce the cause of death and sign a permit so the bodies could be flown out.

We sent Augustine to Jack Miner's, about forty miles away, because we knew Jack had a tri-wheel plane with a radio. When Augustine delivered the message Jack barely had time to get his plane up before dark, and put a message on the air that the Moons had been killed in a plane crash, and that an ambulance was needed to take the injured girl to a hospital, and the two bodies back to the States.

Since it was getting dark Jack did not have time to wait to get confirmation that his message had been received, since he had to get back to his own small landing strip before dark. We had also asked him to go to another town and notify the police and a local doctor to come to Libertad.

Maria opened up a bedroom in the abandoned hotel, and put clean sheets on the bed for the two girls. I put a temporary splint on the injured girl's arm, braced up her broken jaw, then gave her a shot of demerol for pain, and a shot of penicillin.

Nita and I stayed at the hotel to take care of the two girls. We made coffee and stayed up the entire night, taking turns pouring coffee for the people who came and went.

The doctor and the police arrived at midnight. Next morning at seven o'clock, after the bodies were enclosed in plastic bags and fumigated, we loaded them on the plane that had been sent for them. The girl with the broken arm and jaw was flown directly to Tucson.

The mortuary had received a call from Guaymas, about the accident. Two fishermen who were flying across the Sea of Cortez, had intercepted Jack's message. When they arrived at the Guymas airport they reported the message, and it was relayed from there.

That was an exciting, though tragic experience, but it did not end there. Eighteen years after the accident, in 1979, I received a call from the girl that had been flipped out of the plane. She was married and had two children.

She told me that the girl who had been injured, was also married and had two children. I received a call from Dr. and Mrs. Moon, parents of the injured girl, not long ago, who told me that Augustine died of throat cancer. They still go to Libertad to rest, but they said that it is not the same. The local fishermen now use dynamite and long lines to get their catch. It saddened me, since I have so many happy memories of Libertad, and of Augustine and Frankie, and the Seri Indians.

After the excitement of the plane crash had died down we asked some of the local fishermen if they would take the old Seri Indian with the broken hip to Tiburon, and to see if someone would take him from Tiburon to Hermosillo for better medical care.

The Sea of Cortz was quiet then, and I offered them the use of our boat. The fishermen, who had lost their fear of the Blue Goose, offered to take the old woman with the paralysis as well. I gave Mr. Herrera the out-board motor for taking the Seris to Tiburon, and for the use of his ice and ice house, while we were in Libertad.

The Sea of Cotez, was at times rough and fierce, while at other times, it was smooth and calm. The fishing had not been good on our second trip because of the wind and bitter cold. The local fishermen told me the fishing would improve after the first of March.

The natives know their land, because on the first morning of March I looked out and the whole world had changed! Birds were all over the sky, pelicans were diving, and fish were jumping. We were ecstatic.

We quickly got our fishing gear together, and launched the boat. Just offshore, near the hotel, was a hot spring; and beyond that, were some large boulders protruding above the water.

We put on some red-headed plugs and began by trolling among the boulders. The groupers had come back and began to hit, then dive for the back of a boulder. They were large, from ten to twenty pounds, so it was difficult to dislodge them once they were behind the rocks. It was not long before both Floyd and I lost our plugs.

Iva and Nita put me ashore so I could go back and try the blue hole below the bluff where I had had good luck the year before. I took my spinning tackle and drove up to the point, then walked down to the shore. Almost every time I cast a lead jig with a white feather beyond the hole, then retrieved it across the deep water letting it sink just a little, I'd get a strike from a sea trout.

When the sun was overhead I took off my jacket and threw it back on the beach. As I caught the fish I would throw them on the beach near my jacket. The tide began to come in about this time, and my jacket, along with some of my fish, began floating away.

I'd stop just long enough to retrieve my jacket, throw it and the fish farther back on the beach, then go back to my fishing. It was a race between the tide and me. I slipped once, and fell on the rocks, bruising my elbows and my fanny, but even that didn't stop me. I fished until the tide was in, and the fish stopped biting. I was exhausted, and exhilirated. The fish hawks in the Joshua trees acted as though they wished I would give up and go home.

I went to the truck and got two fish strings that we used for bass. With two or three of the fish on the the hooks I found I could barely lift them. The fish were so heavy that the chain cut into my hands while I was carrying them back to the truck.

When I'd get a string of them to the truck; I'd take them off, then lay them on the trunk bed and cover them with a tarp. I had caught almost fifty nice big sea trout.

When I would go back to the truck the fish hawks would try to raid the fish that were still lying on the beach, but the fish were so large that the hawks had difficulty trying to lift them. I would yell and throw rocks to scare them away from my fish.

When I got back to the cabin, the other three were there with a catch of large groupers. Then the fun began, cleaning all those fish, chipping the ice, and packing them for the trip back to Kanab. We had brought one of the old ice boxes that had stood in front of the garage in Fredonia, Arizona, to pack our fish in. It had been used to store ice and Coca Cola, so it made an ideal storage container for our load of fish.

We finished packing by early afternoon, and headed home. When we reached Nogales, we bought dry ice and put it on top of the ice-packed fish, and got them home in good shape.

That night, we camped at a little reservoir between Nogales and Tucson. I was searching through my camping gear and finally asked Floyd if he had seen my potty.

He laughed and said, "Oh Doc, I forgot to tell you, when Frankie was helping us pack I asked him if there was anything he could use, and he pointed to your potty, that was sitting in the unfinished utility room, so I gave it to him."

When Floyd asked Frankie what he wanted the potty for, Frankie said he wanted to use it for a *frijole* pot. I have a friend who fails to see any humor in Floyd not telling Frankie that it should *not* be used as a frijole pot. She tells me that Floyd and I were crude, when Floyd didn't tell Frankie, and when I laughed about it.

CHAPTER TWENTY-SEVEN
Topolabampo and other Ports of Call

After Morris Ervin, Nita's brother-in–law, died in 1955, her sister, Louise, frequently accompanied us on our trips. Louise and Nita were close, so it was a pleasure to have her travel with us.

We made one memorable trip to Baja, in a four-wheel-drive vehicle, camping out along the way. The three of us slept in a pop-up tent. Although we thought we were pretty well equipped, it was still a rough trip.

Our son, Bob, who was an auto mechanic, gave us all the parts he thought we might need along the way, including a catalogue telling us how to use them. He never did have much faith in me as a mechanic.

We first stopped to see Glenna and Jack in Las Vegas, then drove to Mexicali where we crossed the Mexican border. From Mexicali, we drove to San Felipe, on the east coast of Baja.

We pitched our tent, and camped there for three days. We had a short log from someone who had been there before, but no maps. The road was nothing more than a few truck tracks, made by the fishermen, or by trucks of the men who came in to buy the fishermen's catch. We enjoyed large delicious shrimp, while we were there, and ate our fill of them.

The wind began to blow late one afternoon. By the time we got to Oakie's Landing, it was blowing so hard that we decided not to put up the tent. There were a couple of fishermen's shacks there, so we rented one for the night for one dollar.

The wind blew so hard that we were afraid the shack would blow off the bluff, and into the sea. We had our camping equipment with us, so we were able to prepare our supper and breakfast the next morning, in the shack.

After breakfast, Nita and Louise announced they were going on strike. They refused to go any farther. They even refused to get into the truck. I could not change the mind of two determined women, so I wandered down the beach to watch the fishermen bring in their nets. Except for two small octopi, the nets were empty.

I asked one of the fishermen if octopus was good to eat. "Si Senor, muy buena" he grinned, and then showed me how to remove the ink sac. After he removed the sac, he told me to boil the octopus for a long time. He said that I should then strip off the outer membrane, and the suction cups on the tentacles; chop them in small pieces, add peppers and tomatoes, and cook them with eggs.

I followed the fisherman's instructions, taking two hours to prepare my feast. The girls were still sulking, as they sat on a bench outside the shack. They refused to taste the octopus, and watched silently while I prepared, and ate it, by myself. I made a big show of enjoying every bite, smacking my lips and making *mmmnn* sounds, as I ate. They were not impressed.

When I finished eating, I packed the truck, and told the girls to get in. I was getting testy, and said that we were going to drive down to the middle of Baja, or else. I promised to be careful and considerate, but I told them they would have to stop sulking, and come along.

After a few hours of silence from the girls, they finally gave in, and started talking to me. They were good sports, but I must say they enjoyed the trip more after they got home and could talk about their experiences, than they did during the trip.

I had wanted to go to Angel's Landing on an island, but due to our little feud I decided to skip any side trips, and go straight down the peninsula. Sometimes, we didn't set the tent up, but slept on the cots in the open air and cooked our meals on the gas stove set up on the tailgate. It was a lonesome trip - in a lonesome land. It was so barren that Nita and Louise would start cheering when they saw a bird. It was an event when we saw a cow, and a real occasion when we saw another truck!

It took us five days to reach the village of San Ignacio. We turned off the road, crossed a small stream, then drove along a lane lined with date palms planted by the early Catholic priests. There was a large mission that had been built with the help of the Indians.

We drove into town and found the local hotel, which had a large courtyard, covered with grapevines. There was a well, and a stream that flowed along the edge of the courtyard. The public utility (or toilet) was in the corner of the building, opposite our room. A young girl appeared to be in charge of the hotel, possibly the daughter of the owner.

We decided to treat ourselves and eat out that night, so we went to a private house that served Mexican food. I may have eaten too much, or perhaps it was the octopus, because I was the only one of the three of us, who suffered a severe attack of Montezuma's revenge.

It took me twenty-four hours to recover. When I felt able to travel again, we packed and drove through Santa Rosalie to Muleje, where we rented a cabin. Muleje also had an old church and courtyard. After doing some laundry, the girls did some sightseeing. I joined them at the church, which was under repair. There were remains of an old garden, that had once been cultivated in the backyard of the mission. At the upper end of the plot was a large stone cistern, with a headgate at the base. The dirt was graded up to the top of the back side, and by walking up there, we could see the trail that came from the Muleje River, and up the bank to the top of the cistern.

It was easy to visualize the hundreds of Indian converts as they carried jugs of water up the trail to dump in the cistern, for   irrigating the garden, in the early days of the mission.

We stayed in the lovely old town for several days, wandering and exploring the area. When we left Muleje, we drove to Concepcion Bay, making camp at El Cojote. While Nita and Louise were setting up the tent, half a dozen boys and girls who lived near the base of the mountain, came to see the Americans. They pitched in and helped us set up camp, laughing and talking, and making us laugh. They made us feel welcome, and the girls loved it.

There was a shrimp boat anchored in the bay close to where we set up camp. While we were setting up camp, four men rowed over in a dinghy, when they heard the laughter. They wanted to hear us speak English, so we got out our Berlitz dictionary, and enjoyed a two-way language session, punctuated by laughter from the kids.

Three of the men were young, and the fourth man had the bushiest black beard I have ever seen. One of the fathers of the children who were helping us, joined us. He was Mr. Morelia, and his job was to keep a fire going in a metal barrel on the beach to provide a landmark for the men in the shrimp boats, while they were running their nets at night.

The bearded fellow, was the diesel engine operator on the shrimp boat. He invited us to fish with his crew the next day, at no charge. It was a generous offer, and we accepted.

The next morning, the dinghy was sent for us to take us to the shrimp boat. It was raining and windy, when we climbed aboard. We had to climb over the stern, and wade through a load of shrimp, that several boys were busy cleaning.

Pelicans and seagulls were diving and fighting for the parts of the shrimp that were being thrown overboard. The cleaned shrimp were scooped down a hatch, into a hold full of ice.

The crew had been fishing all night and were tired, but first, before taking their rest, they wanted to help me to catch a rooster fish. They had a large basket of bait that they threw over the side as I trolled, but with the wind and rough weather, I didn't catch anything.

The wind died down about two in the afternoon, and the sun came out, making us warm and sleepy. The crew pulled the boat close to a small island, and tied up. They scrambled ashore, found a nice sandy beach, and went to sleep. The engineer did not sleep, but instead, took us on a guided tour around the cliffs and caves, for more than two hours. We were then taken back to our campsite.

The men refused to accept any money from us, waving it aside. The girls insisted that they accept a five-pound box of chocolates and some cigarettes for sharing their time and their boat with us. I contributed a case of beer. They seemed happy with our meager gifts.

Despite the poor fishing and bad weather, we went away with a feeling of warmth and gratitude for the generosity of the Mexican fishermen, and for Mr. Morelia and the children.

The next morning, we packed our camping gear and took to the road again, refreshed by our exploration of the caves the day before, and the time we shared with our new friends.

The road that led away from Cojote Bay climbed high above the Sea of Cortez. We stopped at the top, and looked back at the shrimp boat, and the hundreds of pelicans and seagulls diving for the shrimp parts. We all waved goodbye, then turned south, and followed the ridge that descended and went along the edge of the Sea of Cortez.

We later came to a small island just offshore, with a neck of sand connecting it to the mainland. We parked the truck at the side of the road, and climbed out to look over the area. Near the island, in the sand and gravel, we could see evidence of clams; little squirts of water, as we walked along the beach. I went back to the truck, got a shovel and a bucket, and before long, we had the makings of clam chowder. We decided to stay.

While Nita and Louise were preparing the chowder, I took my spinning rod and went fishing. I looped on a small spinner and cast out over the deep water, losing that spinner, and the next one. I then tied on a thin wire leader, and got a strike immediately. I landed a red snapper that weighed several pounds, more than enough for our supper.

While cleaning and scaling the snapper, I noticed some moss-covered rock oysters, so I collected a basket full of them. That night, I built a fire, and set up the grill. We placed the oysters on the grill, face side up, added salt and pepper, butter and parmesan cheese; and as the moon rose over the island, and the Sea of Cortez, we enjoyed *Oysters Rockefeller.*

While we were camped there, we met a Mexican goat herder, named Alberto. He came into our camp and asked us to read a letter, written in English, from his friend in Los Angeles. I could read the letter, but with my limited Spanish, I had difficulty telling him what the letter said.

Alberto appeared to be very young, but he said he had a wife and nine children back in the mountains. He herded goats to support them.

The next morning, Louise woke up with her legs and ankles swollen. She suffered intense itching, so I decided it must be an allergy to the weeds, or to the oysters we had eaten. There were large blisters on her ankles and the lower part of her legs. Knowing that Louise was allergic to numerous things, I came prepared. I gave her a shot of cortisone, then applied a cortisone ointment to her legs, wrapped them, and instructed her to keep them elevated. She got some relief when we poured sea water over the towels on her legs.

We left the island and followed the Sea of Cortez for awhile, then began to cross the Baja Peninsula, from east to west. That afternoon, we came to a three-way crossroad, with no road signs, indicating where the three roads led.

We had flown down to Loreta a few years before, so by looking at the direction of the roads, we guessed that the road to the left led to Loreta, the middle road to Commodu, and through it, over to Parissma. We knew there was a good road north of La Paz, for a hundred or more miles, and thought that we should come into it at Commodu. There was no one to ask, so we picked the road we thought we should follow. That was part of the excitement of traveling in Mexico, never knowing where we would hang our sombreros that night.

Soon after leaving the crossroads, we began a climb over a granite mountain, where the road was designated by stones. I was proud of our old Chevy as it climbed slowly over that granite mountain in four-wheel drive. There were oil slicks on the road, where previous travelers had knocked holes in their vehicles.

We descended slowly to the bottom of the canyon on the other side of the mountain, only to be confronted with a view of the road climbing steeply upward on loose rock and shale. We made camp for the night, in the bottom of that canyon.

Louise was in a lot of pain, so we made her a cot outside of the tent. We had a piece of red carpet that we placed by the cot, along with a box to put her glass of water on. I gave her a shot of demerol for pain, and our last shot of Canadian Club. (We now know that painkillers and booze do not mix!) We soaked the towels in the last of the sea water we carried with us, and wrapped them around her legs.

The next morning, Nita and I explored some ruins nearby, leaving Louise in camp to rest. We thought we were alone, until we heard a rooster crow. A short time later, a cowboy rode into camp and told us there was a small town just ahead. We gave him a pack of cigarettes.

After we reached the top of the mountain, we could look down on the town of Commodu, which was located in a peaceful setting. When we reached the town, the natives seemed to be more reserved than the ones we had met previously, so we drove on through. Perhaps it was shyness around Americans.

There were signs of new land development along the graded road north of La Paz, and much newly cleared land. We saw vast fields of grain in three periods of growth: some just planted, some mid-way in growth, and some ready for harvest. Diesel pumps were providing water from deep wells, for irrigation. That area is now one of the big oil developments in Mexico.

We camped that night in a newly developed orchard. The next morning, we arrived in La Paz, and after driving around the town, found the LaPerla Hotel by the wharf, and checked in.

When I told the manager about Louise's condition, he clapped his hands, and two young men appeared. They went out to the truck with him to see how they could best transport Louise into the hotel. They went back to the hotel, came out with a Captain's chair, and gently lifted Louise into the chair. They then carried her across the street, through the hotel lobby, and up the stairs into her room. Before leaving, they plumped the pillows behind her back, and asked if there was anything they could do, to to make her more comfortable.

It took five days for the blisters to disappear, after numerous soakings in boric acid water, and keeping her legs elevated. We stayed in La Paz for three of those five days. We had booked first-class passage to Topolabampo, aboard the *Viscosta,* for the three of us and our truck; so before Louise was totally healed, we left for Topolabampo.

First-class passage consisted of a very small cabin, without a door, and three bunks about eighteen inches deep, attached to the other wall. Louise took the lower bunk, I took the top bunk, and Nita slept on the middle one. I could stand on Nita's bunk and slide into mine, but I had to sleep either on my back or my stomach, to keep from falling out.

There were steam pipes just above me that were so close I couldn't turn over; a steady drip-drip of water fell on me as I tried to sleep. If I slept on my stomach, I had to crawl in feet-first, and if I slept on my back, I slid in head-first. There was also an open hatch in the cabin.

That night, as we crossed the Sea of Cortez to Topolabampo, the waves were running north and south; while we were sailing east to west. What a thrill that was!

The boat had unloaded lumber at La Paz when we first came aboard, and I think the lumber was their ballast! With our truck loaded on the top side, and with an empty hold, we really rolled with those waves.

The girls laughed, because we'd first see the moon through the doorless cabin; then on the next roll, the rail would dip in the water, sending several gallons of water across our cabin floor, and down the hatch. We were kept awake most of the night by a Mexican family who sat on the steps outside our cabin, talking.

The next morning, we were served octopus for breakfast, with scrambled eggs in tomato sauce, served over flour tortillas. We also drank black coffee. The cream provided for coffee in most cases, consisted of canned cream.

After following the ever-changing channel into the bay at Topolabampo, we arrived at the dock. The tide was out, so the deck of the *Viscosta* was four feet lower than the dock. This meant that our truck had to be lifted by manpower, at a cost of one hundred American dollars. More than twenty dock-workers got hold of the truck, then by using planks and muscle power, lifted the truck onto the dock. The same method had been used at La Paz when we loaded the truck, and at the same cost.

It felt good to be off the boat, and back onto black-top again. We drove to Guymas, and checked into a motel for the night. We were told by the hotel manager and everyone we talked to, that the fishing had been phenomenal that day. I talked the girls into staying over an extra day, promising them good fishing, but we didn't catch a single fish. I had hired a guide, rented a boat, and fished all day, with no luck, but no one else caught anything either.

We started homeward the next day, stopping at Rocky Point, Mexico, to see my sister, Catherine, her husband, Ted, and Ted, Jr.. They had a trailer at Rocky Point, and loved it; but I thought the place was barren and uninteresting.

We then drove back through Las Vegas to see the girl's sister, Glenna. After an enjoyable visit with Jack and Glenna; we drove back to Kanab, after putting Louise on a plane in Las Vegas to fly home to Springfield, Virginia.

Over the years, Nita and I took Louise with us to explore every corner of Mexico, as well as a one month trip to Guatemala in 1973. We had wonderful times together, but in 1973, I began to have problems with my eyes, and found that I had glaucoma. I was instructed not to drive for two years.

Nita's health began to fail, and for the next three years, she suffered several strokes. She had complained of severe headaches, and a doctor who examined her, said it was simply "nerves."

In September, 1977, Nita woke up vomiting, and complained of an excruciating headache. She went into a coma and did not regain consciousness Three days later, Nita died. We had been married for more than fifty years, and had lived most of that time, in southern Utah.

Nita (Juanita Hauer Aiken), was laid to rest in Kanab, where we had spent so many years together, and where our two sons, Duke and Bob, live with their families.

My eyes were operated on after Nita's death. The surgery helped to restore partial vision for reading, but today, in 1989, I am almost blind. I recently went back to Navajo Lake with friends, and most of what I saw was with my mind's eye, remembering what once was so vivid to me.

A few months before I lost Nita, I underwent surgery for carcinoma of the descending colon. Since there was some metastasis, I underwent chemotherapy each week for one year. The treatment tends to deplete the white count, so I had to have frequent blood tests. Today, almost twelve years later, I am doing well for a ninety-three-year-old.

When Louise came to Kanab for her sister's funeral, she stayed for a couple of weeks. Duke and Sue's son Russ, married Kim, in Beaver, Utah, so Louise stayed to attend the wedding with me.

The loss of Nita was a blow to both of us. As long as Louise was with me, the pain was not as great, but when she left, I missed her terribly. We had known each other for more than fifty years, and with Nita, had shared laughter, anger, and frustration, in our many trips together.

We decided that we would continue the trips, even though Nita, whom we both loved, could not be with us. We knew that she would always be with us in spirit.

In December, 1977, I flew to Washington, D. C. to spend Christmas with Louise, now that both Nita and Morris were gone. Morris had been dead for twenty-three years, and Louise had never remarried.

We booked passage on a cruise ship, the *Fair Wind,* sailing out of Fort Lauderdale, Florida, on December 28, 1977. We spent eleven days, visiting five Carribean islands.

Louise made it plain that she loved me like a brother, and that although we shared a cabin, there would be absolutely no hanky panky!

I laughed, and said that in my time, I had had a tonsilectomy; an appendectomy, prostatectomy, vasectomy, iradectomy, and cataracts removed from both eyes, in addition to a year of chemotherapy, so I was interested only in living, not in cohabitating.

When we were introduced aboard ship, she would say, "I am Louise Ervin, and this is Dr. Aiken. We are living together, but not in sin."

Until Louise's death in 1987, we shared many happy times together. After our first cruise, I became involved in managing the restoration of the Kanab Heritage House. I spent twelve years planting trees, grapes and roses, and guiding visitors through the old house. I have met people from all over the world there.

Friends like Mardean Pugh, her sister Lyall MacDonald, Ina Fae Frost, Pearl Little and Beth Pugh, and other friends too numerous to mention, have made my long life rich; beyond anything I had ever expected out of life.

CHAPTER TWENTY-EIGHT
Comparisons - Then and Now

My book began with the last century, 1896 - and we are now close to the end of another century, 1989. I have lived for more than ninety-three years, and have seen many changes, and many improvements, in the practice of medicine, and in the world in general. Some of the changes are good, and benefit mankind, and some changes we could have done without.

Perhaps I have lived as long as I have because I grew up on a farm where food was grown on soil enriched with natural fertilizers, and the food we ate was grown on land that was not poisoned by sprays.

I speak of sprays, because I was exposed to one of those *"safe"* pesticides on January 8, 1988, when I was told that it was *"perfectly safe;* it was used all of the time,"* by a pesticide company owner. Since then, I have undergone two surgeries on the left ear for carcinoma, and in April 1989, underwent a CT scan, because of swelling on the side of the head, at the site of the cancer. I don't know what the future holds, as far as the cancer is concerned, nor does Kathryn Vilips-Jackson, the editor of The Doc Aiken Story.

Kathryn left her home in California, and was staying in my home during the editing of this book. She was also exposed, and has undergone three surgeries, including the removal of a breast; due to an infiltrating ductal cell Adeno Carcinoma, after exposure to *Dursban*. It has the same base as *Malathion* and is manufactured by Dow C hemical Company. After the book is completed, Kathryn will return to California and to *The City of Hope,* for further treatment.

The book has been a labor of love, as well as frustration. Kathryn checked, and re-checked everything I had written or told her. If there are errors in names or dates, I accept full responsibility. She would sometimes drive me mad with questions to make sure I did not exaggerate on the length of an operation, or how many I did in a day; or how many fish I caught, or how many wild horses we saw. I became so careful about facts, that when I called to find out where Roner was buried I even asked how deep the boys dug the grave!

She was horrified when I said I took out my pocket-knife to open the pus-filled blisters on someone's foot. She wanted to know if I sterilized the knife first. I didn't remember. In the twenties and thirties, we may not have been as sterile as doctors are today. Nurses and medical personnel did not always have the training that is required today for one to work in the medical field.

Sometimes, the janitor gave the anesthesia. The janitor helped most of the time during a surgery. He once said, "Gosh, I can do an appendix operation as good as Doc Aiken can!"

There was a nurse from the deep South, who would sometimes come to work with manure on her shoes. When one of the nurses would tell her she had manure on her shoes, she'd drawl, "But it's *clean* manure!"

The practice of medicine has come a long way since the twenties. I have talked to other doctors about ectopic pregnancies, and why there were so many of them in earlier days, and why there are so few today. The general conclusion is, that before we had antibiotics, if a woman had a pelvic inflammation, it was usually prolonged, and the tubes to the uterus would become scarred.

When the uterus is scarred, a fertilized egg may not reach the uterus, but stay in the tube and begin to grow there. When the placenta attaches itself to the tube, it ruptures in a couple of weeks. If it attaches itself near a large blood vessel, the patient bleeds heavily when the rupture occurs, and suffers extreme pain. Now that we have antibiotics to take care of an inflammation right away, we don't see the scarring that sets the stage for an ectopic pregnancy.

It is the same thing with tonsils. We may have as many tonsilitis cases as before, but we don't see the complications that we used to see. Before antibiotics, inflammation of the tonsils could extend to the adenoids, which are near the eustachian tube, then spread to the middle ear. As a result, there were a lot of kids with earaches; but now, with penicillin and other antibiotics, the initial infection is soon quieted down.

We no longer have to lance eardrums. We didn't open eardrums much in earlier days, probably because most of us were not as skilled as doctors are today. We didn't have the equipment for good visibility either; we just could not see the eardrum as we can now. Nowadays, we have a speculum with a magnifying glass on it, that we lacked in my day.

You can't even recognize the eardrum through that glass if you are looking at it the way we used to. With magnification, the eardrum shows up several times larger than normal. Years ago, a doctor had to take a lance to find out where the pus was gathering, but it is much easier now, simply because you can see better.

In my day, parents simply let an ear abcess, thinking it was just a little earache, and the child would get over it. This sometimes led to infection of the middle ear, up into the antrum, and into the mastoid. We rarely hear of mastoid problems today, but in the past we did many mastoid operations, some in grown-ups. Although it did not happen with any of my patients, I have heard of deaths caused by mastoid problems, and of disfigurement, when a muscle was cut, and the patient's face was pulled upward on one side.

The X-ray equipment is superior today. I used to have a small machine that I had to turn on for ten seconds, but today it is much faster. We were not aware of the dangers of X-ray, and did not wear protective shields. I have set bones, under a flouroscope, many times, and because of it, have had skins cancers removed from my hands.

There were many thyroid problems in the early days, many of them *colloidal thyroids,* called *big neck.* Since this condition contributed to high blood pressure and arteriosclerosis, we referred quite a few patients to specialists for surgery.

After we built our own hospital, one of our patients, Bernice Pugh, had thyroid problems. I suggested she go to Dr. McGregor, or to Dr. McFarlane, for surgery. I treated her for ten days with *Lugol,* in preparation for surgery. Bernice surprised me by saying, "I am not going to either of them. You are going to do it!"

I protested, saying I had not done a thyroid operation by myself. Bernice's husband, Lloyd, spoke up and said, "Well, you are going to do one now. We are not going anyplace else."

This was not the first time I had faced a challenge, so I got out my books and began to re-study the metods of a thyroid operation. I had assisted in thyroid operations before, but had never particularly liked the techniques used by the doctors I had assisted. They never seemed to use the same technique twice, and that bothered me.

It seemed to me that it was always a bloody operation. The doctors just took a big glob of the thyroid, cut it off, then grabbed for the bleeders. By the time they thought they had enough of the thyroid out, there were a dozen or more hemostats hanging on the patient; almost choking the poor patient to death. I felt I could not do surgery that way.

In the first place, I did not have that many instruments. I found, in my research, that there were several ways of doing a thyroid operation. One technique appealed to me; one developed by *Hallstead.* He was gentle on tissue, and anatomically precise. He knew exactly where an artery was before he opened it; so he tied it off, put a couple of small clamps on it, then cut between it and tied it, thereby preventing heavy bleeding. I liked that idea, so that is the technique I used on that first thyroid operation.

I used #6 silk for suturing. The doctors I had assisted in the past, had used *chromic gut*, and put a drain in, but with the silk, I did not put in a drain. I got better looking scars, and certainly better results. There are several women in Kanab who have had their thyroid removed, with little scarring.

When we talk about hypothyroid cases, it should be noted that we also had some babies who were hypothyroid. These babies are very good, and very quiet. They are usually plump, and slow to learn.

One time, I said to a new mother, "I haven't seen your baby in quite awhile. How is she doing?" She beamed, and said, "Oh! She is such a good baby. You know, sometimes I think she is too good!"

That made me jump. I asked her to bring the baby in to see me, and when I saw her, the little six-month old child sat in her seat, her tongue protruding, not making a sound. Her hair was stringy, and I knew then, we had a hypothyroid case; one of five at about the same time.

At that time, the Medical Association in Utah began to realize that many of us country doctors were not keeping up with our education. Most of us had graduated from medical school more than ten years before, and some of us had not gone back for additional training.

While I was President of our Southwest Medical Association, I tried to get speakers who could give us some help on the problems that confronted country doctors. Many of us were too far away to attend medical meetings, where we could listen to information on the latest advances in medicine.

It was decided that a questionnaire would be sent out by the association, and doctors would be asked what problems they had. The plan was to send out a consultant to answer questions on various problems, from pediatrics to surgery. I wrote to the Association, asking for information on hypothyroid conditions. I knew that I should give thyroid, but did not know what dosage to give.

Tony Jenkins was in charge of the State Health Department, and they had hired Amos Christie, Assistant Professor of Pediatrics at the University of California, at Berkeley. He was later Professor of Pediatrics at Vanderbilt, in Tennessee. Christie was sent around the State as a consultant. He had already visited with several doctors around Utah, and made Kanab his last stop. He was accompanied by his wife, and Tony Jenkins.

When I brought the five hypothyroid cases to him, he said he had never seen one before. He said they did not have them on either coast; that there might be some in the Midwest, and suggested that the environment might be the cause.

These cases can be treated sucessfully, if they are treated early enough. One little girl I treated was slowed down just enough to make her beautiful, and with a calm disposition. She became a beauty operator, and the last I heard of her, she was working in Idaho.

One of the theories we came up with, after consultation, was that if the mother is hyperthyroid when she is carrying the baby, her hyperthyroid keeps her baby from developing a thyroid. One sometimes gets a similar thing with diabetes. A mother who is diabetic when she is carrying her child, prevents the baby's pancreas from developing, making the child hypoglycemic. Babies born under these circumstances, must be given glucose intravenously shortly after birth, or they can die.

Dr. Christie suggested, in answer to my question of how much thyroid to give, was to give just enough thyroid to make the patient a little hyper-active, up to the point of being irritable, and with a fast pulse; then we should cut back on the dosage.

You cannot give a child too much thyroid because there is a growth factor involved.The bone grows from the epiphesis, and too much thyroid causes the growth area of the long bones to close, stunting the growth of the child.

During the time the Christies and Dr. Jenkins were in Kanab, Nita was still living. We invited them to join us for dinner at the Grand Canyon. The sun was setting over the canyon, so we lingered at the bar after dinner, and with the manager, we all sang the *oldies,* until some of the other guests objected.

The winter that Dr. Christie visited us, he invited me to attend a pediatric seminar in Berkeley. While we were there, he received a commission as a Colonel, to take care of the English children being sent to the United States during WWII.

Another thing we did not know about years ago, was the Rh negative factor in mothers. We used to get babies who were born jaundiced, but we did not know why. In later years, when more was known, we recognized that some of the jaundiced cases were caused by a sensitivity in the blood. The Rh negative problem arises when the Rh negative mother is married to an Rh positive father. If, in some way, the mother's blood gets sensitized, the baby develops a high *icterus index,* that is sometimes fatal.

The solution to the problem then, was to inject the baby early with Rh negative blood. I never felt I had the ability to inject the blood into the baby's *fontanel* (the soft spot over the brain). I had always been afraid to do that, since I had neither the training, nor the experience.

My method was to take blood from an Rh negative patient, who generously donated blood, when I needed it. I would use between 50cc and 100cc of blood in a dose, and inject it under the skin of the baby's back. Six or seven babies, who were supposedly doomed to die because of the Rh factor, lived, with this treatment.

Some of the blood specialists that I have consulted said that what I did would not do any good; that it only works if you inject the blood into the vein. But, all I have as evidence, is that all of the babies treated with my method lived, and were healthy children.

While the first baby of an Rh negative mother may not develop an icterus, the second child sometimes develops problems. If the mother has a third child, they can be in serious trouble. The child sometimes dies, and if a fourth child is born, it is almost certain the child will die. The babies I used my procedure on were third and fourth babies, so I feel that my method can be considered successful.

When one of my patients, Laura Chamberlain, was expecting her third baby, I sent her to Salt Lake City to see a specialist. His comment to her about my procedure was to tell her that it could not be done, and that if he did not deliver her child, the child would die. This made Laura mad, so she told him that she would go back to Dr. Aiken; that he would take care of her.

After the child was born, we used the Rh negative blood from our donor, Donna Baird. Donna still lives in Kanab, and it is through her generosity, that several babies lives were saved. Laura's baby, Lex, lived, and went on to become a star athlete, and served a mission in South America. Lex Chamberlain is also a strapping six-feet, seven inches tall, and is intelligent, talented, and good looking.

There was an amusing aftermath with a couple of my Rh negative babies. Lois Blair, whose mother was Rh negative, and Sirrie Chamberlain, Laura's daughter, went into nurse's training at Holy Cross Hospital. When the girls began studying about the Rh negative factor in school, they told their instructors about how Dr. Aiken handled it. Every one of the professors said that it could not be done that way. The girls stood up for me, and defended my method of treating Rh negative cases; saying that they were living proof, my method worked.

How did I figure out what to do in those cases? I just reasoned that there was some factor in the blood that counteracted the problem, and I could not see why it had to go into the blood stream. I theorized that the blood could be absorbed into the subcutaneous tissues. Besides, I did not have the nerve to inject blood into the baby's soft spot, and give blood that way.

Later on, when Dr. Sanella and Dr. Reilly came to practice with me, both doctors criticized my method. Dr. Sanella was a blood specialist, and maintained that it would do no good to use my method; so Dr. Reilly and I did a complete blood exchange, on one or two babies. But, the fact remains, the babies I treated all lived, and were healthy. Had the procedure not been done, I am sure they would have died.

We used to have quite a few eclampsias, but today they are rare. Eclampsia has been called a *disease of theories*; and the treatment for the condition, *various theories*. Prenatal care was almost non-existent, when I was practicing medicine. Most women did not call on me until it was time to deliver. A man might approach me on the street and ask if I was going to be home in December; that his wife was expecting a baby. Sometimes, I would not be called until a mother was in labor, perhaps convulsing, or unconscious.

When I arrived to deliver a baby I didn't know what condition the mother was in, or what position the baby was in. I didn't know if the mother suffered from a heart condition, diabetes, or had albumin in the urine. I was always being confronted by the unknown.

In looking back, I am surprised we did as well as we did!

We found, a few years later, that we could give magnesium sulfate hypodermically, to stop convulsions. Some doctors thought it helped, and others disagreed. Aside from medication though, proper care, and rest, took care of some of the eclampsia cases.

It was thought that the eclampsias were brought on by auto-intoxication from the fetus, or from kidney disease, or by poisoning of the mother by the placenta, or infection or infusion of the placenta. But, the fact that there are few cases today, indicates that education and better prenatal care is the answer; just as education about diptheria, smallpox and polio, help to prevent the problems that we had, not that many years ago. Prevention has always been better than trying to cure a disease.

I lost only one confinement case in my more than fifty years of medical practice. The mother was an eclampsia case. She was from Bellview, Utah, and had had several children before this pregnancy.

One evening, her family brought over a urine sample to my office in Hurricane. I was on another call and did not get back for some time. When I ran the sample, I found it loaded with albumin; so early the next morning, I drove to Bellview. When I arrived, she had already started labor, and had started to convulse.

We delivered the baby, although the mother was in convulsions the entire time. Three hours after the delivery, the mother seemed to be quiet, but she had hemorrhaged heavily. I left some ergotrate with her family to give to her. I had given some to her, earlier.

I stayed with her until early afternoon, then went home and returned later in the evening to check on her. When I returned, I was shocked to learn that she had died two hours after I left. They had no telephone, so there was no way for them to call me. I was told that she had another hemorrhage after I left.

Another case was Ruth Lewis, who had already started labor when they left their home in Alton, to come to the midwife, Laura Broadbent, in Kanab. As they drove onto the main highway leading to Kanab, Ruth went into convulsions. I didn't know anything about her condition until I arrived at Mrs. Broadbent's, and found that Ruth had gone blind, and was still convulsing. This was about 1933 or 1934.

The treatment at that time was to give a five to ten percent dextrose intravenously, plus the intramuscular shot of magnesium sulfate. We had no dextrose, so I mixed Karo syrup with boiling water, cooled it, and used that intravenously. These methods seem primitive now, but Ruth had gone blind, and I knew that something had to be done quickly.

After her baby was delivered, Ruth stopped convulsing; but it took another week for her blindness to disappear.

When I was interning, in the twenties, if we had an obstetrical case that required a caesarean section, the surgeon used the *classic cut*, a longitudinal incision from the *xiphoid* (lowest part of the breast bone) to the *symphysis pubis* (pubic bones); and when the uterus was exposed, the surgeon would make a long incision through the body of the uterus, and break the bag of water.

Since the incision was made in the vascular area, we would have a vast amount of blood and water. It was considered to be a dangerous, and serious operation. We had to hurry to get the baby out, and to get it breathing. Then we had to tie off the bleeders, and sew up the uterus and the abdomen. The death rate from these operations was high in the twenties. I have known of several patients who died, while undergoing a caesarean section.

After I began my practice in the West, I assisted Doctors MacFarland and McGregor with sections, a number of times. Later on, the surgical technique changed drastically, with the surgeons using a *transverse incision* low on the abdomen, near the neck of the uterus. With this method there was little blood loss, making the operation a safer one.

With the early caesareans, a woman could only have one or two babies that way, and then the uterus would tend to rupture. The newer technique made the incision in a part of the uterus that wasn't stretched, and this allowed the mother to have more children by section, without the complications.

We did not have Medicare, nor the medical insurance that is available today. If you were a doctor, you took care of people: whether they had money or not. You might hope that you would be paid, but your dedication to saving lives was uppermost in your mind. Somehow, I can't help feeling - it should still be that way!

The End